▶ **bachelor-wissen**
English Linguistics

bachelor-wissen

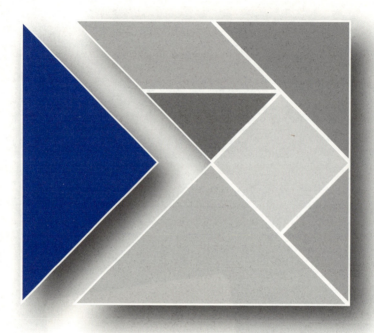

bachelor-wissen ist die Reihe für die modularisierten Studiengänge

▶ die Bände sind auf die Bedürfnisse der Studierenden abgestimmt
▶ das fachliche Grundwissen wird in zahlreichen Übungen vertieft
▶ der Stoff ist in die Unterrichtseinheiten einer Lehrveranstaltung gegliedert
▶ auf www.bachelor-wissen.de finden Sie begleitende und weiterführende Informationen zum Studium und zu diesem Band

bachelor-wissen

Christian Mair

English Linguistics

An Introduction

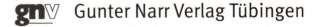
Gunter Narr Verlag Tübingen

Prof. Dr. Dr. h.c. Christian Mair ist Inhaber eines Lehrstuhls für Englische Linguistik der Albert-Ludwigs-Universität Freiburg und Mitglied des nationalen Wissenschaftsrates.

Bibliografische Information der Deutschen Nationalbibliothek

Die Deutsche Nationalbibliothek verzeichnet diese Publikation in der Deutschen Nationalbibliografie; detaillierte bibliografische Daten sind im Internet über <http://dnb.d-nb.de> abrufbar.

© 2008 · Narr Francke Attempto Verlag GmbH + Co. KG
Dischingerweg 5 · D-72070 Tübingen

Das Werk einschließlich aller seiner Teile ist urheberrechtlich geschützt. Jede Verwertung außerhalb der engen Grenzen des Urheberrechtsgesetzes ist ohne Zustimmung des Verlages unzulässig und strafbar. Das gilt insbesondere für Vervielfältigungen, Übersetzungen, Mikroverfilmungen und die Einspeicherung und Verarbeitung in elektronischen Systemen.
Gedruckt auf chlorfrei gebleichtem und säurefreiem Werkdruckpapier.

Internet: http://www.bachelor-wissen.de
E-Mail: info@narr.de

Satz: Informationsdesign D. Fratzke, Kirchentellinsfurt
Druck und Bindung: CPI – Ebner & Spiegel, Ulm
Printed in Germany

ISSN 1864-4082
ISBN 978-3-8233-6393-4

Contents

Preface: how to use this book IX

1 Introduction – linguistic and other approaches to language 1
1.1 Orientation 1
1.2 Demonstration/discussion 8
1.3 Problems and challenges................................... 13
1.4 Practice 17

2 Phonetics and phonology – the sounds of speech............. 21
2.1 Orientation 21
    2.1.1 Sounds and letters: the need for a phonetic alphabet...... 21
    2.1.2 Sounds as sounds, and sounds as elements of linguistic systems: from phonetics to phonology.................. 23
    2.1.3 Stress, pitch, intonation – phonetics and phonology beyond the individual sound.......................... 28
2.2 Demonstration/discussion 30
2.3 Problems and challenges................................... 34
2.4 Practice 37

3 Morphology and word-formation – the structure of the word... 39
3.1 Orientation 39
    3.1.1 Free and bound morphemes 39
    3.1.2 Lexical and grammatical morphemes.................. 43
3.2 Demonstration/discussion: The major word formation strategies of present-day English............................ 44
3.3 Problems and challenges................................... 50
3.4 Practice 54

4 Syntax I/general principles – the structure of the clause........ 57
4.1 Orientation 57
    4.1.1 Words, phrases, clauses and sentences.................. 57
    4.1.2 Form categories and their grammatical functions 61
4.2 Demonstration/discussion 63
    4.2.1 Basic strategies for the expression of grammatical relations 63
    4.2.2 Typological classification of languages.................. 67
4.3 Problems and challenges................................... 68
4.4 Practice 71

5	**Syntax II/the fundamentals of English grammar**	73
5.1	Orientation	73
	5.1.1 Parts of speech	73
	5.1.2 Phrases	75
	5.1.3 The seven basic clause patterns	77
5.2	Demonstration/discussion	79
5.3	Problems and challenges	81
5.4	Practice	85
6	**Semantics and lexicology – the meaning of words**	89
6.1	Orientation	89
6.2	Demonstration/discussion	94
6.3	Problems and challenges	99
6.4	Practice	104
7	**Pragmatics and discourse analysis**	109
7.1	Orientation	109
7.2	Demonstration/discussion	119
7.3	Problems and challenges	121
7.4	Practice	125
8	**Applied linguistics, language teaching and translation studies**	127
8.1	Orientation	127
8.2	Demonstration/discussion	128
8.3	Problems and challenges	134
8.4	Practice	138
9	**A pluricentric language – standard Englishes around the world**	141
9.1	Orientation	141
9.2	Demonstration/discussion	145
9.3	Problems and challenges	151
9.4	Practice	157
10	**Dialectology – regional variation in English**	159
10.1	Orientation	159
10.2	Demonstration/discussion	160
10.3	Problems and challenges	165
10.4	Practice	167
11	**Language in the city – social and ethnic variation, multilingualism**	171
11.1	Orientation	171
11.2	Demonstration/discussion	172

| 11.3 | Problems and challenges | 176 |
| 11.4 | Practice | 183 |

12 Language change and the history of English ... 187
12.1	Orientation	187
	12.1.1 Old English period (c. 500 – c. 1100)	190
	12.1.2 Middle English period (c. 1100 – c. 1500)	192
	12.1.3 Early Modern English period (c. 1500 – c. 1750)	193
	12.1.4 Modern English period (since c. 1750)	195
12.2	Demonstration/discussion	195
12.3	Problems and challenges	199
12.4	Practice	203

13 Past masters, current trends – theorising linguistics for students of English ... 207
13.1	Orientation	207
13.2	Demonstration/discussion	208
13.3	Problems and challenges	217
13.4	Practice	220

14 Linguistics and the public – language myths, language politics, language planning and language rights ... 223
14.1	Orientation	223
14.2	Demonstration/discussion	227
14.3	Problems and challenges	229
14.4	Practice	237

| Glossary | 241 |
| Index | 259 |

Preface:
how to use this book

The present book is obviously not the first introduction to linguistics for students of English. It complements and competes with a number of related titles, some published in Britain and the United States for international audiences, and some published in Germany with the needs of a more local readership in mind. Some of what this book presents is, of course, new and original material not found elsewhere; a fair amount, however, is just the basic stuff which undergraduates in English have to master if they want to understand the complexities of the structure and the use of the (foreign) language they have decided to focus on in their studies.

Nevertheless, the author has a clear justification for publishing just this book at just this time. It is the unified perspective it is written from – a perspective which he hopes will be useful and productive for the intended audience.

A first factor which motivates the present project is an external political one. Currently, in Germany, Austria and Europe as a whole, higher education is being profoundly transformed, the most conspicuous outward sign of reform being the restructuring of entry-level undergraduate courses in the B. A. framework. The present book is a response to this in that it aims to meet bachelor students' needs **without diluting and lowering academic standards**.

Secondly, the book aims to present linguistics not as such, or out of context, but **specifically for students of English,** i. e. students wishing to make productive use of what they learn about language and linguistics in other areas of their academic courses (cultural studies, literature) and in their later professional careers in language teaching, the media, public relations or similar areas of language- and culture-related professional activity.

Thirdly, the book is not designed as a manual of information to be learned and reproduced, but as an invitation to explore the fascinating complexity which the English language, and languages in general, display both in their structure and in their use. The focus is thus on **learner autonomy as an essential first step towards independent research.**

As readers will see, each of the following 14 units has the following structure:

1. Orientation
2. Demonstration/discussion
3. Problems and challenges
4. Practice

The reader's careful attention is invited for the first. The reader's own initiative, activity and creativity are vital prerequisites to the success of the other three. To help readers with basic concepts and terminology, the book contains a comprehensive glossary at the end. If you experience difficulties with some of the exercises, or if you want to check your results, you can consult the web-page accompanying the book at www.bachelor-wissen.de, which gives you the solutions. This site also contains useful additional material and sound samples.

The book will no doubt serve many practical purposes – as a class text, in helping students prepare for their exams, or as a reference work consulted occasionally. Beyond that, however, I hope that readers will retain a few essential insights even after they have forgotten about the inevitable detail, such as the lesser-used symbols of the phonetic alphabet, or some technical definition of a grammatical concept, or the specifically New Zealand realisations of the short front vowel phonemes. These include:

- a fascination with the intricate structural complexity of the English language, and – by implication – that uniquely human endowment, the language faculty;
- an appreciation of the diversity of a global language, of the many varieties of English that have arisen in response to the expressive, social and cultural needs of an extremely heterogeneous community of speakers; and – not least –
- a theoretically grounded understanding of the true role of language in society.

The importance of the part played by language in fostering human community and society cannot be over-estimated. And yet public debates about language issues are still too often informed by half-truths and myths – propagated by educators, politicians, cultural critics. What the trained linguist can bring to this debate is two scientific virtues: a respect for empirical data and a commitment to rational argument. In the public discourse on the shape of English and the role the language plays in the world today, this is still a much needed contribution.

I would not like to close this preface without a few heartfelt words of gratitude – to Dr. Birgit Waibel, English Department of the University of Freiburg, for invaluable help in the final stages of the project, in preparing diagrams, the solutions to the exercises and the web-page accompanying the book, to Luminita Trasca, also of Freiburg, for patient and competent proof-reading, and to Jürgen Freudl, Narr Publishers, who was a stern taskmaster when it came to deadlines and a constructively critical reader of a previous version of the present book.

Freiburg, February 2008   *Christian Mair*

Introduction – linguistic and other approaches to language

Orientation

1.1
What is linguistics?

Any book introducing undergraduate students to a new academic field, its terminology and investigative methods must start by answering the defining question, which in our case is simply: "What is linguistics?"

To say that "linguistics is the rational and systematic scientific study of language, usually based in institutions of higher learning such as colleges or universities" seems a fairly helpful first approximation. Of course, in offering an answer to this first question, I have raised two more. First, it is not at all clear what we mean by "language" in an academic-linguistic context. The every-day English word *language* has multiple meanings (as do its equivalents in other languages), as can easily be demonstrated by comparing its meaning in the following two sentences (see Exercise 1 below for further examples):

> The language of the British press has changed considerably over the past few decades.
> Language is what distinguishes human beings from apes.

In the first example, the word *language* denotes a particular functional variety of one specific language, in this case English, whereas in the second it could be glossed as the "ability to learn and use any of a large number of human languages."

Secondly, while its home in universities as one academic discipline among others is secure, the precise status of linguistics as a science is contested territory (as we shall see in many places throughout this book). Is linguistics part of the humanities, close to literary and cultural studies, with which it shares an interest in the phenomenon of style for example? Is it an empirical social science, using quantitative and qualitative methods to study the communicative networks among people which ultimately constitute society? Is it an experimental science like psychology, studying the role of language in human cognition, or the place of language-acquisition in the development of the human personality? Or is it a natural science, in that it helps us to understand the complex physiology of the human speech apparatus, or the neurological basis of language both in the healthy person and in those suffering from various kinds of language disorder or language loss?

A subfield of the humanities, a social science, an experimental natural science?

This incomplete list of possible orientations in linguistics opens up many vistas which the present introduction will not explore. Its aims are more practi-

Linguistics for students of English

cal and limited. The first is to equip readers with the terminology and methods necessary to describe present-day English, the language they have made the focus of their studies, both in its structure and in its use. The second aim is to introduce students to the major theoretical positions and trends in the field, so as to give them the basis for independent further work. And not least the book aims to show where a knowledge of linguistics can be made productive outside the field, for example in the teaching and learning of foreign languages, or for developing a more sophisticated grasp of language-related issues in literary and cultural studies.

Linguistics – the pre-history of the field

But how did the burgeoning discipline of linguistics arise historically? In answering this question, we cannot help but be struck by an apparent paradox. We find signs of people's keen interest in linguistic issues for practically the whole recorded history of humanity, but dispassionate scientific objectivity in the study of language, the scholarly study of language for its own sake, or – for short – linguistics as an academic discipline, are historically very recent pursuits.

One marvel which seems to have caused people to wonder in many places and at different times in history is the fact that human beings live in a world of many languages, which is obviously impractical. A well-known non-scholarly answer to this puzzle is contained in the *Old Testament* of the Bible (Genesis 11), where multilingualism is explained as God's punishment for the human pride manifested in the attempt to build the enormous Tower of Babel.

Fig. 1.1
Pieter Breughel the Elder, "Tower of Babel" (1563), Vienna, Kunsthistorisches Museum

Within one and the same language community, people are keenly aware of sometimes very slight differences in pronunciation, grammar or vocabulary. In a British context, for example, "aitch-dropping," technically speaking the dropping of initial /h/ in stressed syllables, is a strong social marker. If someone says *'eavy metal music* instead of *heavy metal music*, the contrast is trivial, and any confusion about the intended meaning is unlikely. However, this detail of pronunciation will instantly mark out the speaker as either educated, standard or middle-class (if *heavy* is pronounced with *h*) or uneducated, non-standard or working-class (if the aitches are dropped). Of course, the general public, including literary writers, are aware of this, so that aitch-dropping becomes available as an efficient device for literary characterisation, as it does, for example, in the case of Uriah Heep (from Charles Dickens' *David Copperfield*), who deceptively styles himself as *'umble* (← *humble*) all the time. The motif is taken up by the rock band of the same name, whose best-known album is also called *Very 'eavy, very 'umble*.

Among those fascinated by aspects of language long before the emergence of linguistics as a specialised discipline have been major philosophers. The classical Greek thinker Plato (428/27 BC – 348/47 BC), for example, seems to have thought a lot about the question of whether the name (i. e. the sound of a word) has any natural or logical correspondence to the person, thing, quality, activity or process it refers to, or whether this relation is arbitrary.

Linguistics and philosophy

If we think of verbs such as German *zischen* or English *hiss*, we might tend to give credence to the former view – the sound of the words seems to be motivated by the sound in the real world. If we think about a sound sequence such as /iːgl/, we will tend to favour the latter as this sound sequence corresponds to *Igel* "hedgehog" in German and *eagle* "Adler" in English, and it is difficult to see any connection whatsoever between either animal and the words used to refer to them. In the typical fashion of a dialogical Platonic argument, the philosopher develops a compromise position: Kratylos argues that names are motivated; Hermogenes claims that they are arbitrary; Socrates moderates between the two.

Modern linguists are less circumspect and tend to agree that Hermogenes' position is the appropriate one. First, there are far more words for which the relation between sound and meaning is arbitrary than there are "onomatopoetic" forms in which the sound of the words appears to imitate some natural sound. Secondly, even those words which seem to be imitations of actual natural sounds turn out to be highly arbitrary and language-specific on closer inspection. Note, for example, that the initial letter <z> in German *zischen*, which corresponds to the sounds /ts/, would be a forbidden combination in English (see Exercise 5 below for further discussion).

"Onomatopoeia" – the imitation of natural sounds

Apart from philosophical concerns about language, there have also been practical ones. Language teaching, for example, has a history to look back on which is at least as old as the philosophical debate about language. In fact,

Linguistics and language teaching

two of the seven Classical "liberal arts," which formed the core curriculum of higher education well into the Early Modern period, are language-related, namely grammar (which in the old understanding included the study of pronunciation) and rhetoric.

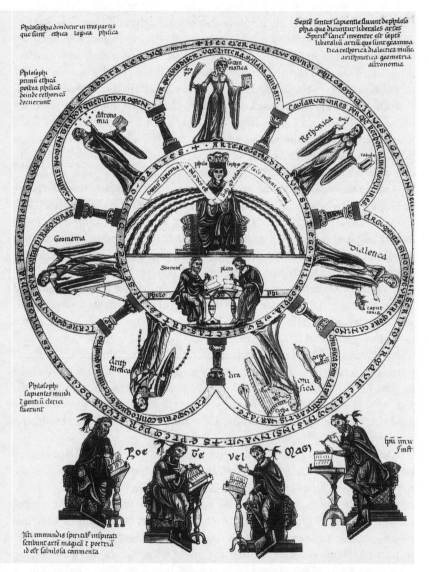

Fig. 1.2 | The "seven liberal arts," with *Grammatica* and *Rhetorica* on the top and top-right (from: Herrad of Landsberg, "Hortus deliciarum" [1180])

For a long time, the foreign languages which were studied and taught most were Latin, Greek and Hebrew, the three "sacred" languages of the Bible. From the 16th and 17th centuries onwards more and more of the modern European languages started developing coherent traditions of producing teaching and reference materials, such as dictionaries and grammar books. Some of the works which have come down to us over the ages clearly reveal a lot of linguistic insight, but as a whole this tradition does not amount to more than a precursor of the scholarly "linguistic" perspective on language. Figure 1.3 presents the title page of one such practical grammar of English, which was presumably produced for the benefit of German immigrants to British North America.

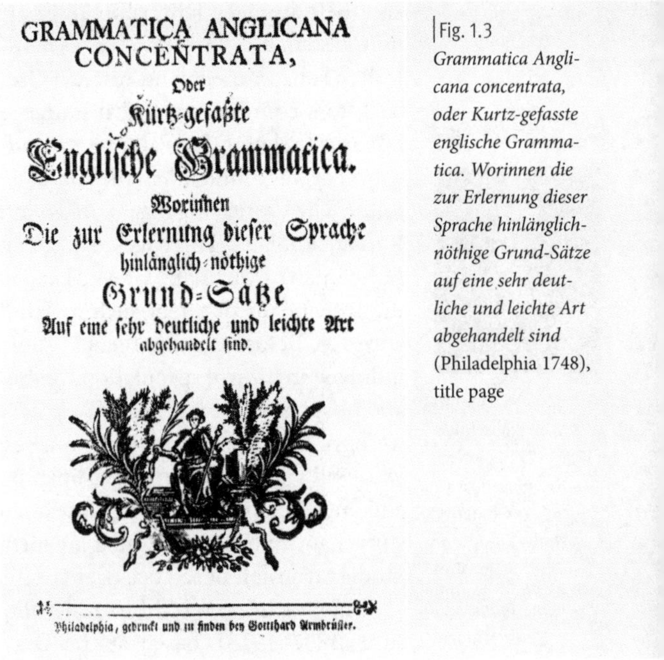

GRAMMATICA ANGLICANA
CONCENTRATA,
Oder
Kurtz-gefaßte
Englische Grammatica.
Worinnen
Die zur Erlernung dieser Sprache
hinlänglich-nöthige
Grund-Sätze
Auf eine sehr deutliche und leichte Art
abgehandelt sind.

Philadelphia, gedruckt und zu finden bey Gotthard Armbrüster.

Fig. 1.3 *Grammatica Anglicana concentrata, oder Kurtz-gefasste englische Grammatica. Worinnen die zur Erlernung dieser Sprache hinlänglich-nöthige Grund-Sätze auf eine sehr deutliche und leichte Art abgehandelt sind* (Philadelphia 1748), title page

Another pre-cursor of academic linguistics is the tradition of textual criticism which first flowered during the Renaissance, when scholars looked at ancient texts from classical antiquity very closely in order to determine their authentic versions, which had often been corrupted in centuries of transmission. Very often, such a comparison of extant manuscript versions was a necessary step to prepare the first printed editions of these texts. This pursuit soon became known as **philology** (from the ancient Greek for "love of the word" or "love of language"). Originally, philology comprised the study of language and literature. Today the term is preserved in expressions such as "Englische Philologie," one of the traditional German designations of English Studies. In a modern linguistic context, the term *philology* refers to the specialist study of language history, especially in the context of editing texts.

Linguistics and textual criticism

Finally, the fact that Europeans conquered and colonised ever growing portions of the world meant that many new and exotic languages were encountered, translated from and into, documented and taught. Arabic, Chinese, Persian and the ancient and modern languages of India thus became of interest to Europeans. This meant that, slowly but surely, a critical mass of knowledge about languages accumulated which led to the birth of linguistics as an academic discipline of study toward the end of the 18th century.

In this early phase, language scholars' orientation was strongly historical. Building on an insight first formulated in 1786 by William Jones (1746–1794), who worked as a judge on behalf of the British East India Company in Calcutta, subsequent generations of scholars traced the history of the various members of what was later to be referred to as the Indo-European family of languages in order to reconstruct their common origin (proto-Indo-European or *Ursprache*)

The birth of linguistics as an academic discipline

and their mutual relationship. In particular, Jones' seminal insight had been to note systematic correspondences between Sanskrit, an ancient language of the Indian subcontinent, and Ancient Greek which made it plausible to trace both back to a common historical source (see Unit 12 for further information on historical relationships among the Indo-European languages, esp. Fig. 12.1).

What was found out in the course of the 19th century still holds in its essence today. The Celtic languages spoken in the very West of Europe, the Germanic, Romance, Slavic languages, some languages of the Baltic region (Latvian, Lithuanian), Albanian, Greek, Persian and some of the major languages of the Indian subcontinent such as Hindi or Punjabi all go back to a common ancestor. Before the emergence of historical-comparative linguistics, people indulged in bizarre speculations on historical relationships between languages and peoples on the basis of a few pairs of words which sounded similar. Today, we have a rigid methodology to assess the value of such claims, and people who will still argue for direct links between the civilisations of ancient Asia and ancient America just because a few place names, names for gods or foodstuffs happen to sound similar are fortunately not taken seriously any more – a modest triumph of science over speculation.

Fig. 1.4
William Jones (1746–1794), pioneer of historical-comparative (Indo-European) linguistics

Diachronic and synchronic approaches to the study of language

One practitioner of historical-comparative linguistics, Ferdinand de Saussure (1857–1913), based at the University of Geneva in Switzerland, was instrumental in bringing about a re-orientation of approach which has dominated the field to the present day. He pointed out that the **diachronic** study of language (i.e. the study of its development through time) did not make it possible to understand how languages worked at any given point of time. The most trivial argument to prove this is, of course, that we can speak and write a language perfectly without knowing anything at all about its history. For example, it does not bother us in the least that the word *nice* meant "difficult" a few centuries ago, as is shown by the following extract from Daniel Defoe's well-known novel *Moll Flanders*:

> I was really with child [= pregnant].
> This was a perplexing thing because of the Difficulty which was before me, where I should get leave to Lye Inn; it being one of the nicest things in the World at that time of Day, for a Woman that was a Stranger, and had no Friends, to be entertain'd in that Circumstance without Security, which by the way I had not, neither could I procure any. (Daniel Defoe, *Moll Flanders*. 1722: ch. 32)

The context here makes clear that the situation is far from *nice* in the present sense of "pleasant." At the time, the word meant "difficult, tricky." Looking around hard enough, we can find some old-fashioned or fossilised usages of *nice* which remind us of this older use even today, for example, a *nice distinction* (i.e. a difficult or pedantic distinction).

De Saussure proposed that the most appropriate approach to the scholarly study of language should be a **synchronic** one, with a focus on how a language functioned as a structural system at any given time. In practice the move from the diachronic approach to the synchronic one often meant that the focus of interest shifted from the oldest stages of the language (in the case of English the Old English period lasting from c. 500 to c. 1100) to the contemporary language, but this does not necessarily have to be the case. We can study Old English from a synchronic perspective, for example, by showing how it worked as a structured system at a given point in time, let's say the well-documented period immediately before the Norman Conquest in 1066. Alternatively, we can take a diachronic approach to present-day English, for example by showing which processes of historical change are going on right now.

Fig. 1.5
William, Duke of Normandy, "the Conqueror," from the Bayeux Tapestry

What unites both historical-comparative ("diachronic") and structuralist-synchronic approaches to language and sets them apart from all the precursor traditions is their explicitly **descriptive** orientation. Where the teacher instructs in how to use a language correctly (that is according to the educated standards prevalent in a community), where ordinary speakers react to linguistic difference primarily emotionally ("I just hate that New York City accent," "all those Anglicisms are ruining the German language"), academic linguists generally do not pass value judgments on the linguistic forms and structures they are studying.

1.2 | Demonstration/discussion

Prescriptive and descriptive approaches to the study of language

In this section we will illustrate the contrast between various judgmental or "prescriptive" perspectives on language and the strictly descriptive take on linguistic phenomena which is the hallmark of academic linguistics. After the discussion of the examples, you will be able to more clearly understand the concerns of linguistics and distinguish them from other ways of analysing linguistic usage.

As a first illustration, consider the general American pronunciation of English, probably the most widely spoken and certainly the most widely heard accent in the world today. In comparison to British English, it is characterised by a number of well-established pronunciation features. Probably most salient among them is the fact that the <r> is pronounced wherever you find it in spelling (unlike British English, where <r> is silent if it follows a vowel). Thus, you hear an /r/ in the American pronunciation of words such as *water*, *car* or *hard*, whereas the <r> is silent in a British pronunciation. Also, the /t/ tends to be weakened in certain positions in American English, in particular between vowels if the first one is stressed (e. g. in words such as *water* or *Betty*). Trivial though these details of pronunciation may seem, they occasionally provoke strong negative reactions. Compare, for example, the following quotation from a letter written by American novelist Henry James (1843–1916):

> There are, you see, sounds of a mysterious and intrinsic meanness, and there are sounds of a mysterious intrinsic frankness and sweetness; and I think the recurrent note that I have indicated – fatherr and motherr and otherr, waterr and matterr and scatterr, harrd and barrd, parrt, starrt, and (dreadful to say) arrt (the repetition it is that drives home the ugliness), are signal specimens of what becomes of a custom of utterance out of which the principle of taste has dropped. (Henry James, "The Question of Our Speech," in *The Question of Our Speech/The Lesson of Balzac: Two Lectures*. Boston and New York 1905: 29)

Fig. 1.6 | Henry James, novelist (1843–1916)

This is an interesting example of linguistic self-hatred, as the famous novelist Henry James was an American by birth (even though he died a naturalised British subject).

The next quotation is not from a famous individual of the past but taken from the present and the World-Wide Web. It was posted by an instructional designer with a British background and shows that some of the prejudice voiced by Henry James has survived:

> How did the T become a D when in the middle of a word? I am a British lady and find this very annoying and hard to understand what was meant. For years I really thought that Nita Lowy's name was spelt NEDA! How do the students manage in dictation (or don't they have that in schools now). It affects everyone, as I just saw in print someone referring to Dr. Adkins, which would be the obvi-

ous spelling if one had only heard the word spoken and did not know that the correct spelling is Dr. Atkins. The sentence below gives an example of problems in understanding the spelling of certain words.

I am writing this as I hear it pronounced: Paddy and Neda attended the innerview and were congradulated on the recipe with the budder badder for the cake they cooked with their dada. (daughter).
(source: http://www.linguistlist.org/~ask-ling/archive-most-recent/msg02452.html)

This statement provides an illustration of the slight animosity which educated British speakers sometimes feel towards American speechways, probably because – as the people who got the language going – they resent the political, economic and cultural pre-eminence of the United States in the world today.

What would descriptive linguists make of the statement by Henry James? The answer is simple. They would dismiss it as a completely unfounded and subjective value judgment. Even worse, some linguists might add, is the fact that this type of negative judgment on linguistic forms usually masks contempt for the speakers who use them. This, they would argue, is socially detrimental, as it is unfair to judge people not by what they do but by how they speak. Historical linguists might point out that among the people who pronounced the /r/-s in this way was one William Shakespeare (1564–1616). The r-less pronunciations of words such as *father*, *mother* or *part* arose only in the 18th century among the lower classes of London and then took some time to become the general British standard.

In the "British lady's" pronouncement, the descriptive linguist would first point out that in the word *congradulated* as spelled here there is a mistake, because of course the stereotypical American would pronounce it as *congraduladed*. Whereas Henry James does not give any rational reasons for his dislike of the American accent, the British lady presents an argument: Americans do not distinguish between certain pairs of words, which makes their English difficult to understand and confusing. To this objection, the descriptive linguist would respond that for every instance in which two words are impossible to tell apart for accent reasons in American English there is at least one comparable case in British English. For example, the words *source* and *sauce* are clearly distinct in their pronunciation in American English but sound completely alike in British English. The reason, incidentally, is to be found precisely in the r-less pronunciation so much favoured by Henry James.

In real life, unlike constructed examples and jokes, the danger of misunderstandings resulting from the identical pronunciation of words with different meanings is, of course, minimal. If the topic of a conversation is urban problems in the United States and we hear *inner city*, we know from the context that we are talking about neglected city centres and do not even think of the theoretical alternative *inter-city*. If in a conversation in Britain somebody says [sɔːs] and the topic is food, we hear *sauce*, and not *source*.

Flapped /t/ in American English

What really might intrigue the descriptive linguist in the case of the American /t/ is the intricate set of rules which governs the weakening or "tapping"/"flapping" of the /t/. The latter terms are intended to capture the fact that in the American articulation of the sound the tip of the tongue just briefly taps or flaps against the palate (on which more will be said in Unit 2). As has been mentioned, such flapped or tapped /t/-s occur between vowels, **but only if the first one is stressed**. Thus we find them in *Italy*, but not in *Italian*, in *atom* (which sounds like *Adam*), but not in *atomic*, and so on. It occurs after /r/, as in *dirty*, *hurting*, and the /t/ disappears entirely after /n/, as in *enter* or *centre*, **but again only if the syllable preceding the /t/ is stressed**. This is why we would not get it in a word such as *entire*, which is stressed on the second syllable. Having been given so many clues, you can further hone your analytical skills as a budding descriptive linguist in Exercise 6 below.

Different definitions of language

Here, we shall return to the question raised at the very beginning – how to define language, the object of linguistic description. As has already been hinted at, it seems to be a much easier task to define linguistics than it is to define its object of study, human language and the diversity of languages – past and present – spoken in the world. To get a flavour of the diverse ways in which great thinkers in the field have approached the problem, consider the following proposals. Note that there is little overlap between the definitions, and that each emphasises a different aspect of the object to be defined:

> Language is a purely human and non-instinctive method of communicating ideas, emotions, and desires by means of a system of volitionally produced symbols. (Edward Sapir, *Language: An Introduction to the Study of Speech*. New York 1921: 8)

> From now on I will consider a language to be a set (finite or infinite) of sentences, each finite in length and constructed out of a finite set of elements. All natural languages in their spoken or written form are languages in this sense. […] Similarly, the set of 'sentences' of some formalized system of mathematics can be considered a language. (Noam Chomsky, *Syntactic Structures*. The Hague/Paris 1957: 13)

> The essence of speech is that one human being, by movements beginning at his diaphragm and involving various parts of his chest, throat, mouth and nasal passages, creates disturbances in the air around him, which within a certain distance from him have a perceptible effect on the ear-drums and through them on the brains of other people, and that the hearers can, if they belong to the same language community, respond to these disturbances, or noises, and find them meaningful. (R. H. Robins, *General Linguistics: An Introductory Survey*. London 1971: 77)

After reading through the three definitions, one might well start wondering whether they actually target the same phenomenon. Sapir's definition comes closest to our common-sense understanding; it emphasises the role of language as a tool for human communication, its symbolic character, and the fact that it is not an instinct or reflex but volitional and conscious. Chomsky's definition, by contrast, is much more narrow and technical, drawing an analogy between the grammar of a language and a mathematical algorithm; nothing is implied about the role of language in society and communication. Robins, finally, approaches language through the sound of speech, emphasising the physical and acoustic sides of the phenomenon and disregarding grammatical function and content.

In view of these various emphases, it is probably not a mistake to have an amateur have the final say. The following definition is by the famous 19th-century American poet and writer Walt Whitman (1819–1892):

> Language is not an abstract construction of the learned, or of dictionary-makers, but is something arising out of the work, needs, ties, joys, affections, tastes, of long generations of humanity, and has its bases broad and low, close to the ground. (Walt Whitman, "Slang in America," 1885)

Fig. 1.7
Walt Whitman
(1819–1892)

Before going on with our defining work, let us pause to consider what it means to "know" a language. It certainly means to be able to speak it fluently and to communicate effectively. In addition, our linguistic intuition ("Sprachgefühl") enables us to make finely grained judgments about nuances in meaning between alternative expressions or about the well-formedness of certain grammatical structures. Thus, an ordinary speaker of English knows with absolute certainty that both of the following sentences are possible utterances in his language:

Linguistic intuition and well-formedness

> Inflation more than merely tripled between 1973 and 1983.
> Inflation will more than merely triple over the next 20 years.

A German speaker, by contrast, will accept only one of the structurally analogous sentences:

> * Die Inflation mehr als nur verdreifachte sich zwischen 1973 und 1983.
> Die Inflation wird sich in den nächsten Jahren mehr als nur verdreifachen.

The *-sign is a widely used convention in linguistics. In synchronic linguistics it indicates that a construction or sentence is ungrammatical. In diachronic linguistics it signals that a form is assumed as a plausible reconstruction although direct evidence (for example in old texts) is missing.

Die Inflation verdreifachte sich zwischen 1973 und 1983, by itself, is a well-formed sentence. The problem thus is to find a place for the modification *mehr als nur*. The sentence given above does not work, and no amount of moving around the parts will make it work: **Die Inflation verdreifachte sich mehr als* nur, die Inflation mehr als verdreifachte sich nur, etc. On the other hand, any structure which has a form of *verdreifachen* in clause-final position is possible:

> Die Inflation hat sich in den letzten Jahren mehr als nur verdreifacht.
> Ich weiß, dass sich die Inflation alle hundert Jahre mehr als nur verdreifacht.

The complexity of language

This is a statement of the most important facts. At this stage in our introduction to linguistics we are not interested yet in a search for possible reasons. However, it is clear that the **rules** which are at work here are not those which are usually taught to foreign learners of English and German as part of their grammar teaching, nor are the sentences of the kind which children would practice massively in the early stages of natural language acquisition. In this sense, the example serves well to illustrate the enormous formal complexity of human languages.

This formal complexity is capable of expressing similarly complex meanings. While it is fairly easy to define the meaning of the verb *triple* ("increase threefold"), the combination *more than triple* raises a problem. Theoretically, this expression covers anything from "increase a little more than three-fold" to "increase a hundred-fold" and beyond. In a natural communicative situation, however, we are very likely to assume that we are talking about an increase which is between three-fold and four-fold. Why? The adverb *merely*, in its turn, introduces another nuance, namely that the increase was less than expected under the circumstances. In other words, it signals the speaker's attitude towards the event reported.

A working definition of language

After this exercise in consciousness-raising, we can now return to the initial question and name a number of features which must figure in any definition of language. Together they make up a good composite working definition of what a human language is.

1) New-born human beings have a genetic or natural predisposition to acquire a language (or languages) spoken in their communities. They are rather free to decide on what occasions and for what purposes they use language (which is an important contrast to many more instinct-based communication systems prevalent among animal populations).

2) Human languages represent meaning symbolically. The relationship between the sound of a word and the concept it denotes is thus arbitrary, as is easily shown by the following words used to denote the concept "bread":

   ekmek (Turkish), *Brot* (German), *pane* (Italian)

3) Words are combined into larger constructions by rules which are language-specific conventions. German *es wurde gesungen und getanzt* expresses roughly the same idea as English *there was singing and dancing*. It is not possible to re-create the German structure in English or vice versa.

4) Human languages are sound-based. For a small number of the world's c. 5,000 languages writing systems have been developed. Deaf people are capable of expressing themselves through signing.

While, as has been hinted at, several animal species have developed very complex systems of communication, the above-named features in their combination ensure that language is a uniquely human achievement. Animals may be able to communicate warnings or directions to their fellows, but only human beings use languages for complex reasoning, to talk about alternative worlds or possible behaviour, or to systematically lie and deceive.

Problems and challenges | 1.3

In Section 1.2 above we had a look at how people developed negative attitudes towards particular ways of pronouncing the English language. Of course, this problem is not restricted to matters of pronunciation. Similar responses are occasionally aroused by grammatical constructions, as well. Again, the linguistic details in question are trivial, but the social consequences may be considerable. This section will introduce you to the use of computerised **language corpora**, i.e. textual data-bases which have been compiled for the purposes of linguistic research. Such corpora are a relatively recent innovation in linguistics. They are powerful tools, not the least of their advantages being that they allow students to gain hands-on research experience very early on in their coursework.

Corpora and the study of language

Consider the following extract from a play by the renowned British dramatist Tom Stoppard (b. 1937):

> Max: [...] if you don't mind me saying so.
> Henry: *My* saying, Max.
> *Max gets up and wants to leave*
> Henry: I'm sorry, but it actually *hurts*.
> (source: Tom Stoppard, *The Real Thing*. London 1983: 34)

Without going too deeply into the details of grammatical analysis at this stage, let us state the problem. Max uses the verb *mind* followed by a pronoun in the object form followed by the participle of the verb. In present-day English, there are numerous instances of this pattern: *I found him reading, I caught them napping*, etc. Henry resents the usage, insisting on a supposedly correct alternative: the verb *mind*, followed by a verbal noun (or gerund) which is modified by the possessive pronoun. Again, there are numerous instances of this pattern: *I hate his singing, I am tired of your complaining*, etc. Max is offended because his partner in conversation comments on the outer form of his utterance rather than the message. This is impolite. As the following examples show, the plain grammatical facts are somewhat in favour of Max. In most cases, both variants are possible, and if only one works, it is in fact Max's and not Henry's:

> She doesn't mind his smoking during lunch.
> She doesn't mind him smoking during lunch.
>
> She doesn't object to Peter's smoking during lunch.
> She doesn't object to Peter smoking during lunch.
>
> ?? Who would have dreamed of such a thing's happening a year ago?
> Who would have dreamed of such a thing happening a year ago?
>
> I can tell you that I'm not looking forward to this happening again.
> * I can tell you that I'm not looking forward to this's happening again.

There just is no genitive or possessive case for the demonstrative pronoun *this*, and the genitive is a rather unusual choice for a noun denoting a lifeless object such as *thing*. In other cases, the contrast is neutralised, because a form such as *her* functions both as object case and as a possessive:

> Nobody objects to her smoking after lunch.

It is in such instances of divided usage that corpora are useful. The British National Corpus (BNC) is an up-to-date database comprising the unbelievable amount of almost 100 million words of running text covering a wide variety of written and spoken genres (see Fig. 1.8).

Mark Davies, of Brigham Young University (Provo, UT, USA), makes this material available in a very user-friendly format at his BNC View homepage (http://corpus.byu.edu/bnc/). For the construction at issue here a search for "mind him" produces 35 hits, of which 14 illustrate the construction under study:

> "Don't you <u>mind him</u> stealing your father's eggs?"
> Therefore I don't <u>mind him</u> hearing the very worst about my past.
> She didn't <u>mind him</u> telling her things, and learned very quickly.
> Diana, Barry's wife of 35 years, doesn't <u>mind him</u> meeting all the great screen goddesses.
> I wouldn't <u>mind him</u> being Heathcliff's son, if only he loved her and could be a good husband to her."
> If he did not know that, I do not <u>mind him</u> admitting it, but it is extraordinary ignorance on his part.
> I wouldn't <u>mind him</u> sitting on top of my Christmas tree," said either Dosh or Freddie.
> The Guardian also says Shearer twisted an ankle avoiding a lunge from Carl Bradshaw on Sat and may miss their game with Pompey on Wednesday, I wouldn't <u>mind him</u> missing sundays game.
> Apparently, she did not <u>mind him</u> being a mop head when occupying other Government positions, but felt it would not be fitting for the role of Chancellor.

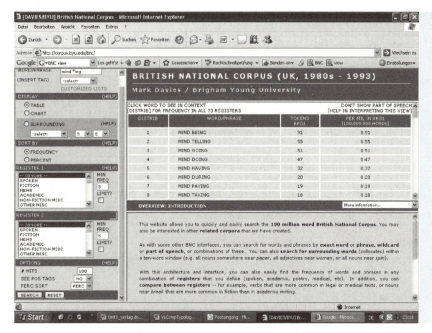

Fig. 1.8
BNC Screenshot – search for *mind* + *VERBing* through the "BNC View" website

ignore her and er <pause> pop next door and <pause> I mean I don't <u>mind him</u> popping out as long as he's

Well, I don't <u>mind him</u> walking across that bit but <pause>

Actually, I don't really mi-- <u>mind him</u> looking after me, he's very good!

Did you <u>mind him</u> going over there, staying over there?

he didn't <u>mind him</u> speaking and as soon as <name> yeah right then he said I'm not I'm not telling <unclear>

Henry's desired alternative occurs less often, a mere six times:

Gullit, of course, is injured and there are still fears for his playing career, never <u>mind his</u> appearing in Italy.

Never <u>mind his</u> scrummaging, or doubts about his fitness round the park, he was worth his ticket for his line-out work.

But I didn't <u>mind his</u> thinking it, his sudden flattering benignity.

No, she didn't <u>mind his</u> ringing so late.

She wanted to tell him they didn't <u>mind his</u> being there, it didn't matter, he wasn't trespassing.

Why did she <u>mind his</u> being hurt so much?

Corpus examples illustrate what we know and have suspected all along. In addition, they alert us to determinants of variation which we have not considered. Note, for example, that the expression *never mind his* + *VERB-ing* occurs twice, whereas *never mind him* + *VERB-ing* is not attested. Is this latter form impossible, or is its absence from the British National Corpus accidental? This would be a question worth further corpus-based inquiry.

Another promising avenue of research would be to tabulate the origins of the various quotations. Are they from written texts – and hence formal? From spontaneous conversations – and hence informal? Systematic study will help us answer these questions – and others which will arise in the course of the work. At the end of our research, we will be in a position to offer a well-documented and comprehensive description of current usage.

References and further reading

Chomsky, Noam. 1957. *Syntactic structures*. The Hague/Paris: Mouton.
Oxford English Dictionary. Second edition. Ed. by **John Simpson** and **Edmund Weiner**. Oxford: OUP. ⟨http://dictionary.oed.com/entrance.dtl⟩
Robins, R. H. 1971. *General linguistics: An introductory survey*. London: Longman.
Sapir, Edward. 1921. *Language: An introduction to the study of speech*. New York: Harcourt, Brace and Comp.

There are numerous introductions to linguistics aimed at student and academic audiences. For a work which has long been in successful use internationally see:

Yule, George. 2006. *The study of language: An introduction*. 6th ed. Cambridge: Cambridge University Press.

For a work geared to the needs of a German-speaking readership and focussed on English compare:

Bieswanger, Markus, and Annette Becker. 2008. *Introduction to English linguistics*. 2nd ed. Tübingen: Francke.
Kortmann, Bernd. 2005. *English linguistics: Essentials*. Berlin: Cornelsen.

In addition, there are numerous books on language, languages, and the English language in particular which are addressed to a non-expert readership. Many of them do not even pretend to objectivity but represent their authors' personal prescriptive agenda. For a point of view which is presented forcefully, and not without entertainment value, but would be considered as plain reactionary by most linguists, compare:

Amis, Kingsley. 1997. *The King's English: a guide to modern usage*. London: Harper-Collins.
  [Kingsley Amis (1922–1995) was a major 20th century English novelist.]

A popular treatment which professional linguists would sneer at because it is sometimes rather superficial is:

Bryson, Bill. 1990. *Mother tongue: the English language*. London: Hamish Hamilton.

Popular treatments which aim high intellectually and successfully combine expert knowledge, clear exposition and a broad inter-disciplinary horizon are:

Crystal, David. 2003. *The Cambridge encyclopedia of the English language*. 2nd ed. Cambridge: CUP.
Pinker, Steven. 1994. *The language instinct: how the mind creates language*. New York NY: Morrow.

Practice

|1.4

1. Consider the meaning of the word *language* in the following expressions and paraphrase it in such a way as to bring out the contrasting usages clearly:

   Example:

   The language of the British press has changed considerably over the past few decades.

   The word *language* here denotes a specific way or style of using the English language in a particular written genre.

   Language is what distinguishes human beings from apes.
   She teaches sign language in a school for the deaf.
   Sally can conduct fluent conversations in at least four languages.
   Watch your language, kid!
   As a teacher I sometimes feel that the children speak a completely different language from me.
   Lëtzebuergesch used to be a dialect of German but has been one of the three official languages of Luxemburg since 1984.
   Who was the guy who got the Nobel Prize for decoding the language of the bees?
   If you know how to read the language of graffiti, they tell you a lot about life in the city.

2. Why did the instructional designer quoted in Section 1.2 above refer to herself as *a British lady* rather than *a British woman* or an *Englishwoman*? What are the differences in meaning between the words *lady* and *woman* in present-day English?

   a) As a first step, note down your intuitions about – say – the contrast between *Ask the lady over there* and *Ask the woman over there*.
   b) Discuss your intuitions with a native speaker of English and consult entries for *woman* and *lady* in a dictionary of your choice.
   c) Collect a largish number of authentic uses of the two words from corpora and discuss the material.

3. To prove the point made above that knowledge of language history (diachrony) is irrelevant to the working of language as a structured system (synchrony), look up the words *woman* and *lady* in the *Oxford English Dictionary* (OED). This is the largest and most comprehensive dictionary ever produced for any language. It occupies almost two metres of shelf-space in its printed version, and is likely to be on hand in your departmental or university library. Alternatively, if your institution has a subscription, you may check the regularly updated online version (http://dictionary.oed.com/entrance.dtl). One special feature of the OED is that it charts the history of English words beginning with the first attested uses and through all subsequent expansions and changes of meaning. What do the entries for *woman* and *lady* say about the earliest meanings of the words? Is this knowledge useful in any way?

4   Consult a native speaker of English about his or her response to the following forms:

> We don't need no education.
> Hopefully, the war will soon be ended.
> Let me assure you that I am not actuated by mercenary considerations.
> Had I in the least surmised that it was her husband's rash purchase of an expensive automobile that she was going on about I would have told her to shut up and get her act together.

5   Return to the "Platonic" problem of the appropriateness of the name to the thing and consider it in the light of the following data:

1) The conventional representations of the sound of a sneeze are *hatschi* in German, *atishoo/atchoo* in British English, and *ah-choo* in American English.
2) The conventional representations for a cock crowing are *kikeriki* in German, *chicherichi* in Italian, *cocorico* in French, *cock-a-doodle-doo* in English, *kukuriku* in Russian, *kokekoko* in Japanese, and *kong-shi* in Chinese.

6   Indicate which of the following /t/-s are candidates for flapping in American English.

> quantum physics, quantity, quantitative, quantitatively
> I go to school every day
> If he goes, I go too

7   Consulting linguistic corpora

This is a brief extract from a conversation among working class speakers from Central Northern England (source: BNC KB1 4334ff.).

Corrinne	She's not interested.
Albert	No.
	I think she'll be married shortly.
June	I can see her marrying him.
Corrinne	<unclear>
June	Yeah.
	But he's one of them lads where she'll never have owt, cos he don't do, he won't bloody work will he?
Corrinne	Well he's doing taxis.

And this is an extract from a scientific paper included in the Freiburg-Lancaster-Oslo/Bergen (F-LOB) corpus of written British English (text J 09):

> In a recent paper (Kemball-Cook *et al.*, 1990), we demonstrated a modified sodium dodecyl sulphate polyacrylamide gel electrophoresis (SDS-PAGE) method for visualization of factor VIII heavy chain (FVIII HC) polypeptides. This approach, based on that first described by Weinstein *et al.* (1981) enables

FVIII structure to be studied in a wide range of samples without further purification. We have therefore used this technique to study the proteolytic breakdown of FVIII HC in plasma and concentrates when exposed to a range of coagulation enzymes.

Which text is easier to understand, and why?

8   As you have worked hard, it is time for some relief. "What the writers say" is an occasional feature in this book highlighting some of the more bizarre and unexpected ways in which linguistics figures in English literature. The passage quoted below is from a novel by Anthony Burgess (1917–1993). Edwin is a professional linguist who all of a sudden finds himself in a psychiatric hospital and has to explain his job ...

Text 1.1
Anthony Burgess, *The Doctor is Sick*, Penguin ed., 15

What the writers say

"Let's sit down, shall we," said Charlie, and Edwin, feeling that he was a bad host, led his visitors over to his bed. "Now," said Charlie, "what is it your wife here says that you do?"

"Linguistics."

"Aha." The three of them sat, leg-swinging, on the bed. "I've never heard of it," said Charlie, "and that's a fact. Mind you, I'm not saying that there's no such thing, but no mention of it has ever come my way before."

"Oh," said Edwin, "it does exist."

"That's as may be, but, if it does exist, it'll be above the heads of people like me and her." He jerked his head towards Sheila. "Me, I clean windows. Anybody can understand what that is, and you don't get put into places like this [the hospital ward] if you do a job like that. Mind you, you can get put into a hospital, if you're a window-cleaner, but not into a hospital like this one, because window-cleaning doesn't affect the brain."

Having worked your way through Unit 1, could you do a better job than Edwin at explaining what linguistics is about?

Unit 2

Phonetics and phonology – the sounds of speech

Orientation | 2.1

Sounds and letters: the need for a phonetic alphabet | 2.1.1

In the linguistic analysis of the sounds of spoken language, beginners usually have to make a conscious effort to break the mould of spelling, particularly in a language such as English, in which there is such an obvious discrepancy between orthography and pronunciation. Of course, there is a correspondence between letters, the graphic signs of writing, and the sounds articulated in pronunciation. For example, the letter <p> fairly regularly corresponds to a particular sound, and so do most other **consonants** (that is sounds which usually cannot form the nucleus of a syllable, see p. 29). However, there are irregularities even here in this simple case: for example, the <p> is silent in the words *psychology* or *pneumonia*. The correspondences between sound and spelling are much more complex for most **vowels** (that is sounds which usually form the nucleus of a syllable). For example, the words *people*, *beat*, *seed* and *perceive* all have the same vowel [iː], but it is spelled in four different ways. If two vowels are pronounced together, we have **diphthongs**. The correspondence between sound and spelling is similarly complex for English diphthongs. The three words *pair*, *pare* and *pear*, for example, have the same diphthong [ɛə], which however is spelled in three different ways depending on the meaning.

This list could easily be extended – and might culminate in asking whether *fish* could not equally well be written *ghoti*: *gh* as in *laugh*, *o* as in *women*, and *ti* as in *nation* (a witticism probably wrongly attributed to the famous dramatist and campaigner for spelling reform George Bernard Shaw (1856–1950)).

Clearly, before embarking on the serious study of speech sounds, we have to get rid of the complexities caused by the spelling system, which – in English as in most other languages with a long writing tradition – is the result of a historical evolution and often rather arbitrary when seen from a synchronic perspective. The problem was recognised by the pioneer **phoneticians** (a word derived from the Greek word for "sound" and describing linguists studying speech sounds) of the 19th century. To put the study of speech sounds on a firm footing, the International Phonetic Association (IPA), founded in 1886 and thus one of the oldest professional associations in linguistics, developed a phonetic alphabet designed to enable linguists to unambiguously **transcribe** the sounds of all human languages. Used in this sense, to transcribe means

The difficult relationship between spelling and pronunciation

| Fig. 2.1
George Bernard Shaw (1856–1950), writer, social activist and spelling reformer

Transcription and the phonetic alphabet

not just to write but to really represent the spoken language on the written or printed page.

Vowels and consonants

As has already been hinted at, the two major classes of speech sounds are vowels and consonants. In order to produce the different vowels, we position our speech organs in certain specified ways but we do not block the air-stream by causing friction or complete closure. If we block the air-stream in some way, the result is a consonant. The IPA transcription symbols for vowels and consonants are represented in Figures 2.2 and 2.3 respectively. Since this **phonetic alphabet** is designed to capture the sounds of all languages of the world, or all the possible speech sounds which human beings can produce, it contains many more symbols than the student of English has need for. Therefore, you need not be intimidated by the complexity of the symbols. To the extent that they are relevant for English, they will be explained in further detail below.

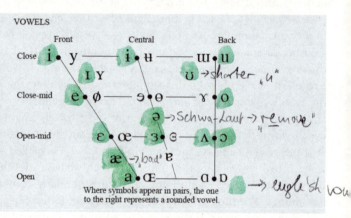

Fig. 2.2 | IPA symbols for vowels

In this diagram, [i] figures as a "close and front" vowel because it is articulated in the front of the mouth and with the front part of the tongue close to the palate. The vowel [ɑ], by contrast, is a "back and open" vowel because it is articulated at the back of the mouth, with the tongue lowered (more on these physiological details below).

Fig. 2.3 | IPA symbols for consonants

THE INTERNATIONAL PHONETIC ALPHABET (revised to 2005)

CONSONANTS (PULMONIC) © 2005 IPA

	Bilabial	Labiodental	Dental	Alveolar	Postalveolar	Retroflex	Palatal	Velar	Uvular	Pharyngeal	Glottal
Plosive	p b			t d		ʈ ɖ	c ɟ	k g	q ɢ		ʔ
Nasal	m	ɱ		n		ɳ	ɲ	ŋ	ɴ		
Trill	ʙ			r					ʀ		
Tap or Flap		ⱱ		ɾ		ɽ					
Fricative	ɸ β	f v	θ ð	s z	ʃ ʒ	ʂ ʐ	ç ʝ	x ɣ	χ ʁ	ħ ʕ	h ɦ
Lateral fricative				ɬ ɮ							
Approximant		ʋ		ɹ		ɻ	j	ɰ			
Lateral approximant				l		ɭ	ʎ	ʟ			

Where symbols appear in pairs, the one to the right represents a voiced consonant. Shaded areas denote articulations judged impossible.

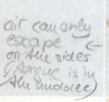

22

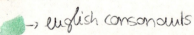

Orientation

Unit 2

To facilitate comprehension of this complex diagram, these are the consonants needed for the transcription of Standard British English. In addition to the IPA categories, the following Table also lists **affricates**, which occur when a plosive consonant, e.g. [t], merges with the fricative, e.g. [ʃ], produced in the same place of articulation.

plosives (or stops)	p, b, t, d, k, g
affricates	tʃ, dʒ
fricatives	f, v, θ, ð, s, z, ʃ, ʒ
nasals	m, n, ŋ
other	l, r, j, w, h

Table 2.1
List of English consonants

The terms appearing in the horizontal axis of the IPA chart (s. Fig. 2.3) – from "bilabial" to "glottal" – refer to the **place of articulation**, the terms appearing in the vertical axis – from "plosive" to "lateral approximant" – refer to the **mode of articulation**. They will be explained further below. The term *pulmonic* means that an air-stream exhaled from the lungs is involved in their production. This is the statistically normal case in all languages, and most languages in the world have only pulmonic consonants. (The best-known examples of non-pulmonic consonants are the click sounds of the South African Khoisan languages, for which the air-stream is started by a downward movement of the tongue. They have been popularised by South African singer Miriam Makeba's "Click Song," available from several web-sources, for example YouTube (http://www.youtube.com/watch?v=OHxkiXALQjU).

Beginning students are frequently overwhelmed by the complexity of the phonetic alphabet and fail to see the relevance of this degree of detail for their studies. However, the connection to everyday life is real enough. Just pronounce the German word *viel* and use this pronunciation for the English word *feel*. You will immediately hear that it does not sound right, and the reason is simply that in German we have a clear or "palatal" [l], whereas in English in this position the [ɫ] is dark or velar. Similarly, you can pronounce the German loanword *crashen* the German way – as in *das Auto ist in die Wand gecrasht* –, and you see that a German [kr] sounds very different from an English one.

2.1.2 Sounds as sounds, and sounds as elements of linguistic systems: from phonetics to phonology

The aim of **phonetics** is a precise description of the sounds of human languages from three perspectives:

- **articulatory** (how are they formed in the mouth, the glottis and the nasal cavity?)

Phonetics – the physiological and physical attributes of sounds

- **acoustic** (what are they like when measured while travelling through the air?), and
- **auditory** (how are they perceived by the listener?)

In phonetics, sounds are described for their own sake and in their own terms. Factors such as meaning and grammar are not relevant.

From among the three perspectives named in the above paragraph, it is the articulatory one that provides the most useful starting point. Figure 2.4 below represents the parts of the human body which play a role in the production of sounds.

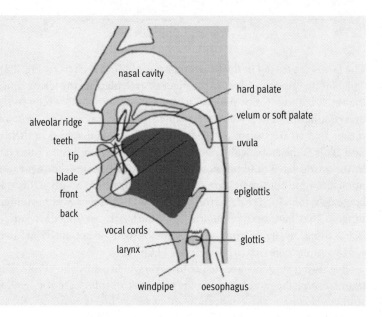

Fig. 2.4 | The human articulatory apparatus (source: www.universalteacher.org.uk)

The production of vowels

The single most important factor in the articulation of vowels is the position of the tongue in the mouth, schematically represented in the **vowel quadrilateral** shown in Figure 2.2 above. To properly "read" this figure, you imagine a cross section of a human mouth looking to the left, with the teeth and the lips being at the "front," and the velum being at the "back." In an open mouth, the tongue obviously occupies positions ranging from "close" to the palate to "open" (i.e. maximally lowered). This is why we distinguish front vowels from back vowels (depending on whether the front or the back of the tongue is involved in their articulation) and high (or close) vowels from low (or open) vowels (depending on whether the tongue is raised or not). The vowel [i], which – as can be seen – occupies the top left end of the quadrilateral, is a "front high" vowel because it is created by raising the tip of the tongue as high as possible.

Unlike consonants, where we can usually tell pretty clearly whether we have a [p] or a [t], transitions between the different vowels are smooth and gradual.

By convention and for better orientation, the most extreme or typical realisations of the various positions are referred to as **cardinal vowels**. For example, if we raise the front end of the tongue as high as possible, the result would be the cardinal vowel [i], which is in fact pretty close to the English long [i:] that we find in words such as *beat* and *seed*. The central vowel /ə/ requires least effort, because the mouth is relaxed and open, and the tongue remains in neutral position. This is why this particular vowel is very frequent in unstressed words and syllables. In the phrase *for the painter*, we would get it in [fə], [ðə] and the second syllable of *painter* ([peɪntə]). If we lower our tongue as far as possible, the result is "ah" ([ɑ]), which is why patients are encouraged to produce this sound for medical examinations in which the doctor wants to have a look "all the way down." Diphthongs are produced by movements of the tongue from the starting point to the end point, for example from [ə] to [ʊ] in [əʊ]. (Vowel sounds such as [ʊ] or [i:] which consist of just one element are also called **monophthongs**.)

Secondary factors which have an impact on vowel quality are lip rounding and nasality. The contrast between English *earl* and German *Öl*, for example, is due to the fact that this particular central long vowel [ɜ:] is produced without lip-rounding in English but not in German. If the velum is lowered during articulation and a part of the air-stream thus allowed to escape through the nose, the result is a nasal vowel. Such nasal vowels are rare in English except in loanwords from languages such as French, which have them.

For consonants, the crucial three dimensions are:

- **place of articulation** (i.e. which parts of the mouth are involved in obstructing the air-stream)
- **manner of articulation** (i.e. is the obstruction total, that is a brief stop, or partial, that is some kind of friction), and
- **voicing** (i.e. do the vocal cords vibrate during articulation, as they do in voiced consonants or vowels, or do they not vibrate, as they do in voiceless consonants).

The production of consonants

With these hints it is now possible to return to the IPA symbols presented in Figure 2.3 above and read the diagram with an understanding of the principles underlying it. The possible places of articulation are given in anatomical order from left to right, as in the vowel quadrilateral, starting with the lips and ending with the glottis. A bilabial consonant is, thus, a consonant which is produced by some obstruction caused by both lips. A palatal consonant is produced by an obstruction caused by the tongue and the palate, and so forth. The various manners of articulation are listed from top to bottom, from the strongest to the weakest. Thus, "plosives" are produced by blocking the air-stream completely for a brief period. Fricatives are produced by partially obstructing the air-stream, and approximants, finally, are produced without audible friction. Just as the simple vowel quadrilateral in Figure 2.2 does not represent diphthongs, the consonant chart does not indicate various types of "mixed" manners of articulation, such as the very common combination of a plosive and the corresponding fricative (as in [tʃ] or [dʒ]).

The limit(ation)s of the phonetic approach

The phonetic approach to the sounds of speech raises an interesting problem. The more refined our instruments of analysis are, the more sounds we can distinguish. This is – satirically – pointed out in George Bernard Shaw's play *Pygmalion* (first performed in 1913). Pygmalion is a mythical sculptor who is said to have carved the woman of his dreams in ivory and was rewarded for his labour by the Goddess Venus breathing life into the statue. This motif is transferred to contemporary England. In the play, it is Professor Higgins, practitioner of the then new science of sounds, who wants to transform the Cockney flower-girl Eliza Doolittle into his feminine ideal by training her to speak like a lady. This is bound to go hilariously wrong, as the change of accent does not go hand in hand with a change of Eliza's sturdy East London proletarian attitudes. The play subsequently inspired a highly successful musical and movie (*My Fair Lady*). The character of Professor Higgins was apparently inspired by the real-life figure of Henry Sweet (1845–1912), pioneer linguist and phonetician.

Fig. 2.5 Henry Sweet (1845–1912)

Here is Prof. Higgins, talking to his associate Pickering:

Text 2.1 George Bernard Shaw, *Pygmalion* (1913)

Prof. Higgins: Tired of listening to sounds?
Pickering: Yes, it's a fearful strain. I rather fancied myself because I can pronounce twenty-four distinct vowel sounds, but your 130 beat me. I can't hear the difference between most of them.
Prof. Higgins: Oh, that comes with practice. You hear no difference at first; but you keep on listening, and presently … they're all as different as A from B.

Higgins' argument is convincing, but it nevertheless goes against a deep-seated intuition we have about sounds. If we ask a speaker of English how many sounds there are in his language, we won't usually get a precise answer, but most people will settle on a figure in the range between 20 and 50. Claims that English or any other language might have 130 different vowels would be met with disbelief.

Important and less important attributes of speech sounds

Let us explore this intuition on the basis of an example. A phonetic analysis of the English sound [k], for example, shows that there are several different realisations of this consonant in English words. As you can easily hear by speaking the words aloud, the [k] in *cool* or *crude* is rather different from the [k] in *kiss*. Putting the former into the place of the latter, or the other way round, makes the words sound funny indeed. By consulting the IPA chart, we can even pinpoint the source of this difference: it is largely a matter of the place of articulation. In front of a palatal or "front" vowel such as the [ɪ] in *kiss*, the place of articulation of the [k] is pulled forward a little, to make articulation easier. In extreme cases, we might even think about transcribing the result of this fronting by using the [c]-symbol of the IPA alphabet.

Coming back to our initial question – namely how many sounds there are in a language –, how can we reconcile such facts with our intuition that in spite of these differences in articulation there is just one *k*-sound in English? The solution to this apparent paradox requires a change of perspective – from **phonetics**, the self-contained study of speech sounds, to **phonology**, the study of speech sounds seen as basic units in a structural system.

In human languages, the basic function of sounds is to help us distinguish meanings. Which of the many possible contrasts between sounds are used for this purpose differs considerably across languages. The branch of linguistics concerned with the study of sounds as elements in such language-specific sound systems is called phonology. Any element in such a system which serves to distinguish between meanings is called a **phoneme**. To find out the phonemes of a particular language, we need to look for **minimal pairs**, pairs of words which differ in exactly one sound and in their meaning. The following minimal pairs, for example, show that the voiceless plosive consonants of English ([p],[t],[k]) are phonemes.

Sounds as basic units of phonological systems

pack	–	back
pack	–	sack
cap	–	cab
town	–	down
done	–	sun
rude	–	root
crane	–	grain
rack	–	rag
bicker	–	bigger

Table 2.2
Minimal pairs

Each pair of words conveys two distinct meanings, and each pair is distinguished by exactly one sound – no more and no less. Never mind how different the spellings are: *write* and *right* would not qualify as minimal pairs; they are different in meaning but pronounced exactly alike. *Pack* and *bag* are not minimal pairs, either; they are distinct in meaning but differ in two sounds rather than one.

The phonetically distinct kinds of [k] which we distinguished above will never show up in minimal pairs of this kind because, at least within the sound system of present-day English, they are in **complementary distribution**. That is: where one **allophone** (or realisational variant), for example, the back or velar one, occurs, the other one (in our case the front or palatal one) is ruled out. If we put a velar [k] into a palatal environment such as *kin* or *kid*, the result is a funny accent but never a confusion about meanings. This is not to say

Complementary distribution

that such distinctions cannot be phonemic in languages other than English. Arabic, for instance, distinguishes between a velar /k/ and uvular /q/ plosive phoneme.

Phonetic and phonemic levels of transcription

In the linguistic study of sounds it is therefore essential to make clear which level of description is intended. The following conventions are widely accepted in writing on phonetics and phonology (and have thus far been used in the present book without explicit explanation). Orthographic signs (or letters) are represented in angled brackets (e. g. <p>), sounds viewed as phonemes between slashes (/p/), and sounds viewed phonetically between square brackets ([p]). Phonemic or broad transcriptions confine themselves to the phonemically relevant contrasts and are therefore relatively simple to read. Phonetic or narrow transcriptions, by contrast, can be enriched with large amounts of detail and therefore often appear very complex by comparison. For example, the unitary English phoneme /t/ has several positional allophones varying in degree of aspiration. This comes out if we place narrow and broad transcriptions of the following words alongside each other:

tin	[tʰɪn]	/tɪn/
neat	[niːt]	/niːt/

The raised little *h* in the narrow transcription of *tin* indicates that this sound is articulated with "aspiration," that is a greater degree of force, at the beginning of a syllable but not at the end. You can test this easily by holding a sheet of paper in front of your lips and then pronouncing the two words *tin* and *neat* in succession. The paper should blow away when you pronounce *tin*, but not move after *neat*.

Similarly, /r/ is a phoneme in all varieties of English. However, its phonetic realisations and distribution differ across varieties. British English Received Pronunciation (R. P.) has [ɪ], American English a more retroflex (tip of the tongue curled backwards slightly), and Scottish English even has an apical or trilled [r].

2.1.3 | Stress, pitch, intonation – phonetics and phonology beyond the individual sound

So far the discussion in this Unit has centred on individual speech sounds, which have been approached either from a phonetic or from a phonological perspective. But even an introduction must at least briefly mention the **supra-segmental** domain, that is all those many interesting phenomena which extend beyond the single segment in the sound chain.

Phonotactics – which sounds can combine with which others?

The sounds of a language do not occur in any possible sequence or combination. There are clear language-specific constraints that regulate which sounds can occur in which position in the word or syllable. The study of such constraints is the domain of **phonotactics**. For example, an initial cluster of

/ʃn/ is a common occurrence in German (*Schneider, Schnitzel, schnell,* …), but most unusual in English. The reverse holds for /sn/ (as in *sneak, snail, snow,* …).

Languages differ considerably with regard to which syllable structures they allow or prefer. If we use the symbol C to refer to any consonant, and V to refer to any vowel or diphthong, the structure of the very simple syllable *go* could be represented as CV. Compared to many other languages in the world, English allows very complex clusterings of consonants syllable-initially and finally – for example syllables of the abstract pattern CCCVCCC or, if we allow grammatical endings such as the plural *s*, even CCCVCCCC, as in *strengths*. However, the type of consonant admissible in such clusters and the order in which they are arranged is severely restricted. While the syllable-initial sequence /str-/ is common, /tsr-/ or /rts-/ are not.

Another important supra-segmental phenomenon is **word stress**. Every English word of more than one syllable has at least one main stress, indicated by ' in the transcription. The word *graphical*, for instance, has a stressed first syllable and two unstressed syllables following it: ['græfɪk(ə)l].

Word and sentence stress

The word *photograph*, on the other hand, has a stressed syllable at the beginning but the last syllable is not entirely unstressed: it bears a secondary stress, indicated in the transcription by ˌ ['fəʊtəˌgrɑːf].

The placement of word stress in present-day English is extremely complicated. Owing to a history of extensive language contact, the English language contains elements of three partially incompatible stress systems today, a Germanic one which usually favours stress on the root syllable (in practice often the initial syllable), a French one which calls for accent on the final syllable (*de'scend*), and one influenced by the movable stress of Latin and Greek (e. g. *'photograph, pho'tographer, photo'graphical*). Note that over time many borrowed words from French and the classical languages have adopted "Germanic" initial stress (e. g. *nature, category*), and some are variable (e. g. *address, garage*).

In addition to word-stress, there is, of course, also **sentence stress**. Sentence stress is best treated together with **intonation** as both interact in highlighting important content in an utterance. In spite of its immense importance to the spoken language, linguists have not yet been able to agree on a generally accepted notational system comparable to the IPA symbols used for the individual sound segments. But in principle the basic **intonational unit** is structured around a stressed nucleus on which a pitch movement occurs (spelled in capitals in the following example), a pre-nuclear onset, and a coda. In the most neutral reading of the following sentence, *friend* is the nucleus, showing a falling intonation, *he's your* is the onset and *then* the coda:

Intonation

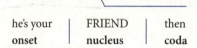

he's your	FRIEND	then
onset	nucleus	coda

In an appropriate context, for example if we want to emphasise that the person in question is *your* friend rather than someone else's, the nucleus can, of course, shift back to *your*, and *friend then* together will be the coda.

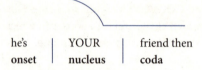

he's	YOUR	friend then
onset	nucleus	coda

In yet another context, even the very first word of the tone-group might receive stress: *HE's your friend then*.

Full and weak forms

Note in this connection that words such as articles, prepositions, conjunctions and pronouns (i. e. all words which have primarily grammatical function) are usually unstressed in connected speech. Our example contains two relevant items – the auxiliary verb *is* and the possessive pronoun *your*. In our example, the word *is*, which would be pronounced [ɪz] in isolation, is reduced to [z]. Other possible reduced pronunciations encountered in connected speech are [s] (after voiceless consonants) or [əz]. *Your* is pronounced as [jʊə] or [jɔː] in isolation in British English. The most common American pronunciation is [jɔr]. These are also the pronunciations which will be used in connected speech, if the word is stressed. In other instances, however, [jə] would be expected. The reduced pronunciations of such grammatical words are also known as **weak forms**. Many of them contain the vowel [ə], which also happens to be the only English vowel which does not occur in stressed syllables.

Assimilation

A final phenomenon worth mentioning on the supra-segmental level is **assimilation**, the influence exercised by one sound on the articulation of another one occurring in close proximity. This is also a phenomenon characteristic of rapid and colloquial speech. Our example *he's your friend*, for instance, might be pronounced as [hɪʒə frend], with the two separate segments [z] and [j] merging into [ʒ]. As the IPA chart in Fig. 2.3 shows, the postalveolar fricative [ʒ] is a good compromise between the alveolar [z] and the palatal [j].

2.2 | Demonstration/discussion

"Foreign" accent as a learner problem

For students of English, phonetics and phonology will become an academic pursuit and thus an aim in itself only in a minority of cases. A basic knowledge of the field is, however, essential for every student as it affects two issues central in any undergraduate course in English. First, accent and pronunciation are what distinguishes speakers of different varieties of English most comprehensively and far more systematically than lexical or grammatical peculiarities. The phonetic characteristics of the major varieties of English will therefore feature prominently in the relevant portions of Unit 11. Secondly, accent, or more precisely a foreign accent, is also a major problem at all levels of competence in foreign language learning. Of course studying a contrastive description of the sound systems of English and German will not make a student learner's accent go away, but it is a helpful first step in diagnosing one's level of competence and in raising one's awareness about what still remains to be practiced. For the language teacher, an understanding of the linguistic mechanisms responsible for a foreign accent is helpful for designing appropriate teaching materials and strategies for various groups of learners.

In this spirit, consider the following list of the phonemes of English (British Received Pronunciation = R. P.) and German. Here are the consonantal phonemes, represented by their IPA symbols except for the German palatal-velar fricative – <ch> in spelling –, which is not represented by a unitary symbol but by its two positional allophones commonly known as "*ich*-Laut" and "*ach*-Laut":

The phonemes of English and German: contrastive survey

A: consonants

	English (R. P.)	German
plosives	/p, b, t, d, k, g/	/p, b, t, d, k, g/
affricates	/tʃ, dʒ/	/tʃ, pf, ts/
fricatives	/f, v, θ, ð/ „th"	/f, v, ⟨CH⟩ [x, ç]/
sibilants	/s, z, ʃ, ʒ/	/s, z, ʃ/
nasals	/m, n, ŋ/	/m, n, ŋ/
other	/l, r, j, w, h/	/l, r, j, h/

Table 2.3
List of English and German consonants and vowels

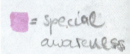 = special awareness

And here are the vowel phonemes, including diphthongs:

B: vowels:

Aal	/ɑ:/	/ɑ:/	car
alle	/a/	/ʌ/	bud
Esel	/e:/	/e/	bed
Ernte	/ɛ/	/æ/	bad
		/ɜ:/	earth
ihn	/i:/	/i:/	seat
in	/ɪ/	/ɪ/	sit
offen	/ɔ/	/ɒ/	hot
Ofen	/o:/	/ɔ:/	caught

Unzeit	/u/	/ʊ/	book
Ufer	/u:/	/u:/	boot
öffnen	/œ/		
Öfen	/ø/		
üppig	/ʏ/		
über	/y/		
Leere	/ə/	/ə/	about
Lehrer	/əɹ/ /ɐ/		
Eimer	/aɪ/	/aɪ/	time
auch	/aʊ/	/aʊ/	house
Europa	/ɔɪ/	/ɔɪ/	boy
		/eɪ/	same
		/əʊ/	home
		/ɪə/	here
		/ɛə/	there
		/ʊə/	poor

For the consonants, the situation is identical in American English at the phonemic level. Phonetically, we would need an extra symbol for the 'flapped' realisation of the /t/ phoneme as [ɾ] (as in *bitter*). For the rather more serious contrasts in the vowel and diphthong phonemes see Exercise 2 below.

What are the major learning difficulties faced by a speaker of German when trying to master the new phonemic system of English? At the risk of some simplification, there are three types of obstacles:

1) Phonemic gaps

Consonants

As the lists show clearly, there are phonemes in English which are absent from German. Among the consonants, the most obvious cases are the dental fricatives ([θ, ð]) and the semi-vowel [w]. What beginning German-speaking learners will do is to substitute what they consider the closest German equivalent to the English sound. For the voiceless dental fricative this is usually either [s] or the labio-dental fricative [f]. However, as is shown by minimal pairs such as *sink* – *think* or *thought* – *fought*, this is not a suitable strategy. For English [w], a common substitution is [v], so that learners might pronounce [wɪliəm] as [vɪliəm], using the same sound which occurs in the German name *Wilhelm*. Substitution is made even easier by the fact that the same letter – <w> – is used to denote the different sounds in the two languages.

Vowels

For the vowels, the comparison between English and German shows several contrasts. For example, there are more phonemic front vowel distinctions in English than in German, and this leads to learners of English often collapsing the distinction between [e] and [æ] by articulating both in the same way – roughly as German [ɛ]. Minimal pairs such as *bet – bat* or *celery – salary* are then no longer kept distinct.

2) Distributional constraints

Even if a particular phonemic contrast is present both in the English and German systems, there may still be pronunciation problems because the rules for the distribution of the phonemes in the syllable are different. Consider, for example, the distinction between voiced and voiceless <s>. This is a phonemic contrast both in English and German, as is easily apparent from minimal pairs such as the following:

final: rice – rise
medial: racing – raising   heißer – heiser
initial: sink – zinc

Note, however, that while in English the opposition is found syllable-initially, medially and finally, in German it is restricted to medial position. Whether in German we pronounce a word such as *Sonne* with a voiced [z] or a voiceless [s] largely depends on our regional background: initial [z] is found in the North and recommended in the standard pronunciation; initial [s] tends to be preferred in the South. In syllable- or word-final position, German only has [s]: *Haus* (but compare *Häuser*, with [z]), *Glas* (but compare *Gläser*, with [z]). It is therefore particularly difficult for beginning German learners of English to articulate [z] in syllable-final position in English words. This will lead to a noticeable accent, as some of the most common words in English (e.g. *has, is, does*) happen to end in [z].

The problem of final devoicing (or "Auslautverhärtung") is not restricted to <s> but encompasses all fricatives, affricates and plosives. Any of the following English minimal pairs are thus potential problems for German learners:

Syllable-final devoicing

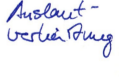

cap – cab   leaf – leave
right – ride   teeth – teethe
leak – league   rich – ridge

In all, final devoicing, or the neutralisation of the voicing contrast in syllable-final position, in German learner English is thus probably the most massive single contributing factor to this particular foreign accent.

3) Contrasts in the allophonic realisations of phonemes

Sometimes there is no contrast between the two languages at the phonemic level, but nevertheless the auditory impression is rather different. This affects the consonant /l/, for example. German /l/ is "clear" in all cases. That means it has a front vowel resonance. In British English, this clear [l] is found only word-initially and between vowels. Before consonants or at the end of words, the /l/ is "dark" [ɫ] because it has a back vowel resonance. In most varieties of American English, velar or "dark" /l/ is the common realisation in all phonetic environments. Thus, the phonemic or "broad" transcription of German *fiel* and English *feel* is identical: /fi:l/. However, the phonetic or "narrow" transcription is [fi:l] for German and [fi:ɫ] for English.

Word-stress

In addition to these three sources of error, there are of course numerous further difficulties at the supra-segmental level. Foremost among them is probably the highly intransparent word-stress system of present-day English. For example, there is no logic behind the fact that *apple-cake* is pronounced with a stress on the first element (like the German *Apfelkuchen*), whereas *apple-pie* generally has level stress (that is equal stress on both elements). Similarly, there are so many polysyllabic words in English which have their stress on the "antepenultimate" (= third syllable counted from the end) – *co'rollary*, *peni'tentiary*, etc. – that it is difficult to see why *category* should not be in this class and be pronounced as *ca'tegory*. (The correct pronunciation is, of course, *'category*, with the stress on the first syllable.)

2.3 | Problems and challenges

PRAAT – doing phonetics by computer

The "problems and challenges" sections of the present introduction are usually constructed around some corpus-based task. As most widely available corpora of present-day English reduce the live complexity of speech to orthographic transcription, this procedure is difficult to follow here. Instead, readers are encouraged to explore the opportunities for computer-aided work in phonetics, for example through PRAAT, a software suite developed by Paul Boersma and David Weenink of the University of Amsterdam (http://www.fon.hum.uva.nl/praat/).

The problem chosen for illustration here is the pronunciation of the diphthong [aɪ] in Canadian English. Whereas speakers of British or American English have broadly the same diphthong realisation in *white* and *wide* (that is before a voiceless and a voiced following plosive), many Canadians have [əɪ] in *white* and [aɪ] in *wide*. This is important, and many people are aware of it, because it is one of the very few phonetic characteristics distinguishing a Canadian accent from a United States one. In linguistic field-work, it is of course possible to consult informants in a purely auditory analysis. The linguist listens carefully to what he or she hears and transcribes accordingly. With PRAAT, however, it is possible to subject the recorded data to instrumental-phonetic analysis. The screenshot below shows you what a diphthong looks like in this perspective. (If you have the opportunity, you may want to consult the accompanying web-page for this book in order to get it in full colour.)

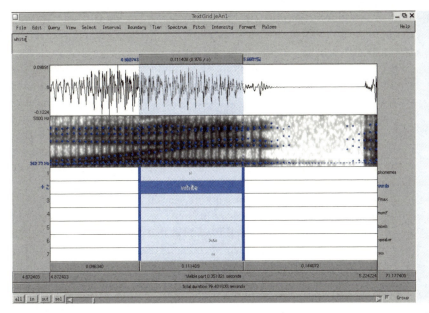

Fig. 2.6
PRAAT – illustrative screenshot "white" (screenshot and explanatory text kindly provided by Ingrid Rosenfelder, University of Freiburg)

The screenshot shows a so-called *Text Grid Editor window*, which displays a sound file together with its corresponding *TextGrid*. This is basically a text file containing annotation text in combination with time information from the sound file. A TextGrid consists of one or several **tiers**, which appear as rows below the speech waveform, and into which information can be entered. This can be very useful for research, as it allows you to mark the phonemes (or any other phenomenon) that you are interested in analysing, add your own comments or background information, and easily retrieve all instances thus marked.

What you can see in this window is the realisation of the diphthong /aɪ/ in the word *white*, as pronounced by a speaker of Canadian English. Time is running along the x-axis, or from left to right, and is indicated in seconds. A portion of the sound file corresponding to the interior part of the diphthong /aɪ/ has been shaded dark. In the upper window, the speech **waveform** is displayed, i.e. the varying air pressure that has "hit" the membrane of the microphone during the recording. The lower window shows a **spectrogram**, which indicates the frequencies that the waveform is made up of at a certain point of time, with darker shading indicating higher intensities of the frequency components in question. Frequencies range from 0 to 5,000 Hertz and are displayed along the y-axis (i.e. from bottom to top) of the spectrogram.

Underneath the spectrogram, the various tiers of the TextGrid are shown, together with their names on the right-hand side. Note that boundaries (solid vertical lines) have been inserted into these tiers to demarcate the extent of the diphthong, and that information about the sound in question (phoneme: /aɪ/, first tier; word: *white*, second tier) has been entered. The last two tiers (without any boundaries) contain information about the speaker, namely speaker ID and speaker sex.

Superimposed on the spectrogram are a number of dots, which show the location of the vowel **formants**. These are the resonance frequencies of the vocal tract, and the first and second formant correspond roughly to the high-low and front-back dimensions of the vowel quadrilateral, respectively, with higher vowels having a lower first formant (F1) and fronter vowels a higher second formant (F2). Note that all formants are located along the darkest areas of the spectrogram, i.e. they belong to those frequency ranges that contribute the most to the intensity of the overall sound.

As you can see, the first two formants are very far apart at the end (**offglide**) of the diphthong /aɪ/, the first formant having a very low, the second formant a very high value. This means that the vowel at that point of time is both high (low F1) and front (high F2), which of course agrees with the position of the sound [ɪ] in the vowel quadrilateral. At the beginning (**onset**) of the diphthong, F1 is higher, and F2 considerably lower. This corresponds to a lower and backer onset, [ə] in this case, because of the special Canadian pronunciation noted above. (The phenomenon demonstrated here is commonly called **"Canadian Raising,"** because the onset of the diphthong is "raised" from [a] to [ə].) Also, note the large blank area to the right of the diphthong. This is the closure phase of the following plosive /t/, during which the air stream is blocked completely and no sound is emitted from the vocal tract.

Had this diphthong been pronounced by a speaker of British or American English, or had the diphthong been followed by a voiced instead of a voiceless

Fig. 2.7 Canadian raising

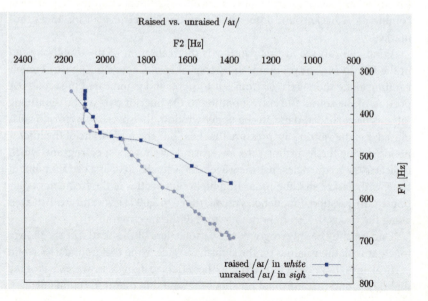

consonant, the onset of the diphthong would not have been raised. Thus, the first formant (F1) would have been higher at the beginning of the highlighted area. Using acoustic analysis techniques allows researchers to assign precise measurement values to statements like these. Each dot in the spectrogram above corresponds to exactly one formant measurement (e.g. F1 = 563 Hz at the beginning of the diphthong). This makes it possible to more accurately compare vowel realisations, for example, by plotting formant trajectories in F1/F2 space, as in Fig. 2.7, which shows the diphthong realisations in *white* (raised) and *sigh* (unraised).

Further reading

A convenient introduction to English phonetics and phonology, with a useful accompanying compact disc, is:

Skandera, Paul, and Peter Burleigh. 2005. *A manual of English phonetics and phonology.* Tübingen: Narr.

For more advanced treatments, consult:

Cruttenden, Alan. 1997. *Intonation.* 2nd ed. Cambridge: CUP.
Giegerich, Heinz J. 1992. *English phonology.* Cambridge: CUP.
Gimson, Alfred C. 1996. *An introduction to the pronunciation of English.* 5th edition. Rev. by Alan Cruttenden. London: Arnold.

Gimson 1996 is an authoritative reference on Standard British "Received Pronunciation". If you are unsure about the pronunciation of individual words, you can consult pronouncing dictionaries such as:

Jones, Daniel. 2003. *English pronouncing dictionary.* 16th ed. Cambridge: CUP.
Upton, Clive, William Kretzschmar, and Rafal Konopka. 2001. *The Oxford dictionary of pronunciation for current English.* Oxford: OUP.
Wells, John C. 2000. *The Longman pronunciation Dictionary.* Harlow: Longman.

Jones is a standard work of reference on British pronunciation which has been around since 1917. The Oxford and Longman dictionaries provide alternatives and additional coverage of American English.

PRAAT (software for acoustic analyses): http://www.fon.hum.uva.nl/praat/

Practice

|2.4

1   Ask a native-speaking informant to read the following sentence for you:

*Sooner or later, she is **going to want to talk** to you.*

Transcribe the portion of the statement spelled in bold italics and comment on the relation between the spelling as 'going to want to talk' and the corresponding pronunciations. Ask your informant to read the sentence carefully first, then rapidly. What do you notice?

2 Consult a reference work of your choice for a list of the vowel phonemes of standard American English and try to map them onto their British R. P. equivalents given above. What major differences do you note?

3 Consult one of the pronouncing dictionaries mentioned above to find out which of the following are minimal pairs in British and American English.

collar – caller, don – dawn, shot – short, can't – cant, winter – winner

4 The pronunciation of the following words is variable in modern English:

dispute (noun), *controversy, applicable, to address, address, adult, leisure, data*

Find out what guidance you are given in the three pronouncing dictionaries mentioned above. Does the advice given by the various sources differ, or do they all agree?

5 Transcribe a slow and rapid version each of *ten bottles*, *what do you want* and *Smith is your boss* and comment on the differences.

6 Consult reference works on the phonetics of British English R. P. or the General American accent to determine the allophones of the /r/ phoneme in these two varieties. Where there is more than one variant, give the rules for their distribution. How do the various realisations of English /r/ differ from German?

7 Consult one of the bigger dictionaries of the English language for words starting in 'shn' or 'schn'. What do you find? Go to your departmental library and consult the Oxford English Dictionary, or OED, the biggest of them all, for the entry for *s(c)hnozzle*. Try to account for the exceptional phonetic structure of this particular English word.

8 Give a list of three-consonant clusters which may occur in English.

9 In their book *Kontrastive Linguistik deutsch/englisch: Theorie und Anwendung* (München: Hueber 1974) Ernst Burgschmidt and Dieter Götz suggest the following diagnostic text for use in assessing German learners' pronunciation skills.

> Yesterday I went to the grocer's. My mother had told me to buy eggs, some salad and tomato ketchup. Then I realized that I had forgotten my money. I had to run back, but my mother had already left the house when I arrived […] (Burgschmidt/Götz 1974: 224)

Indicate the likely pronunciation problems in the text. Which mispronunciations would you expect?

Unit 3

Morphology and word-formation – the structure of the word

Orientation | 3.1

Free and bound morphemes | 3.1.1

While speakers of a language are not usually aware of the complexities of the phonological system of their language, everybody has a common-sense notion of what a "word" is. If asked, speakers of English, for example, would in all likelihood agree that in spite of the considerable differences all of the following qualify as words:

"Word" – problems of definition

> she, look, looking, onlooker, type, write, typewriter, (to) type-write

This common-sense understanding of what a word is may suffice for practical purposes. It is not sufficient, however, for the purposes of linguistic analysis. Consider just some of many more problems that we would have to solve:

> Phonetic contractions: Is the form *I'm*, contracted from *I am*, one word or two? The same question could be asked for *don't*, *gonna* – a common colloquial pronunciation of *going to*, and hundreds of similar cases.

> Sequences of nouns: Sequences of nouns can be of three kinds. (1) They can be spelled as one unit (e.g. *nutshell*), in which case it is uncontroversial to accept them as words. (2) They can be spelled with a hyphen (e.g. *apple-pie*), in which case there are also good grounds for considering them as words. (3) They can be spelled separately, and these are of course the difficult cases to classify.
>
> Does the expression *London broker* consist of two words, because the meaning of the entire phrase is the exact sum of the meaning of its parts, i.e. a broker based in or coming from London? Then what about *insurance broker*, which incidentally would be translated as one word in German (*Versicherungsmakler*)?

> Variable spellings: The spelling of many complex words in English is notoriously variable. The noun-noun sequences discussed above are one example. Some of them are found in all three possible variants: as *motorcar* and *wordformation*, as *motor-car* and *word-formation*, and as *motor car* and *word formation*.

To get out of such dilemmas, linguists studying the structure of words have created a precisely defined technical term, the **morpheme**. In analogy to the term *phoneme* (= smallest linguistic unit capable of distinguishing between meanings), the word *morpheme* refers to the minimal unit capable of express-

The morpheme – minimal unit capable of expressing meaning

39

ing a meaning of its own. Metaphorically speaking, we could refer to morphemes as atoms of meaning.

By notational convention, a morpheme is placed between braces ({}). Thus the graphic word <high> consists of the morpheme {high}, while the graphic word <higher> is a combination of the morpheme {high}, which provides the specific word meaning, and the morpheme {-er}. The meaning of this morpheme is more difficult to specify than that of the word <high> because it is more general, expressing a greater degree or, to use the technical term for this grammatical category, the **comparative** form of adjectives.

Free and bound morphemes

This example already makes it clear that we need to distinguish between various types of morphemes. There are morphemes such as {high} which are "free" in the sense that they can stand on their own, and there are "bound" morphemes such as {-er}, which require a free morpheme to attach to. The free morpheme which the bound morpheme attaches to is commonly referred to as the **base**. Bound morphemes are also called **affixes**. The following list illustrates some common bound morphemes of English:

Table 3.1
Bound morphemes

bound morpheme	examples	function
{-s}	two dogs, toys	turns nouns from singular to plural
{-ed}	looked, desired, played	turns verb into past tense
{un-}	untie, undo, unhappy, unpleasant	"negative" morpheme: denotes the reversal of an action if used with verbs, and the opposite quality if used with adjectives
{-ness}	happiness, tiredness	turns adjectives into nouns
{-er}	Londoner, New Zealander, New Yorker	denotes inhabitant of a city, region or country

Inflectional and derivational morphemes

Bound morphemes chiefly serve two functions – an **inflectional** one and a **derivational** one:

1) A bound morpheme is inflectional if it gives us information about how the word is used in a phrase or a sentence. To return to our initial example *higher*: if we have this form of the word, we know that we can continue the sentence with *than* (e. g. *prices are higher than last year*).
2) A bound morpheme is derivational in function if it helps speakers to derive or create new words from an existing base, for example the word *highness* from *high*. (In addition, there is another form, *height*, which is the result of a highly irregular process of derivation.)

An easy test to distinguish between inflectional and derivational processes is to look up forms in a dictionary. Dictionaries usually list the products of derivation as separate entries, but not the inflectional forms of one and the same word.

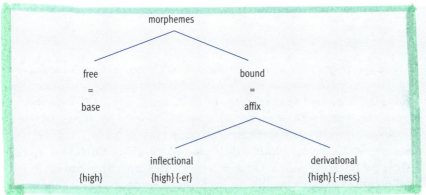

Fig. 3.1
Types of morphemes I

Apart from the comparative morpheme already illustrated, typical inflectional morphemes of present-day English are the 3rd-person-singular {-s} in the present tense, the {-ed} marking past tense, or the plural {-s} in nouns. The derivational morphemes of present-day English number in the hundreds and illustrate various degrees of regularity and productivity. The most important of them will be discussed below.

Note that form-function mapping in morphology is very often rather complex. Rarely do we have a situation where one bound morpheme performs exactly one function. The {-er} which we illustrated in its function of an inflectional morpheme indicating comparative (e.g. *high* → *higher*) also serves as a derivational one, used to turn verbs into agentive nouns indicating the person or thing which performs an activity denoted by the verb (*to bake* → *baker*, *to compute* → *computer*). But this is not the only derivational process this morpheme is involved in. As examples such as *London* → *Londoner* show, it also denotes inhabitants of a place, and in a few irregular cases such as *old-timer* (somebody, especially an elderly person, with long experience in a place or position) the meaning is even more general.

Just as one and the same phoneme may have several contextually conditioned allophonic realisations, so one and the same morpheme may have different **allomorphs**, that is realisational variants. Thus, the {-s} indicating plural or genitive in nouns or third-person singular of the present tense in verbs comes in three different phonetic realisations: [s], [z], [ɪz]. The voiceless *s* is used after all voiceless consonants except [s, ʃ, tʃ]. It would be found, for example, in *cats*, *beliefs* or *baths*. The voiced *s* occurs after vowels and voiced consonants except [z, ʒ, dʒ] – for example in *boys*, *girls* or *bathes*; and the syllabic [ɪz] is found after [s, z, ʃ, ʒ, tʃ, dʒ] – for example in *races*, *buzzes*, *washes*,

"Allomorphs" – realisational variants of morphemes

watches or *judges*. Similar allomorphy can be observed in derivation. The derivational morpheme {-tion}, for example, which turns verbs into nouns, has two allomorphs: [eɪʃn] and [ʃn], as can be seen in the following examples:

    to detain → detention
    to retain → retention
    to realise → realisation
    to organise → organisation

Productivity of morphological processes

Bound morphemes are also highly variable with regard to their **productivity**. The regular inflectional morphemes are in principle fully productive. For example, the plural {-s} attaches to any noun except a very small number of exceptions. Some of these are historical fossils. For example, the plural of *ox*, *foot* or *mouse* is not, as would be expected **oxes*, **foots* or **mouses*, but *oxen*, *feet* and *mice* – older forms which, unlike hundreds of others, have so far refused to die out by regularisation. Other exceptions are more difficult to explain. It is difficult to see, for example, why English speakers do not accept nouns such as *information* or *advice* in the plural (**informations*, **advices*).

There are vast differences in the degree of productivity displayed by derivational morphemes. At the lowest end of the cline of productivity, there are forms which are recognisable as transparent instances of derivation, but we cannot use these morphemes to derive any new words today. This is the case, for example, with the {-th} morpheme, which is occasionally encountered in English as a derivational morpheme turning adjectives into abstract nouns:

    warm → warmth
    wide → width
    merry → mirth
    foul → filth

Note, for example, that [faʊl] becomes [fɪl-] in [fɪlθ]. This irregularity is due to the fact that this pair were related by *umlaut* (or i-mutation) in Old English, much like *faul* and *Fäulnis* still are in present-day German. The stock of such forms is limited to these and a few more (e. g. *length*, *strength*, *dearth*). But new ones cannot be added. Thus, we are unlikely to encounter:

    clean → * cleanth
    round → * roundth

At the other end of the cline of productivity, there are derivational morphemes whose productivity approaches that of inflectional ones, for example the morpheme {-ness}, which does the same job as {-th}, albeit far more readily, and with none of the phonetic complications which are found in most examples containing {-th}.

happy	→	happiness
concrete	→	concreteness
interconnected	→	interconnectedness
busy	→	business [bɪzɪnɪs] …

Note that the last-named example illustrates the productive and regular derivational process. *Business*, in the pronunciation given, is the noun corresponding to the adjective *busy* and means "Geschäftigkeit" in German. *Business*, in the pronunciation [bɪznɪs] and meaning "Geschäft," though originally due to the same process, has by now established itself as a separate word through a process of **lexicalisation**.

Lexicalisation

In lexicalisation, the meanings of words are specified by convention beyond that which is predictable from the regular and productive derivational process. The regular form [bɪzɪnɪs] is not lexicalised to any great extent, and its meaning is very close to what can be predicted on the basis of what we know about the meanings of the base form *busy* and the derivational morpheme {-ness}; it could be paraphrased as "the quality of being busy."

Similarly, the {-er} morpheme, when added to verbs, in very general terms denotes the "person or thing performing an activity." The fact that we "know" that a baker is a person, but a cooker an object is due to lexicalisation. For further examples of lexicalisation see Task 4 below.

Lexical and grammatical morphemes

|3.1.2

Above, we have classified morphemes by a simple formal criterion – whether or not they can appear on their own. Another way of classifying morphemes (and words) is by function and meaning. For this, we need to determine whether they have a concrete and specific lexical or a more abstract and general grammatical meaning. There is an obvious correlation between the two classification schemes employed so far. Most free morphemes (formal criterion) are also lexical (function-meaning criterion), and vice versa: *table, rapid, happy, sit*, etc. Many bound morphemes perform grammatical functions, and many grammatical functions are performed by bound morphemes: {-s}, {-ed}, etc.

However, the correlation is not perfect. In English there is a considerable number of free morphemes with grammatical rather than lexical function. In the following utterance:

Free grammatical morphemes

   Not in the kitchens!

only *kitchen* is a lexical morpheme in that sense. {-s} is a bound morpheme which expresses the inflectional notion of "plural." *Not, in* and *the* are free morphemes, but the meanings they express are akin to those expressed by bound derivational and inflectional morphemes – in this case the generalised notions of "negation," "locality" and "definiteness." While the slot:

   Not in the _____!

could be filled with a very large number of words (e. g. *garden, swimming pool, house*, etc.), there is only a limited number of contrasts available in the other three cases:

Not in the kitchen!	In the kitchen!
Not **in** the kitchen!	Not into/out of/above … the kitchen!
Not in **the** kitchen!	Not in a/some/this … kitchen!

We can thus see that in present-day English grammatical relations are not only expressed by bound morphemes but that this job is done also by a number of free ones (as is typical of languages of the analytical type – a concept which will be explained in Unit 4).

Bound lexical morphemes

Just as there are free morphemes with grammatical function, there are bound morphemes with lexical status. For example, English has a large group of neo-classical compounds, words formed from Greek or Latin elements in the modern European languages. The following are typical examples: *photography, radiography, thermography.*

The second element ({-graphy}) in each of these examples goes back to the ancient Greek root for "write," whereas the first elements ({photo-}, {radio-}, {thermo-}) go back to the Greek for "light," "ray" and "heat" respectively. The compounds thus have the concrete and specific meanings of "light-writing" (= writing with light), "X-ray writing" and "heat-writing." Nevertheless, neither of the four elements involved can stand on its own in the relevant sense. *Graphy* and *thermo* do not occur except as elements in such neo-classical compounds. *Photo* and *radio*, by contrast, are attested as lexical morphemes, but of course not in the senses relevant here.

Table 3.2 Types of morphemes II		lexical	grammatical
	free	{table}, {happy}, {sit}, {radio}, {photo}, …	{the}, {a/an}, {any/some}, {no}, {in}, {to}, {from}, {not}, …
	bound	{photo-}, {radio-}, {thermo-}, {-graphy}, {-er}, {-ness}, {-tion}, …	{-s}, {-ed}, {-ing}, {-er}, {-est}, {-ly}, …

3.2 | Demonstration/discussion:
The major word formation strategies of present-day English

The creation of new words

In this section we shall have a look at the strategies which are available in present-day English to coin new words. Note that one possible strategy, namely to create new words by assembling sounds, is an option which is exercised only very rarely. A recent (20th-century) example is the noun/verb *vroom*, also spelled *varoom*, which echoes the roaring sound of an engine and is also used to refer to reckless and speedy driving. In a way the relative scarcity of such examples is surprising, because there are countless phonotactically possible combinations in English which have not been used yet.

The vast majority of new words is thus formed by modifying existing ones. Thereby, it is useful to distinguish between major strategies which account for large numbers of words and minor ones, which are not necessarily very frequent or general but interesting because of the linguistic creativity they imply. The three major processes used in English are **compounding, derivation** and **conversion**.

Major word-formation processes

Compounding

A compound is a combination of at least two free morphemes. Compounding has been a mainstay of the English word-formation system since Old English times, with the most common case being noun + noun compounds of the modifier-head type.

Compounding

> apple pie
> street lamp
> motor vehicle accident

In *apple pie*, *pie* is the head, modified by *apple*. The head can be modified by numerous other modifiers, for example *cherry pie, pecan pie* or *pumpkin pie*. Similarly a *street lamp* is a kind of lamp, and *a motor vehicle accident* is a kind of accident. Note that in the latter example *motor vehicle*, the modifier of *accident*, is itself a compound, with *vehicle* as its head and *motor* as its modifier. In contrast to German, spelling is not a reliable indicator of compound status in English.

Apart from noun + noun compounds there are numerous other types, which however tend to be much rarer. Here are some examples:

> adjective + noun: *blackboard, medical student*
> adjective + adjective: *blue-green*
> noun + adjective: *power-hungry, power-crazy, trigger-happy*
> verb + noun: *pickpocket*
> verb + verb: *to kick-start, to stir-fry*

As far as the relationship between the component parts of compounds is concerned, most of them display the familiar modifier-head structure. A *medical student* is a student in the field of medicine and not another one. A *power-crazy* individual is crazy about power and not some other pursuit. However, *blue-green* and *stir-fry* are different, as none of the two components modifies or is subordinate to the other. *Blue-green* denotes a colour combining blue and green in equal measure, and *to stir-fry* means stirring and frying food simultaneously. Modifier-head compounds are often referred to as **endocentric** compounds; this latter type, on the other hand, is also known as copulative compounds.

Fig. 3.2 | (Left hand writing) skills? (Left hand) (writing skills)? Left (hand writing skills)?

Pickpocket, finally, illustrates a third (and rare) type, namely **exocentric** compounds. None of the component parts of this compound refers to the referent directly. A *pickpocket* is not a type of pocket, nor is the corresponding verb *to pickpocket* a type of picking (as would be the case in *pocket-picking*). Rather, the compound refers to a person who picks other people's pockets ("Taschendieb").

Derivation

Derivation involves combinations of at least one free morpheme and at least one bound morpheme whose function is not inflectional. The following are examples:

Derivation

unhappy, happiness
density, electricity, audacity, monstrosity
establishment, disestablishment, anti-disestablishmentarian

Sometimes it is useful to distinguish derivational morphemes with regard to their position in the word. If the derivational morpheme precedes the base, it is a **prefix**; if it follows the base, it is a **suffix**. (**Infixation**, that is the placing of a suffix inside the base, is largely restricted to swearing: *absolutely* → *abso-bloody-lutely*.)

Most prefixes preserve word-class. Thus, both *happy* and *unhappy* are adjectives, and both *establishment* and *disestablishment* are nouns. Most suffixes, on the other hand, change the word class, for example from adjective to noun, as in *happy* → *happiness*. In word-formation more so than in other branches of linguistics, there are, of course, exceptions. In *careerism*, suffixation turns a concrete noun into an abstract one, and in *befriend* the prefix *be-* turns a noun into a verb.

Compounding and derivation can easily be combined. The word *user-friendly*, for example, is a compound made up of a noun and an adjective which are both complex internally (*use* → *user, friend* → *friendly*). If there are several suffixes attaching to one root, their order is usually not free, and the number of possible combinations is restricted. Thus, as our list shows, the derivational morpheme {-ity} clearly favours roots of Romance and Latin origin (e.g. *scarcity, magnanimity,* etc.). *Happity is not possible. The functionally similar {-ness} does not display a corresponding constraint: *denseness* is normal, and *monstrousness* or *audaciousness* are plausible words of English.

Also note another important contrast between these two derivational morphemes. Whereas the Germanic suffix {-ness} attaches to its root without any phonetic complications, this is only exceptionally so in the case of {-ity}. If the root has more than one syllable, the stress shifts to the ante-penultimate (third from the back) syllable (*'monstrous* → *mon'strosity*), unless it happens to be there already (*au'dacious* → *au'dacity*). But even in the latter case, the pronunciation of the adjective differs considerably from the noun: [ɒˈdeɪʃəs] vs. [ɒˈdæsɪtɪ].

Conversion

Conversion is the creation of a new word without any formal or external change to the base. Here are a few examples, starting with the most common type, noun-to-verb conversion, and then moving on to some slightly more unusual examples:

source word	type of conversion	converted word	example
bottle	noun to verb	to bottle	This mineral water is bottled at the source.
carpet	noun to verb	to carpet	I had the whole house re-carpeted.
partition	noun to verb	to partition	You can get a spare room if you partition one of the bigger ones.
car-pool	noun to verb	to car-pool	We took turns car-pooling the kids to school.
down	adverb to verb	to down	Workers at the factory downed tools in protest last night.
up	preposition to verb	to up	They kept upping the price.
narrow	adjective to verb	to narrow	How can we narrow the gap between rich and poor?
heavy	adjective to noun	a heavy	The door was guarded by a pair of heavies with a threatening look on their faces.
up	preposition to noun	up	No doubt there have been ups and downs in this relationship.

Table 3.3 Conversion processes

This process, extremely productive in present-day English, is also referred to as "zero-derivation" or "syntactic homonymy." The term *zero-derivation* suggests that such instances of conversion should be regarded as a borderline case of derivation, namely derivation by a zero-morpheme {ø}. The term *syntactic homonymy* emphasises that the part-of-speech class of many English words is not clear out of context and emerges only when the word is used in a particular grammatical or syntactic environment. This is the best way of accounting for cases such as *love* (noun and verb) where it is not clear which of the two is the primary form and which is the converted or derived one. The reason for this uncertainty is that such cases usually go back to pairs of words which were kept distinct by inflectional endings in older stages of the English language. In our example, the noun was *lufu* in Old English, and the verb *lufian*, and the two forms collapsed into one after the loss of inflectional endings.

Some word-formation processes which at first look very much like conversion do not fully meet the criteria on closer inspection. For example, there is a pattern of the following type:

to object (verb)	object (noun)
to import	import
to record	record

Note, however, that in each case the verb has the stress on the second syllable, whereas the noun has it on the first:

/tʊ əbˈdʒekt/	/ˈɒbdʒəkt/
/tʊ ɪmˈpɔːt/	/ˈɪmpət/
/tə rɪˈkɔːd/	/ˈrekəd/

A similar case of borderline conversion is represented by examples in which the nouns end in a voiceless consonant, and the related verbs in a voiced consonant:

to believe	belief
to prove	proof
to teethe	teeth
to house [z]	house [s]

In some instances, finally, adjectives functioning as nouns fail to develop the full range of nominal properties, such as for example the ability to form plurals. In contrast to *heavies*, *the blind*, *the rich* and *the poor* have no plural ending in spite of their indubitably plural reference:

> There are too few specialists on the education and training of the blind.
> Why don't the rich help the poor more?

Apart from the forms cited here, *blinds* and *riches* exist as independent nouns with different senses.

Further word-formation strategies in modern English

Minor word-formation processes

In addition to the major strategies illustrated above, there are a number of processes which are all based on shortening a base form (rather than adding to it). **Clippings**, for example, involve the removal of the beginning or end of a longer word:

Clippings

demonstration	→	demo
professor	→	prof
omnibus	→	bus

Blends, or **portmanteau words**, represent the phonetic merger of two words:

Blends

breakfast + lunch	→	brunch
information + entertainment	→	infotainment
modulator + demodulator	→	modem

Acronyms, made up of the initial sounds/letters of the component parts of a complex word or phrase pronounced as a syllable, have experienced a veritable boom in the recent past, presumably because they are a convenient strategy to cope with long, complex and impenetrable scientific and bureaucratic terminology in everyday communication. The longer an acronym has been current in the language, the less likely people are to be aware of its origin, and the more likely they are to spell it in lower-case letters.

Acronyms

light amplification by the stimulated emission of radiation → LASER → Laser → laser
acquired immuno-deficiency syndrome → AIDS
anti-social behaviour order → ASBO → Asbo/asbo

While the words *laser* and *AIDS* can by now be assumed to be familiar, *Asbo/asbo* probably still requires an explanatory gloss: "a court order obtainable by local authorities which places restrictions on the movements or actions of a person who persistently engages in anti-social behaviour. Introduced under Section 1 of the Crime and Disorder Act in 1998 and first applied in 1999" – see OED, s.v. *asbo*.

If the initial letters of the complex word or phrase are pronounced as such, we have **initialisms** or **alphabetisms**. Spelling may vary:

Initialisms and alphabetisms

disc jockey	→	DJ/dee-jay/deejay
television	→	TV

Back-formations, finally, are cases in which the final part of a word is misconstrued as a derivational ending and speakers construct a base-form which works synchronically but has no historical or etymological justification. Thus on analogy with pairs such as:

Back-formations

governor	← govern
dictator	← dictate
perpetrator	← perpetrate

speakers construct the "missing" verb *to edit* from the noun *editor*.

editor → edit

Note that the symmetry is perfect synchronically, although the direction of the arrow is of course reversed, in accordance with the historical evidence, which shows us that *editor* was first attested in English in 1649, whereas the verb followed only in 1791 (OED, s. v. *editor* and *edit*).

3.3 | Problems and challenges

The categories and classifications presented above provide useful orientation in a notoriously messy field of linguistic description. The sophisticated student, however, should bear in mind that the boundaries between practically all the processes and categories are fluid. This should not come as a shock or be cause for worry. Rather, it is a sign of the creativity and flexibility with which speakers use their languages, and for linguists such exceptions or problematical cases should serve as challenges to hone their analytical skills.

Inflection or derivation?

Consider, as a first illustration, the apparently simple boundary between inflectional and derivational morphemes, the two types of bound morphemes distinguished above. The adverb-forming suffix {-ly} was introduced as a bound grammatical morpheme, and there are two good reasons for doing so. The derivation of adverbs of manner from adjectives appears to be a very regular process, and it is grammatically conditioned.

a rapid talker	–	to talk rapidly
slow motion	–	to move slowly
beautiful singing	–	to sing beautifully
…		

However, closer inspection reveals a number of exceptions. Adjectives ending in *-ly* (*silly*, *deadly*, etc.) lack the corresponding adverb. In a considerable number of other cases, usage is variable, especially in spoken and informal English. While I would not recommend that students write any of the following forms, they are all widely current in actual usage:

come quick, drive slow, speak louder …

With *fast*, the "exceptional" *walk/run/move fast* is in fact the only acceptable option, and the "regular" *walk fastly* is no longer current usage. The adverb form *fastly* is found in combinations only (as in *I am steadfastly opposed to your proposal*).

Even more importantly, the meanings of adjectives and corresponding adverbs may differ. This is most obvious in the case of *hard*, where the adjective and the formally corresponding adverb *hardly* have almost nothing in common in terms of meaning. Less conspicuous discrepancies in meaning are numerous: *natural – naturally, virtual – virtually*, etc.

If, finally, we recall that there is a well-established derivational pattern in which {-ly} serves to create adjectives from nominal bases or other adjectives – as in *friend → friendly, mother → motherly, kind → kindly, sick → sickly* –, it becomes plausible to re-consider the status of the adverb-forming strategy in terms of word-formation. It would stand alongside these two processes as a more productive third one.

There are many other notoriously difficult-to-define boundaries discussed in any introductory work on English word-formation. When, for example, is a sequence of adjective and noun a compound, and when is it a phrase (i.e. a grammatical construction, see Units 4 and 5)? We can easily see the difference between *a black bird* and *a blackbird*. The spelling and the stress pattern differ, the adjective can be modified in the phrase (*a very black bird*) but not the compound, and so forth. But what about the status of expressions such as *golden handshake, silver lining, whispering campaign, running mate, separated fathers*?

Similarly permeable is the boundary between derivation and compounding. Historically, many former free lexical morphemes have travelled down the road to become bound derivational morphemes. A prominent example is, in fact, the {-ly} suffix discussed above, which in Old English meant something like "appearance, shape, body" and rapidly generalised its sense to "having the qualities of," which provided the transition to the present use. We can see stages of the process repeating themselves in present-day English forms such as *child-like* or *war-like*. Traffic in the reverse direction – from bound morpheme to free morpheme – is also attested. For example, forms such as *super, hyper* or *mega* entered the English language in Latin and Greek loan words such as *superfluous, hyperbole* or *megalomania*, then became productive as prefixes (*superman, superhuman; hyper-inflation; megaton, mega-city, mega-good looking*) and finally ended up as free lexical morphemes (*you're super, it was just mega*).

Derivation or compounding?

Corpora are essential tools for the study of word-formation in contemporary English. Students are probably most likely to search the resources in order to find out what forms are attested and to analyse them.

Linking up to the final remarks of the preceding section, here are 10 (of a total of 239 different) word forms in the British National Corpus starting in *mega* and not separated from the rest by a hyphen:

Mega – from prefix to free morpheme

> megabid, megabucks, megabyte, megachiroptera, megaflop, megageomorphology, megajoules, megalith, megalopolis, megamix

These words illustrate established usage in contemporary English. There are the learned terms of Greek origin mainly restricted to scientific/academic English, in which *mega* refers to great size: *megachiroptera* ("big bat" = flying foxes), *megalith* (= "big stone"), *megalopolis* (= "big city"), and – possibly – *megageomorphology*. Other terms, also belonging to scientific/academic registers, denote units of measurement in which *mega* indicates a million: *megabyte*, *megaflop* (in one of two possible senses, denoting units of computational processing capacity: "Floating Point Operations Per Second"), *megajoules*. The rest comprises examples of a more recent usage, in which *mega* combines with ordinary English words such as *bid* or *mix* and has a very general intensifying meaning "larger than usual" or "huge." These words could easily be spelled with a hyphen: *mega-bid*, *mega-bucks*, *mega-flop* (in the non-technical sense), *mega-mix*. It is these forms which provide the basis for an even more recent use of *mega* as a free morpheme. These are the first 25 instances of *mega* spelled as a separate word (from a total of 208) in the British National Corpus:

Table 3.4 *mega* as a separate word, 25 instances from the BNCweb

1	A14 661	The new **mega** brewers introduced new techniques and they were conscious of the raw materials handled in the brewery.
2	A1S 82	Headland believes Multisoft's experience, especially in open systems – computers of different makes that integrate with each other – can be married with systems developed by **Mega**, Headland's own accounting software house which produces larger systems sold directly to clients.
3	A55 22	SCOTTISH & Newcastle Breweries starred again yesterday as the stock market was gripped by rumours that a **mega** takeover bid was imminent.
4	A6A 644	They may get to one of these people if they get a record deal without a manager, and if their record is a **mega** hit, but that is very unlikely.
5	ABW 270	And he had a status-symbol **mega** car which he drove very slowly in the middle lane, his knuckles white with the strength of his grip on the steering wheel.
6	ADR 839	Later in the girls' see-sawing search for stardom it was Dannii who gained the upper hand when she landed the plum job singing and dancing in Australia's **mega** popular Young Talent Time .
7	ALJ 289	"I just hate it," he growled, drooling between yellow teeth, "when people misuse the suffix **mega**."
8	AM0 647	The S'Amfora is a 15 minute walk to the centre of San Antonio and is a **mega** lively hotel, with the bar, which serves snacks all day at reasonable prices, and pool area, as the central focal points.
9	AM0 1047	**MEGA**
10	AM0 1048	Because of its ideal position with the beach and the watersports centre just across the road and a host of bars, shops and clubs on either side, we've used the **Mega** as our Club base in Ipsos for many years.

11	AM0 1049	The focal point of the **Mega** is the large outdoor bar overlooking the seafront which opens at 8.30 am to serve a good English breakfast and snacks throughout the day; it closes well after midnight.
12	AM0 1057	The apartments we've selected, exclusive to Club guests, include the Palmyra, **Mega**, Yannis and Minos and are all close to each other and just across the road from the beach with fabulous views over the bay of Ipsos.
13	AM5 1544	"**Mega** Orange Star"
14	ANX 2374	The references to "kilo" and "**mega**" in the context of computer technology are misleading simplifications; kilo is 2 to the power of 10, not 1000, and mega is 2 to the power of 20, not a million.
15	ANX 2374	The references to "kilo" and "mega" in the context of computer technology are misleading simplifications; kilo is 2 to the power of 10, not 1000, and **mega** is 2 to the power of 20, not a million.
16	ART 1873	As The Smiths grew in commercial stature, so they encountered more and more professional people, especially in America, and these people constantly told the band to think big, to think **mega**, to evolve into a major international unit.
17	AT8 177	Otherwise the only solution would be the resurrection of the synfuels **mega** projects and, barring the unexpected, oil price projections for the rest of the century appear to rule this out.
18	BM5 711	Windsor has already tried to set up a team of his own in F1 and knows the problems involved, not least of which is the **mega** money needed to gain a foothold, never mind putting together the technical talent needed to build his own car.
19	BMF 838	After a **mega** portage up the beach, camp was made high in the sand dunes, giving a spectacular view of the thundering surf.
20	BNP 225	**Mega** Establishment cred but not blue-blooded
21	C87 1456	**MEGA WALLY!**
22	C87 1462	That same stupid person got a Master System 2 for his birthday and went out and bought two £33 games for the **Mega** Drive.
23	C87 2299	**MEGA** MEGATAPES ...
24	C88 1972	Mel Brooks' glorious bad-taste comedy starring Zero Mostel as a crooked Broadway producer who co-opts a timid accountant (Gene Wilder) to help mount a **mega** flop that will make their fortune.
25	C8A 969	Right Said Fred have made it **mega** big in Japan – and as a result, the hit-making trio were keen to please while rehearsing for a TV show there.

Analysing these examples, we are working at the cutting edge of change in contemporary English. There will be great differences among individual speakers with regard to what they accept or produce themselves. Example 7 even formulates objections to the new usage in question here.

On the strength of such evidence, can we put forward the claim that *mega* is now an adjective and adverb in English? The answer to this question is a guarded yes, and much rests on the careful interpretation of the examples. For instance, there is no reason to consider forms such as "mega brewers" (1) or "mega popular" (6) as particularly innovative. They could easily be respelled as *mega-brewers* or *mega-popular*. Note, though, that sometimes it would be possible to add material in between *mega* and the following word: *the mega commercial brewers, a mega and utterly exhausting portage*, and this is only possible on the assumption that *mega* has been reanalysed (cf. p. 68) as an adjective. In our list, there is at least one clear example which shows that such a reanalysis is possible: "think mega" (example 16).

As usual in corpus-based work, finding the answer to our initial question leads to the formulation of new ones. How common, for example, are combinations such as "mega and," "really mega" or "rather mega," in which *mega* may or must be an adjective?

Further reading

Bauer, Laurie. 1983. *English word-formation*. Cambridge: CUP.
Bauer, Laurie. 2001. *Morphological productivity*. Cambridge: CUP.
Haspelmath, Martin. 2002. *Understanding morphology*. London: Arnold.
Plag, Ingo. 2003. *Word-formation in English*. Cambridge: CUP.
Schmid, Hans-Jörg. 2005. *Englische Morphologie und Wortbildung: eine Einführung*. Berlin: Schmidt.
Spencer, Andrew, ed. 1998. *The handbook of morphology*. Oxford: Blackwell.

3.4 | Practice

1. Use the three past-tense forms *attacked, insulted, frightened* as a starting point to find out the allomorphic realisations of the past tense form {-ed} and the rules for their distribution.

2. In addition to those mentioned above, there are a number of further exceptions to the productive {-s} pluralisation of present-day English, for example forms such as *houses* (with voiceless [s] in the singular and voiced [z] in the plural), or *wives* and *wolves* (instead of the expected *wifes* and *wolfes*). Consult reference grammars of English to find out about the extent of this problem.

   Consider s-genitives such as *boys', children's, Dickens', wife's, Bob's, Pat's, Jones's*. Is the genitive {-s} subject to the same allomorphic distribution as the plural? Where are the similarities and contrasts?

3 In addition to the nouns ending in -tion given above (*organisation, realisation, detention, retention*), there are others, such as *action, destruction, obstruction, recuperation, designation*. Which additional problems do these new examples pose for a linguist attempting to find out the rules for the distribution of the various allomorphs?

4 One of the most productive derivational processes in present-day English is agent-noun formation by means of {-er}. Look up the meanings of the following examples in a dictionary:

   painter, baker, (pencil-)sharpener, computer, teller, goer, printer, sitter

   Now try to separate that part of the meaning of these forms which is predictable from the mere word-formation process involved and then go on to specify which additional components of meaning have been lexicalised by convention in each case.

5 Staying with the {-er} suffix, discuss the following complex forms. Try to extend the list by adding similar examples. Discuss issues such as the placement of the derivational morpheme and possible differences in meaning between the agent nouns used alone or in combination.

   cinema-lover, movie-goer, story-teller
   make-upper, maker up
   a maker up of fantastic tales

6 Applied morphology: graffiti on the London Underground:

"OBSTRUCTING	THE DOORS	CAUSES DELAYS AND CAN	BE DANGEROUS"
OBSTRUCT	THE DOOR	CAUSE DELAY	BE DANGEROUS

   Presumably, the person obliterating some morphemes in London Transport's original notice to passengers was not a professional linguist but followed his spontaneous linguistic intuition. Having studied Unit 3, however, you should be in a position to give an explicit account of the strategy employed.

7 In the following extract novelist Will Self, renowned for his occasional tendency towards rhetorical over-drive, sings the praises of a particular kind of cigar. Analyse the morphological structure of the highlighted words and discuss the productivity of the word-formation processes involved. Comment specifically on problems posed by the form *raunchy*. Is *trumpet-type* a noun compound or an adjective derived from the noun with the help of the derivational morpheme {-type}?

   "I smoke the Toscanelli, a **unique** kind of cigar or cheroot, which is a **cut-down** version of something called a Tosca. It's a kind of **great, flaring, trumpet-type** thing of very, very **dark black** tobacco. I think that they are **hand-rolled** – I can't conceive how machines could make them so **idiosyncratic**. Even in a pack of five you will get some that are kind of **spindly and fox-turdy** ... They have a very **strong** flavour, they are sort of **tetanus-ey** and **meaty, raunchy** and **dead bodyish**." (Will Self, *Independent Magazine*)

8 Can you help Clarisse, a character from Robert Musil's novel *Mann ohne Eigenschaften*, with her problem?

Text 3.1
Robert Musil, *Der Mann ohne Eigenschaften*. Reinbek ²²2007: 711

What the writers say
Ein Brief von Clarisse trifft ein

Ulrich hatte keinem seiner Bekannten seine Adresse hinterlassen, aber Clarisse wußte sie von Walter, dem sie so vetraut war wie seine eigene Kinderzeit. Sie schrieb:
"Mein Lieb*ling* – mein Feig*ling* – mein *Ling*!
Weißt du, was ein *Ling* ist? Ich kann es nicht herausbekommen. [...]"

Unit 4

Syntax I/general principles – the structure of the clause

Orientation | 4.1

Words, phrases, clauses and sentences | 4.1.1

The present Unit is concerned with the **grammatical structure of sentences**. For the time being, and for the purposes of a first definition, the term *sentence* is used here in its every-day understanding of "grammatically complete portion of an utterance, usually closed off by a full stop, a question-mark or an exclamation-mark in writing." This, incidentally, hints at the three basic functional types of sentences, namely (1) **declarative** sentences or statements, (2) **interrogative** sentences or questions, and (3) **imperative** sentences or commands, as illustrated by the following examples:

Sentence types

> Sue lost my copy of Huddleston's grammar.
> What did Sue lose?
> Don't lose my copy of Huddleston's grammar.

One important component of grammar, **inflectional morphology**, has already been mentioned in the preceding Unit. The other component, to be dealt with here, is **syntax**. The term is derived from a Greek word originally meaning "arrangement," for example the arrangement of troops in battle. In linguistics, it is the traditional term used for the study of the rules which help us combine words into sentences. The relationship between morphology, syntax and grammar can thus be conceived of as follows:

Grammar = inflectional morphology and syntax

> morphology = word formation + inflectional morphology
> syntax   = grammar – inflectional morphology
> grammar   = syntax + inflectional morphology

So far, the term *sentence* has served us well enough in our introductory definitions. For the purposes of detailed syntactic analysis, however, it is often not precise enough and therefore raises a number of problems. In spite of their differences, for example, all of the following would qualify as sentences:

Sentence versus clause

> Off with you!
> Don't leave now!
> I'm going home.
> If only I had remembered her phone number!
> … because I don't want to lose you as a friend.

57

[No political party in France can afford [to be suspected [of neglecting [to defend the classical heritage of the language]]]], [because [in so doing] it would run a genuine risk [of being accused of cultural treason by the small coterie of opinion makers [who on the strength of their prestige as intellectuals wield considerable influence in publishing]]].

If we want to capture the specific structural features of each of these six sentences, we'd better focus on the **clause** as the basic unit of description. A **clause** can be regarded as the linguistic representation of a state of affairs, usually (but not always) built around a verb as a nucleus and a varying number of constituents. In the list given above, the first five sentences are made up of exactly one clause each. The sixth, by contrast, contains eight clauses which are integrated into a complex hierarchical structure.

Finite, non-finite, verbless clauses

With regard to their outer form, clauses are divided into three categories: (1) **finite clauses**, in which the verb is marked for tense and person, (2) **non-finite clauses** (which are built around an infinitive, gerund or participle), and (3) **verbless clauses** – depending on the form of the verb (or its presence or absence).

(1) finite clauses: Where **are** you **going**?
   … because everybody **wanted** to hear more.
(2) non-finite clauses: **Made** in England.
   … in order **to keep** track of the latest developments.
   With more and more people **taking up** a vegetarian diet
   …
(3) verbless clause: Off with you!

Main and subordinate clauses

With regard to their function, clauses are divided into **main clauses**, capable of standing on their own (e.g. *I'm going home*), and **subordinate clauses**, which expand or otherwise modify a main clause or another subordinate clause (e.g. *[I'm only putting up with this] because I don't want to lose you as a friend*). While finite clauses are unrestricted in their occurrence, non-finite and verbless clauses tend to occur in subordinate function (although, as the survey above shows, there are exceptions to this rule).

It should be noted that the loose definition of syntax given above ("… combine words into sentences") remains imprecise in one important regard even after we have introduced the notion of *clause* as the basic unit of analysis. A clause is not a hierarchically unstructured sequence of words; between the level of the word and the clause there is the intermediate layer of the **phrase** or **constituent**. The following example shows how, strictly speaking, words are combined into phrases which then combine into clauses.

Phrases and constituents

The professor gave every student a copy of the exam paper.

This is not just a sequence of eleven orthographic words, but a clause which comprises eleven words which are grouped into four phrases or constituents.

[the professor] [gave] [every student] [a copy of the exam paper]

In traditional grammar, these constituents would be referred to as the subject, the predicate, the indirect object and the direct object, respectively. A detailed survey of **phrase types** in English will be given in Unit 5. Here, we merely need to distinguish between three major types of phrases, **noun phrases** or **NPs** (with a noun at their centre), **verb phrases** or **VPs** (with a verbal nucleus), and **prepositional phrases** or **PPs** (phrases depending on a preposition).

> Noun phrases, verb phrases, prepositional phrases

There are various grammatical operations which change the order of elements in the sentence, and such changes most often affect the order of constituents rather than the order of words. For instance, we can change our example sentence into:

[the professor] [gave] [a copy of the exam paper] [to every student]

Constituent number three in the original version has now become the last, and been changed from a noun phrase into a prepositional phrase in the process.

Note that while the existence of the phrase level of structure (i.e. a level between the word/morpheme, on the one hand, and the clause, on the other) is uncontroversial, there may be disagreements as to how precisely we should segment a clause into its constituent phrases. There is one widely used model of syntactic analysis in which the verbal predicate is considered the nucleus of the clause, and all three nominal constituents (NPs) would be regarded as in some way dependent on this nucleus. We could visualise the relation between them and the predicate as follows:

> The verb as the centre of the clause

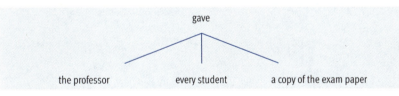

> different approach
>
> Fig. 4.1
> Syntactic analysis – verb as nucleus of the sentence/clause

An alternative approach wants to do justice to the fact that the subject is less directly under the control of the verb than the objects. Accordingly, the first step in a grammatical analysis of a clause is to distinguish between the subject and the rest (which would be analysed as one big verb phrase, consisting of the verb and its objects). This assumed relationship of dependency can be represented by double bracketing or, more conveniently, in the shape of a tree diagram in which S stands for sentence/clause, NP for noun phrase and VP for verb phrase:

> The subject and the verb as equal partners

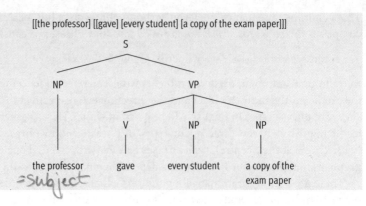

Fig. 4.2 | Syntactic analysis – structure represented through bracketing and through tree diagram

Constituent analysis in ambiguous sentences

The crucial importance of the phrase or constituent level of structural organisation becomes apparent particularly in sentences which are ambiguous, i.e. which have two different interpretations depending on the analysis one adopts:

I bought him a book about medieval sculpture in Ireland.

Here the meaning and the constructional potential of the sentence entirely depend on the phrase structure or constituent structure which is assumed. If we proceed from:

[[I] [[bought] [him] [a book about medieval sculpture in Ireland]]]

or – to represent this in the more accessible shape of a syntactic tree:

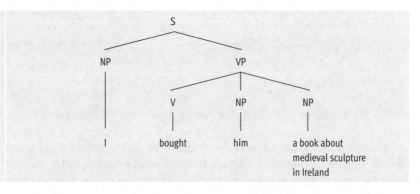

Fig. 4.3 | Ambiguous syntactic structure – interpretation I

– we are talking about a book whose subject is medieval sculpture in Ireland. On this analysis, we could not move "in Ireland" to the beginning of the sentence:

* In Ireland I bought him a book about medieval sculpture.

This sentence is not wrong, but changes the meaning of the original fundamentally. Likewise, we couldn't ask a question about "in Ireland," because – in our current analysis – this prepositional phrase is part of a longer noun phrase which cannot be broken up through questions:

* Where did I buy him a book about medieval sculpture?

Again, the sentence is formally correct, but the meaning is not related to the original.

Now let us assume the following structure:

[[I] [[bought] [him] [a book about medieval sculpture] [in Ireland]]]

or:

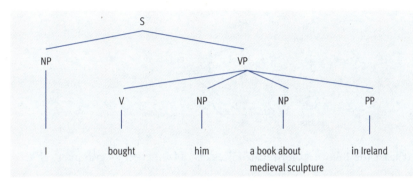

Fig. 4.4
Ambiguous syntactic structure – interpretation II

Here, *in Ireland* is a constituent in its own right, on a par with the other four. And instantly it can be moved to the beginning of the sentence and made the focus of a question, without any interfering changes in meaning:

In Ireland I bought him a book about medieval sculpture.
Where did I buy him a book about medieval sculpture?

Form categories and their grammatical functions

4.1.2
The relation between form and function

One form, different functions

Most approaches to syntactic/grammatical description are based on a distinction between **form** (or **category**) and **function** (= the task a form performs in its grammatical context). In languages, there is no easy one-to-one mapping between category and function. Normally, one linguistic form may have several different functions:

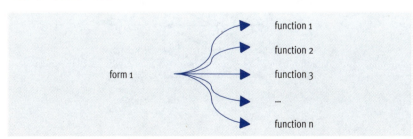

Fig. 4.5
One syntactic form can perform several functions

For example, *to every student* is an example of the form-type (or grammatical category) **prepositional phrase**. In our example above (*[the professor] [gave] [a copy of the exam paper] [to every student]*), it functioned as a prepositional object. Besides that, it can serve a whole range of other functions:

- complement of adjective: ... *a book useful* **to every student**
- modification of noun: ... *an urgent appeal* **to every student**
- adverbial of place: ... *go* **to every student**

One function, different forms

Conversely, a specific grammatical function within the sentence, for example the subject function, can be realised by many different form categories:

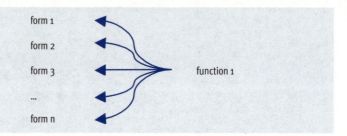

Fig. 4.6 | One syntactic function can be realised by several forms

At least the following form categories can all function as grammatical subjects:

noun phrase (the usual case): **The holiday** was a disaster.
clause (common enough): **That she was willing to forgive him** is a little miracle. [finite subject clause]
To wait any longer would be a waste of time. [non-finite subject clause]
prepositional phrase (rare): **From Stratford-upon-Avon to Luton Airport** takes longer than the flight from London to Rome.

As such diverse form-function mapping is the rule rather than the exception, the grammar of a language ultimately reveals itself to be a complex web of the following type:

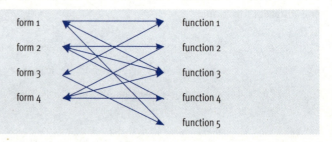

Fig. 4.7 | Complex correlations between forms and functions in natural languages

This looks complicated. Ultimately, though, this is what makes human languages such powerful, flexible and expressive tools for creating and expressing meaning or – as the English idiom goes – for "making sense."

Demonstration/discussion

| 4.2

Basic strategies for the expression of grammatical relations

| 4.2.1

Probably nowhere is the difference between languages greater than in their grammatical systems. Regardless of these differences, however, all languages use the same four fundamental strategies for the expression of grammatical relations, and the differences among them are thus merely due to the fact that the relative prominence of each strategy is variable across languages. Before studying the design features of the grammar of present-day English in detail in Unit 5, we will therefore look at what these basic strategies are and how they work.

Four basic strategies for expressing grammatical relations

Grammatical relations can be expressed through:

1) word order
2) inflection
3) function words, or free grammatical morphemes
4) intonation.

1) Word order

In modern English word order (or, to put it more precisely, the order of constituents or phrases) is one of the most important ways of coding grammatical relations in a sentence. Changes in the order of constituents are almost always associated with changes in meaning or lead to ungrammaticality:

Word order

> the girl forgot the boy
> the boy forgot the girl
> the boy the girl forgot
> the girl the boy forgot

> I had smashed my car-window
> I had my car-window smashed
> * my car-window had I smashed

As the following comparison shows, movement for emphasis in order to produce a balanced information structure in the clause is highly restricted in English, but fairly common in German:

> I wouldn't give him another chance.

In this sentence, the constituent order is fixed. We can change the order of objects, but only if we turn one of them into a prepositional phrase.

> I wouldn't give another chance **to him**.

We can front both objects, but only if we put an emphatic sentence accent on them (indicated by capital letters). This works better for the first example than for the second:

> HIM I wouldn't give another chance.
> ? ANOTHER CHANCE I wouldn't give him.

If we retained the normal intonation (*him I wouldn't give another chance*), this wouldn't work, and the remaining possible orders are out of the question in any kind of intonation:

> * HIM/him wouldn't I give another chance.
> * ANOTHER CHANCE/another chance wouldn't I give him.

This is very different from German, where a much larger number of constituent orderings is possible, and the contrasts in emphasis are often minimal.

> Ich würde ihm nicht eine/keine zweite Chance geben.
> Eine zweite Chance würde ich ihm nicht geben.
> Ihm würde ich nicht eine/keine zweite Chance geben.
> ? Nicht geben würde ich ihm eine zweite Chance.

While, out of context, some people may not like the fourth option, a little twiddling makes even this acceptable – for example by inserting *aber*:

> Nicht geben würde ich ihm aber eine zweite Chance, denn die verdient er nicht.

2) Inflection

Inflection In the course of its history, English has shed most of its inflectional endings. Today, we find inflection used to form the plural and genitive of nouns, the 3rd-person singular and past tense of verbs, and the comparative and superlative forms of monosyllabic and some disyllabic adjectives:

one book	–	two book**s**
the director	–	the director**'s** decision
I play the guitar	–	she play**s** the guitar
I play the guitar	–	I play**ed** the guitar
hot, simple, narrow	–	hot**ter**, simp**ler**, narrow**er**/hot**test**, simp**lest**, narrow**est**

Demonstration/Discussion — Unit 4

Comparing German and English, we often note that grammatical relationships expressed through inflection in the former are expressed by grammatical function words (*to, of, on*) in the latter:

> sie widmete ihre Dissertation ihren Eltern
> she dedicated her thesis to her parents

> das musst Du Deiner Freundin erklären
> that's something you've got to explain to your girl-friend

> die giftigen Abgase der Fabriken
> the poisonous fumes of the factories

An **English** noun (such as, say, *eagle*) has the following forms:

	Singular:	Plural:
Common case:	eagle	eagles
Genitive:	eagle's	eagles'

The equivalent paradigm in **German** is:

	Singular:	Plural:
Nominative:	der Adler	die Adler
Genitive:	des Adlers	der Adler
Dative:	dem Adler	den Adlern
Accusative:	den Adler	die Adler

Fig. 4.8
Nominal inflection in English and German

Note that the noun has only three distinct inflectional forms – *Adler, Adlers* and *Adlern* – but the combination of definite article and noun tends to uniquely identify a particular case-number combination. German nouns come in fairly arbitrary gender classes: *die Krähe*, for example, is feminine, *das Huhn* neuter. But even if the name of a bird is masculine, it may still belong to a different declension class from *Adler*.

	Singular:	Plural:
Nominative:	der Falke	die Falken
Genitive:	des Falken	der Falken
Dative:	dem Falken	den Falken
Accusative:	den Falken	die Falken

3) Function words

Function words, or free grammatical morphemes, are usually identical in form to prepositions, but differ from them in that they have lost their concrete spatial or temporal meanings and are used to express purely grammatical relations. This is obvious in the examples given above for *dedicate something to someone* and *explain something to someone*, where the original directional meaning of

Function words

65

to has been lost. As a result, *to* does not contrast with *from* any longer, as it would in the original prepositional use of these words. Compare:

>I am going **to** Norwich.   I'm just coming back **from** Norwich.
>Explain it **to** me.   *Explain it **from** me.

Similarly, *on* in the following example does not mean that somebody literally collapsed on top of us but merely that we were adversely affected by the event:

>he was so drunk he passed out **on** us
>["er war so betrunken, dass er **uns** ohnmächtig wurde"]

Other common grammatical function words in present-day English are *of*, expressing a wide variety of grammatical relations in noun phrases, and *more* and *most*, which are used in the comparison of some disyllabic and all polysyllabic adjectives.

>the children **of** a widely respected local dignitary
>a novelist **of** considerable reputation
>an ounce **of** pure gold
>the City **of** London
>this execrable fool **of** a student

>humid, wonderful   –   **more** humid, **most** humid/**more** wonderful, **most** wonderful

4) Intonation

Intonation plays a minor role both in English and German in coding grammatical structure. Both languages, for example, have the option of turning a statement into a question through a change from falling to rising intonation (although of course the usual way of forming a question involves a change of word order in addition to a change in intonation):

>Sie sind Student?   You are a student?
>[cf. Sind Sie Student? Are you a student?]

In English, intonation helps to distinguish between restrictive relative clauses (which are integrated into the contour of the higher clause) and non-restrictive relative clauses (which are pronounced as a separate intonation contour – with a short break that is usually represented as a comma in writing). Thus:

>the students who were waiting in the lobby were sent home

implies that there is a larger number of students and only a portion of them, namely those who were waiting in the lobby, were sent home, whereas:

>the students, who were waiting in the lobby, were sent home

means that a group of students, all of whom were waiting in the lobby, were sent home.

Typological classification of languages

| 4.2.2

Languages can be classified into diachronic "families" on the basis of their common origin and historical relationship. In this historical-comparative approach, English turns out to be related to German or Dutch, more distantly to Latin or Albanian, and even more distantly to the ancient Indian Sanskrit language (see Unit 12 and Fig. 12.1 for further discussion). However, languages can also be classified from a synchronic point of view. Such a **typological** classification is usually based on a limited number of parameters and allows for historically unrelated languages to end up in the same typological group. For example, it might turn out that English shares some basic grammatical properties with Chinese. The pioneers of this approach to language study include August Wilhelm Schlegel (1767–1845), Wilhelm von Humboldt (1767–1835) or Edward Sapir (1884–1939) – all scholars who shared an interest in "exotic" languages – whether Indian, Far Eastern or Native American. One of the earliest typologies was based on the dominant shape of the word in a given language and distinguished three (later four) types of languages.

Diachronic language families

Typology – synchronic language families

| Fig. 4.9
August Wilhelm Schlegel (1767–1845)

The **isolating type** tends towards maximally simple words, i.e. a situation in which most words consist of one morpheme only. Languages of the **agglutinating type** may have long and complex words, but these are structured transparently and can be assembled and disassembled easily. The **inflectional** (or **fusional**) **type** has words which are complex and show signs of fusion, i.e. words are much less transparent than in the agglutinating type. Languages of the **polysynthetic** (or **incorporating**) **type**, finally, have words which are extremely long and complex and very often encompass almost the entire information in a clause. Some languages correspond rather closely to one or the other of these ideal types. Thus, classical Chinese is said to be a near perfect illustration of the isolating type. Turkish illustrates the agglutinating type, Latin or Russian the inflectional type, and Inuit (= "Eskimo") or some Aboriginal Australian languages the polysynthetic type. Consider, for example, the following Turkish words, which show agglutination at work:

Isolating languages
Agglutinating languages
Inflectional languages

Polysynthetic languages

| Fig. 4.10
Edward Sapir (1884–1939)

```
evler
ev      +  ler
'house' +  PLURAL

evlerimde
ev      +  ler     +  im    +  de
'house' +  PLURAL  +  'my'  +  'in' (LOCATION)
```

Latin, English, German

Most languages, however, represent mixed types. Consider, for example, the following English expressions and their German and Latin translations:

> he/she would have said
> er/sie hätte gesagt
> dixisset
>
> to the king
> dem König
> regi

Latin clearly instantiates the inflectional type here: the words are complex with regard to their internal structure, and much more difficult to disassemble than the Turkish examples above. English reveals itself to be close to the isolating type. Assuming that *would* is not synchronically analysed as the past of *will* but as an independent modal verb, the expression *he/she would have said* contains three words which consist of one morpheme only (*he/she*, *would*, *have*) and only one word (*said*) which is internally complex. The same is true for *to the king*: the lexical morpheme *king* occurs on its own, and the grammatical information, "dative" and "definiteness" is coded on two separate words each. German is in between Latin and English in both cases.

Analytical and synthetic languages

On the basis of this word-based typology, a simpler two-way classification has been proposed into **analytical** and **synthetic** languages. The parameter of comparison here is clause structure. Analytical grammars code grammatical relations through word-order rules and free grammatical morphemes (or function words), whereas synthetic languages rely on inflection to do the job. Clearly, languages with a lot of inflected or fused words will end up in the synthetic type, whereas isolating languages will be highly analytical. Again, most languages stay away from the extremes and represent various types of mixture. Thus, English is clearly more analytical than German, although there are languages which have even fewer inflections than modern English. Also, as we have noted above, there is language-internal variation within English, for example in the case of di-syllabic adjectives, which allow both analytical and synthetic comparison: *narrow – more narrow – most narrow* vs. *narrow – narrower – narrowest*.

4.3 | Problems and challenges

No rule without exception

An obvious challenge to grammatical descriptions is the fact that there are hardly any rules which have not got numerous exceptions. If a rule is formulated badly, the exceptions that we find may lead us to discard, or at least to refine, the rule. However, the situation is rarely so simple. Exceptions will remain even after several cycles of such refinement, and the linguist will have to get used to the idea that grammatical rules are not as fixed and immutable as mathematical algorithms or the laws of nature but closer to human social conventions, which remain binding even while they are violated occasionally.

In a natural human language a rule must be a tendency strong enough to give the speaker and listener orientation, but a margin of flexibility is desirable if only because it allows flexible responses to new communicative challenges. In other words: exceptions should not trouble the analyst; they are to be expected, and there are usually good reasons for an apparent violation of a rule. As an example, consider the strict S-V-O (Subject-Verb-Object) constituent order of modern English. It is conformed to in the following sentences, and inserting the adverbial between the verb and the object results in ungrammaticality:

> They speak English really well.
> Did Shakespeare write any of his plays in Stratford?
>
> * They speak really well English.
> * Did Shakespeare write in Stratford any of his plays?

In the following sentence, by contrast, the "violation" of the rule is tolerated:

> I speak well only those foreign languages which I started in school and then practiced on the job.

In fact, the technically correct version – *I speak only those foreign languages which I started in school and then practiced on the job well* – would be avoided because it could give rise to misunderstandings. In the trade-off between grammatical correctness and communicative effectiveness speakers are unwilling to pay a price which is too high.

As a second example, consider a form category, the English adjective. A typical English adjective such as *happy* or *tired* displays the following four properties.

1) It can be used as an attribute of a noun: *the happy prince, a tired excuse*
2) It can be used predicatively: *we're not too happy about it, I am tired*
3) It has comparative and superlative forms: *happier – happiest, more tired – most tired*
4) It can be premodified by adverbials: *very happy, extremely tired*.

The tests show that *tired*, while historically originating as the participle of the verb *to tire* and still displaying the relevant ending (*-ed*), has now lost its verbal status.

Note, however, that not all adjectives in English are syntactically well-behaved. Consider, for instance, *mere* and *utter*. *Mere* fulfils criterion (1) – *a mere hint of a foreign accent* – and, at least partly, criterion (3): the superlative *the merest hint of a foreign accent* is o.k., while the comparative **a merer hint of a foreign accent* would be difficult to imagine. It clearly fails, though, on criteria (2) and (4): * *the hint of a foreign accent was mere*, * *a very mere hint* *of a foreign accent*. The adjective *utter* does even more badly, failing all but the first test: *utter nonsense*, but not * *the nonsense was utter*, * *utterest nonsense*, * *very utter nonsense*.

In dealing with apparent exceptions to grammatical rules or instances of variable usage, students will find linguistic corpora immensely helpful. For example, the following is one of hundreds of similar examples from the British National Corpus in which the adjective *interesting* is used to qualify the subject of a sentence and in which it follows this subject:

> But her face was interesting and intelligent and attractive.

We would be unlikely to find the variant *But interesting and intelligent and attractive was her face*, with the subject complement **preceding** the subject it describes. Alongside the hundreds of regular cases, however, we do find a fair number of exceptions which instantiate precisely this sequence. Here are five of them:

Fig. 4.11 Exceptional inversion of subject and verb	CJ4 162	Even more **interesting was** the fact that over 300 cars were parked at the Park and Ride facility at Harman's Cross which obviously reduced the level of traffic along the road to Swanage by that amount.
	HH3 14136	Most **interesting was** an interview with Mark Tolliver, a freelance pilot and convicted drug smuggler.
	A1B 651	Particularly **interesting is** the fact that, after backing so many winners, Pound in The Exile backed unmistakably at least one loser.
	APH 820	Perhaps the least **interesting is** the possibility that the change of context modifies the way in which the CS is perceived, either because of some change in the physical nature of the signal (the properties of an auditory cue, for instance, are likely to change according to the shape of the space in which it is presented) or because there is some change in the way the cue impinges on the animal (if different contexts promote different patterns of orienting behaviour, the same cue, defined physically, may be experienced differently in the contexts).
	BNV 145	Equally **interesting is** the inclusion of some informative footage showing how a Concorde captain is type-converted.

Even these five cases will give you a pretty good idea for the conditions in which we tend to accept this unusual order of constituents. Formulate your hypotheses and use a corpus of your choice to test them.

References and further reading

Baltin, Mark, and Chris Collins. 2000. *The handbook of contemporary syntactic theory*. Oxford: Blackwell.
Downing, Angela, and Philip Locke. 2002. *A university course in English grammar*. London: Routledge.

Huddleston, Rodney, and Geoffrey Pullum. 2005. *A student's introduction to English grammar*. Cambridge: CUP.
Hurford, James R. 1994. *Grammar. A student's guide*. Cambridge: CUP.
Matthews, Peter H. 1981. *Syntax*. Cambridge: CUP.
Matthews, Peter H. 2007. *Syntactic relations: a critical survey*. Cambridge: CUP.
Quirk, Randolph, and Sidney Greenbaum. 1990. *A student's grammar of the English language*. Harlow: Longman.

Practice   4.4

1 Pick out the inflected forms in the following sentences:

John works for IBM.
These days, my mother reads a lot of historical novels.
We liked it there a lot last year, but this year we are looking for a cheaper hotel.
Can you identify the person to whom you handed the parcel?

2 Replace the bold-printed passages in the following sentences by more analytical constructions:

*He's the **politest** person that you can imagine.*
*I find the **book's cover** very misleading.*

3 Replace the bold-printed passages in the following sentences by more synthetic constructions:

***The children of John's sister** are joining us for part of the trip.*
*The door is now even **more narrow** than before.*

4 The discussion in Section 4.3 above has assumed that, unlike *merest*, the superlative *utterest* is not current in present-day English. Test this assumption by:

a) consulting major dictionaries, such as the *Oxford English Dictionary* (OED) or *Webster's Third New International Dictionary of the English Language*;
b) consulting reference grammars such as Quirk/Greenbaum's *Student's Grammar of the English Language* or Huddleston/Pullum's *Student's Introduction to English Grammar*;
c) consulting standard reference corpora of present-day English such as the Freiburg-Lancaster-Oslo/Bergen corpus (1 million words) or the British National Corpus (100 million words);
d) the World Wide Web as the "corpus of last resort".

What do you make of the evidence you find? Which cautions would you recommend when using evidence from the World Wide Web?

5 Classify the following clauses into simple sentences (i.e. those consisting of one clause only) and complex sentences (those consisting of at least two clauses). Group the clauses which you have identified into the finite, non-finite and verbless categories described above:

Long live the Emperor!
Down with the Emperor!
I don't want you to be present at my birthday party.
Living in Scotland, you pick up one or two words which would not be used South of the Border.
Would you believe it?
He just upped and left.
I arranged for an old friend of mine to meet me at the airport.
Students wishing to take the exam before the end of the summer term must register by 30 April.
The committee's report was not expected to be published before the elections.

6 On the basis of the analysis of *evler* and *evlerimde* given in Section 4.2, gloss the meanings of the Turkish words *evlerde*, *evim*, *evde* and *evimde*.

7 Consult a dictionary of linguistics or a reference work on linguistic typology for a good example of a language of the polysynthetic type. Give one example of a word in this language and provide a gloss along the lines of that given for Turkish *evlerimde* above.

Unit 5

Syntax II/the fundamentals of English grammar

Orientation

While Unit 4 was devoted to the study of some important general principles of syntax, the present Unit focuses on a more practical and mundane task – to identify and name the parts or **constituents** of English clauses and establish the structural relationships that hold between them. In line with the framework established in Unit 4, we will start with a look at the **parts of speech** in English, i.e. the word classes which we arrive at when we categorise English words on the basis of their differing grammatical potential. We will then move on to a discussion of **phrases**, semi-autonomous grammatical constructions which are the immediate building blocks or constituents of other more complex phrases or of clauses.

| 5.1

From general linguistics to the grammatical description of present-day English

Parts of speech

The grammarians of ancient Greece and Rome have left us a grammatical classification of words which, in spite of its known weaknesses, has turned out to be surprisingly robust and is still at the heart of most modern taxonomies. They suggest a distinction between nouns (e.g. *organisation, Peter, table*), pronouns (e.g. *he, them, who*), adjectives (e.g. *happy, sad*), prepositions (e.g. *in, on, from*), verbs (e.g. *govern, assimilate*), adverbs (e.g. *rapidly, here, yesterday*), conjunctions (e.g. *because, so that*) and interjections (e.g. *Oh!, Ouch!*). To this we might add the category of articles (*the, a, an*), which is a useful one for the description of English but was not really needed for Latin.

Parts of speech come in two major classes. **Autosemantic words** are those which have a fairly precise meaning by themselves, whereas **synsemantic words** express very general concepts such as spatial, temporal or causal relations and acquire specific meanings only in conjunction with autosemantic words. Thus, we do not need any context to get the meaning of the autosemantic noun *railway station*, whereas the preposition *from* or the definite article *the*, two synsemantic words, do not convey meaning in the same degree of specificity by themselves. They do so, however, in conjunction with *railway station*; *from the railway station* is very different from *above* or *over the railway station*, and *from the railway station* is different from *from a railway station*. Autosemantic words generally form open classes, which contain large numbers of members and can be expanded easily. Synsemantic words tend to form closed classes, with few members and only very occasional expansion or contraction.

| 5.1.1

Word classes

Autosemantic and synsemantic words

These are the major part-of-speech classes of present-day English.

Table 5.1 | Autosemantic parts of speech

	Autosemantic parts of speech
Nouns	English nouns are inflected for number (singular/plural: *one girl – several girls*) and, particularly but not exclusively for nouns denoting human referents, for genitive case (e.g. *the girl's book, the girls' books, the book's cover*). Noun phrases (*the girls, the two American girls, all the girls who attended the course, ...*) typically function as subjects or objects in simple clauses. So do German nouns, but owing to the comparatively more synthetic design of German grammar, German nouns show considerably more inflectional complexity (number, case, gender inflection specific to declension classes).
Verbs	English verbs are inflected for tense (present/past), moderately also for person (3rd person singular in the present tense) and for mood (indicative/subjunctive: *God saves the Queen* vs. *God save the Queen*). In addition to these purely inflectional forms there are many further complex analytical structures expressing tense, aspect and modality. In comparison to German, the obligatory aspect distinction (simple vs. continuous form: *What do you read? – What are you reading?*) is a striking feature of the verbal grammar of present-day English.
Adjectives	English adjectives are inflected for comparison if they consist of one syllable. They are graded analytically, with *more* and *most*, if they consist of three or more syllables, with some variation between synthetic and analytical comparison for di-syllabic adjectives.
Adverbs	Most English adverbs, in particular those derived from adjectives by adding *-ly*, function as autosemantic words: *rapidly, unexpectedly, happily*, etc.

Table 5.2 | Synsemantic parts of speech

	Synsemantic parts of speech
Adverbs	A small number of morphologically simple adverbs, e.g. *more* or *therefore*, express more abstract concepts than the open-class adverbs discussed above.
Articles	Present-day English has a definite (*the*) and an indefinite article (*a(n)*). Whether forms such as *no* – as in *he's **no** fool* (= *he's **not a** fool*) – should be included in this category is an open question.
Pronouns	Pronouns largely overlap with nouns in their grammatical function. Commonly distinguished sub-classes of pronouns are personal pronouns (*I/me, you, he/him, she/her, it, we/us, they/them*), demonstrative pronouns (*this, that, these, those*), indefinite pronouns (*somebody, anybody, ...*), reflexive pronouns (forms ending in *-self* and *-selves*) or reciprocal pronouns (*each other, one another*).
Prepositions	Prepositions usually express relationships between nouns and noun phrases. The most common prepositions are morphologically simple and phonologically very light: *for, from, in*, etc. In addition, there are complex prepositions, which are morphologically complex and usually express more specialised relations: *during, notwithstanding, on account of*, etc.

| Conjunctions | Conjunctions typically express relationships between clauses. There are co-ordinating (*and, or, but*) and subordinating conjunctions (*because, that, while, ...*). |

Where are the weaknesses of this classification which have been alluded to above? One category which is a messy one if applied to present-day English is the pronoun. If defined as a "pro" or replacement form for a noun, the category works only for some of the pronouns mentioned above, for example the personal pronouns. Many indefinite pronouns function as pronouns in this sense but in addition they also display adjectival or adverbial properties to varying degrees. Compare, for example, the following uses of *some*:

Pronouns and determiners

> What about the students? Did any turn up?
> Yes, **some** did but not many in fact.
>
> **Some of** the students even wore three-piece suits.
> **Some** students even wore three-piece suits.
>
> There is **some** interest in this subject, but it is limited.
> There were **some** five-hundred people present at the lecture.
> That was **some** party we had last night, wasn't it?

The first two examples are pronouns in the narrow sense – *some* stands in for the noun *students*. All following uses, however, display additional properties: for example, *some* in *some five-hundred* is an adverbial qualification, and *some* in *some party* is practically synonymous with *a great party* or *a terrific party*.

In view of the obvious overlap between articles, pronouns and adjectives functioning in pre-nominal modification, new types of part-of-speech categories have been suggested in recent linguistics, for example a class "**determiner**" which comprises items such as *a(n), the, all, both, each, some, many* and others which all help to specify, quantify or otherwise determine the general meaning of the following noun.

Phrases

|5.1.2

As has already been pointed out, it is not words which combine into clauses and sentences but **phrases** or **constituents**. The most common types of phrases are **noun phrases (NP)**, **prepositional phrases (PP)**, **verb phrases (VP)**, **adjective phrases (AdjP)** and **adverb phrases (AdvP)**. The phrases are named after their heads and include the heads and their dependents or modifiers. This is simple enough in the case of NPs, PPs, AdjPs and AdvPs, as is illustrated in the following examples, in which the respective heads are printed in bold:

NP:	the **boy**	a **boy** who was playing in the sand
PP:	**to** another famous city	**notwithstanding** the problems involved
AdjP:	**better**	extremely **keen** to take part
AdvP:	right **here**	much more **easily** than expected

A verb phrase (VP) typically consists of a main verb, the auxiliaries which modify it, and those phrases or constituents other than the subject which are necessary to form a basic clause (see 5.1.3 below). These are some examples, in increasing order of complexity.

VPs: the roof [collapsed]$_{VP}$ last night
the roof [could have collapsed]$_{VP}$ last night
I [finished my term paper]$_{VP}$ last night
I [put the alarm clock on the shelf]$_{VP}$ last night

The phrase *last night* is not bracketed as part of the preceding VP because it can be dropped without making the sentence structurally incomplete. By contrast, *my term paper, the alarm clock* and *on the shelf* are bracketed because these phrases need to be there to make the verb phrase complete.

In terms of the category-function distinction outlined in the previous unit, phrases, like words, are form-categories, and their function only becomes apparent in the context of the clause. For example, the prepositional phrase *to another famous city* functions as an object in the first of the two following examples, but as an adverbial of place in the second:

this passage of the book refers [to another famous city]$_{PP}$
the coach took the tourists [to another famous city]$_{PP}$

The difference between the functional status of the PP in each case clearly comes out in the two different questions we can form: **What** does this passage of the book refer to? and **Where** did the coach take the tourists (to)?

As the following example shows, phrases can be expanded to a considerable degree of complexity. The longish sentence:

[the man]$_{NP}$ [read [an interesting book about the history of abstract painting in early twentieth-century Britain]$_{NP}$]$_{VP}$

Heads and modifiers of phrases

consists of just three phrases – as bracketed. *the man* illustrates a simple type of noun phrase, consisting of the noun itself and a determiner, the definite article. The dependency relation is such that the noun is conventionally seen as the head of the phrase and the determiner as the modifier. In principle this modifier-head structure is no different from that found in the long and complex noun phrase *an interesting book about the history of abstract painting in early twentieth-century Britain*. The noun *book* is the head of this noun phrase. It is premodified by the indefinite article *an*, the adjective *interesting* and postmodified by the prepositional phrase *about the history of abstract painting in early twentieth-century Britain*, whose structure is internally complex, as well. Similar expansion strategies can be applied in verb phrases, adjectival phrases or adverb phrases.

The seven basic clause patterns | 5.1.3

Identifying the phrases which make up a clause (or any other complex construction) is the necessary first step in a proper grammatical analysis. By identifying a noun phrase, for example, you have identified a particular formal category. You have not said anything yet about its function in the clause. In this section, we will therefore look at the ways in which NPs, PPs, AdjPs and AdvPs serve to complement the verb (which, as has been pointed out in the preceding Unit, we assume to be the structural nucleus of the clause). In this way we can offer a full grammatical analysis. The technical terms used are largely those found in traditional grammar (e.g. *subject, object*) or in widely used reference grammars of English (e.g. *complement of the subject*), but care is taken to define them in such a way that they suit the facts of English.

Superficially, there is an immense variety of different clause structures, and if you start analysing the clauses in any given text you might come to the depressing conclusion that no two are structured alike. Fortunately, this first impression is deceptive, and closer inspection reveals a relatively simple underlying mechanism. All simple sentences in English correspond to one of the seven basic clause patterns which are discussed and illustrated below:

Basic clause patterns

1.	subject + predicate	SP
2.	subject + predicate + subject complement	SPC$_S$
3.	subject + predicate + adverbial	SPA
4.	subject + predicate + object	SPO
5.	subject + predicate + object + object	SPOO
6.	subject + predicate + object + object complement	SPOC$_O$
7.	subject + predicate + object + adverbial	SPOA

Table 5.3
The seven basic clause patterns

The patterns differ with regard to the number and type of constituents which are needed in addition to the subject to form a grammatical sentence.

The simplest pattern (SP) is illustrated by examples such as the following:

S	P
We	left.
Tom	snores.
The children	are sleeping.

As can be seen in the second and third examples, the grammatical relationship between the subject and the verbal predicate manifests itself not only on the level of meaning but also of form. The singular noun *Tom* agrees in number with the following verb (*snore + s*), and *the children* agrees with the present plural form of the verb *to be* rather than one of its singular alternatives. Subject-verb agreement or concord of this type is, of course, marked much more richly in languages which are more inflectional (or less analytical) than English.

The three-element patterns (SPC_s, SPA, SPO) all have another obligatory constituent in addition to the subject. If this constituent refers to the same person, thing or state of affairs as the subject, it is a complement of the subject, and we analyse the pattern as SPC_s. Such subject complements are usually adjective phrases or noun phrases:

S	P	C_s
Sally	is	a student.
Sally	is	intelligent.
Sally	became	very interested in sports.

If the constituent following the verb does not refer to the same entity as the subject but introduces a new participant in the verbal activity, this is usually an instance of the pattern SPO. "Direct" objects follow the verb directly, whereas prepositional objects are linked to the verb by means of a preposition.

S	P	O
My sister	is reading	the paper.
Arsenal	beat	Manchester United.
Many people	talk	about Professor Smith's latest book.

In the pattern SPA the verb phrase is followed by an adverbial, usually indicating the place or time of the verbal situation:

S	P	A
The film	lasts	two hours.
I	ran	down a steep hill.
We	are going	home.

Object or adverbial? Occasionally, for example if a plain noun phrase or certain kinds of prepositional phrases follow the verb, doubts may arise as to whether the postverbal constituent is an object or an adverbial. This uncertainty can usually be resolved quite easily by means of a few grammatical tests. Objects can be made the focus of questions starting with *who, whom* or *what*, whereas adverbials are usually asked for with *when, where, how, why* or some more specific variant of these. Also, objects can become subjects of passive clauses, whereas adverbials cannot. On the strength of these two tests, *at the railway station* can clearly be analysed as an adverbial in the following clause:

We finally arrived at the railway station.
Where did we finally arrive (at)?
* What did we finally arrive (at)?
* The railway station was arrived at.

By contrast, in the metaphorical use of *arrive at* illustrated in the next example, the constituent following the verb phrase has got all the properties of an object:

We arrived at an acceptable compromise.
* Where did we arrive (at)?
What did we arrive at?
An acceptable compromise was arrived at.

Of the three three-constituent-patterns discussed (SPC$_s$, SPA, SPO), one (SPO) can be expanded further by adding another object, an object complement or an adverbial. The double-object pattern is illustrated by the following examples:

S	P	O	O
Who	gave	you	this book?
The guide	explained	everything	to us.
Many of them	rely	on the state	for support.

In the *give*-type example, the first object is usually called the "indirect" object and almost always refers to an animate referent who is affected by the verbal transaction. The second object, in our example *the book*, is the "direct" object. Objects realised as prepositional phrases are usually referred to as "prepositional" objects.

The characteristic feature of the SPOC$_o$ pattern is that the second post-verbal constituent does not introduce a new participant but further specifies the object in some way:

S	P	O	C$_o$
You	make	me	nervous.
Everybody	considers	Sally	the best choice.

In the SPOA pattern, the object is followed by an adverbial:

S	P	O	A
He	put	the book	on the shelf.
We	couldn't get	the piano	through the narrow door.

Demonstration/discussion 5.2

Is it really possible to assign any given clause that we might find in a text to one of the seven basic clause types? The answer is yes, if we take into account a few simple expansion strategies which provide the link between the simple basic system and the multiplicity of structures encountered in "live" data.

1) Addition of optional adverbials indicating circumstances in the clause

Optional adverbials Unlike the obligatory adverbials in the SPA and SPOA patterns, which are needed to make the clause grammatical, there are optional adverbials – (A) – which can be added to any of the basic clause types without any formal restrictions as long as such an addition makes sense. (These optional adverbials are also often referred to as adjuncts.)

Thus, a sentence such as:

> Peter yawned a lot at the meeting last night.

reduces to a case of SP (*Peter yawned*), expanded by three optional adverbials which indicate the manner, the place and the time of the yawning:

S	P	(A)	(A)	(A)
Peter	yawned	a lot	at the meeting	last night.

2) Expansion of constituents through pre- and postmodification

Pre- and post-modification Constituents can also be made more complex and longer internally through elaborate pre- and postmodification. Consider, for example, the following example – taken from the scientific texts assembled in the F-LOB corpus:

> In a recent paper (Kemball-Cook et al., 1990), we demonstrated a modified sodium dodecyl sulphate polyacrylamide gel electrophoresis (SDS-PAGE) method for visualization of factor VIII heavy chain (FVIII HC) polypeptides.

This is a straightforward case of (A)SPO. *In a recent paper (Kemball-Cook et al., 1990)* is an optional adverbial, and *a modified sodium dodecyl sulphate polyacrylamide gel electrophoresis (SDS-PAGE) method for visualization of factor VIII heavy chain (FVIII HC) polypeptides* is one single (admittedly very complex) object.

3) Clause embedding and clause combining

Embedding It is also possible to replace any constituent phrase except the verbal predicate itself by a clause. In this way, an object, for example, may be expanded into an object clause (which itself may contain further embedded clauses).

S	P	O
I	cannot believe	this.
I	cannot believe	that you never noticed it.
I	cannot believe	that you never noticed that he was in love with you.

In a similar way, we might add a further adverbial, in the form of a clause, to the three existing ones in another one of our example sentences:

S	P	(A)	(A)	(A)	(A)
Peter	yawned	a lot	at the meeting	last night.	
Peter	yawned	a lot	at the meeting	last night	because the financial secretary read out hundreds of figures in a droning voice.

If there is a hierarchical relationship between the clauses of a sentence (i.e. one is superordinate and the other is subordinate or dependent – cf. Unit 4, p. 57–59), we speak of a **complex sentence**. If we coordinate independent clauses (by means of conjunctions such as *and*, *or* or *but*), we produce a **compound sentence**. Actually attested sentences are often the result of both processes applying simultaneously.

Complex and compound sentences

> [There is a modern tendency to regard Mozart's lively buffo music as deliberately cynical], but [I find it hard [to believe [that this high-spirited, joyous music was meant to be taken at anything other than face value]]].

The second of the main or independent clauses coordinated by *but* here is complex in its internal structure. (Note, incidentally, that the distinction between simple sentences, compound sentences and complex sentences is the one area of syntactic description in which the every-day term *sentence*, whose use was discouraged above, still retains a proper technical sense.)

Problems and challenges

5.3

One fragment of the grammar in which present-day English develops extreme degrees of complexity is non-finite clauses, that is dependent clauses organised around non-finite (that is tense-less) forms of the verb such as infinitives (*sing*, *to sing*) or gerunds and participles (*singing*, *sung*). In many cases the use of such non-finite clauses tends to blur the boundary between superordinate and subordinate clauses. Compare for example:

Non-finite clauses

> People in the region expect that the new high-speed railway will boost the local economy.
> People in the region expect the new high-speed railway to boost the local economy.

In the variant featuring the *that*-clause, the boundary between main and subordinate clause is clear, and so is the status of all constituents:

> [people in the region expect [that [the new high-speed railway] [will boost [the local economy]]]]

The sequence *that the new high-speed railway will boost the local economy* is an embedded object clause dependent on the verb *expect*, and *the new high-speed railway* is the subject of this finite clause. In the non-finite alternative construction, which basically means the same, there is, however, some ambiguity about the status of *the new high-speed railway*. In terms of meaning it seems to operate as the "subject" of the following infinitive, as the sentence does not really say that people in the region expect the railway but the effect resulting from its inauguration:

>people in the region expect [the new high-speed railway to boost the local economy]

Assuming that *the new high-speed railway* is a subject and that *the local economy* is the object of *boost*, we can derive the following passive:

>people in the region expect [the local economy to be boosted [by the new high-speed railway]]

This passive is in fact possible. However, in terms of form, *the new high-speed railway* looks exactly like any other object of *expect*, which suggests an alternative bracketing:

>[people in the region expect the new high-speed railway] to boost the local economy

Assuming that *the new high-speed railway* is the object of *expect*, we can derive the following passive:

>the new high-speed railway is expected to boost the local economy [by people in the region]

This passive is possible too. As we do not want to give up the "passive test" for determining objects which works so well otherwise, we are forced to draw the following conclusion. The construction which we are dealing with is a "fused" one in which one constituent has an unclear grammatical status, allowing two equally legitimate analyses. For the grammarian, this may be a messy situation, for speakers using the language in practice it allows freedom and flexibility, including the option of forming a compound passive of the following type:

>The local economy is expected to be boosted by the new high-speed railway.

Similar analytical problems are posed by superficially similar structures such as the following:

>She is looking for an au-pair speaking English and Portuguese.
>She found the au-pair reading her diary.
>She insisted on the au-pair staying in all evenings of the week.

In the first example, the participle clause *speaking English and Portuguese* can plausibly be replaced by a finite relative clause: *who speaks English and Portuguese*. The possibility of replacing one structure with another without a clear change in meaning is usually considered a grammatical test of functional equivalence. We are thus in a position to argue that the participle clause here functions as a relative clause. Such an analysis is ruled out in the other two cases, however. In *she found the au-pair reading her diary*, the participle clause (*reading her diary*) seems functionally equivalent to a complement of the object (*she found the au-pair useless*) or an adverbial (*she found the au-pair in the kitchen*), which suggests treating it as either an adverbial or as an object-complement clause. Either analysis badly fits the third example, in which the whole sequence *the au-pair staying in all evenings of the week* seems to function as one unit in replacement and question tests and is therefore best regarded as an object, realised as a non-finite clause. This essential unity can also be made explicit by putting the *au-pair* into the genitive – an option which is, incidentally, ruled out in the other two examples:

> She insisted on it.
> What did she insist on?
> She insisted on the au-pair's staying in all evenings of the week.

As in most other Units, students wishing to pursue these questions on the basis of corpora will find ample opportunity to do so. For example, corpus data often make clear where the subtle meaning differences are between competing patterns of complementation. For illustration, consider the following use of *find* (from a text about Keith Douglas' poetry included in the F-LOB corpus):

> His work involves both authenticating and statement-supporting sound-patterns, while his truly programmatic effects are subtle, much more so than, for example, those of Wilfred Owen. While we may feel some of his various effects, we need to dissect them and to work out how and where they connect with his meanings, and we may also try to guess which were conscious and which not. **We shall find them to be** far richer, more intricate, and more apposite, in certain poems, than can be appreciated in a single reading or hearing, or even in many.

Competing complementation patterns – semantic contrasts

Why *find them to be*? And not any of the possible alternatives, such as:

> We shall find that they are far richer ...
> We shall find them far richer ...

Find that something is good/bad is a neutral statement of a fact, without any overtone of personal judgment. *Find something good/bad*, on the other hand, expresses a general or permanent opinion rather than a personal judgment on a specific occasion. And expressing such a personal judgment on a specific occasion is precisely what motivated the writer of this text to choose the original construction rather than any of its alternatives.

Competing complementation patterns – stylistic contrasts

Sometimes, constructional variants differ from each other less in their semantic overtones than in their stylistic values, as markers of informal/spoken or as markers of formal/written usage. Informal spoken language, for example, is particularly rich in devices which help move material to the beginning or the end of an utterance for reasons of focus or emphasis. Compare, for example, the following two constructions with their more formal or "written" alternatives in brackets:

> The fool, he did it again! (*The fool did it again.*)
> I find it very hard, remembering all the details. (*I find remembering the details very hard./It is remembering the details that I find hard.*)

Conversely, passives of the following type would be extremely unlikely to turn up in spontaneous speech but are typical for formal written textual genres, such as academic writing.

> The new production process was shown to be industrially viable.

This can be shown easily by the systematic analysis of corpus data. The following diagram illustrates the frequency of the *shown to*-passive in various textual genres sampled in the British National Corpus:

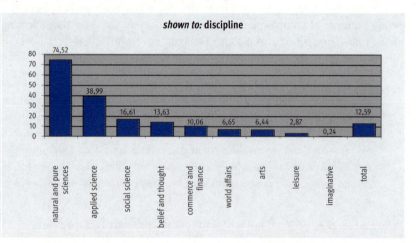

Fig. 5.1 | *Shown to* across written genres (normalised frequency of the construction expressed as instances per million words)

The gradient could not be clearer: the natural sciences, at least with regard to this particular variable, represent the core area of science writing, with applied sciences/engineering following in (a distant) second position. The humanities and the social sciences are the other two genres which narrowly exceed the 12.59/1,000 000 average for written English. In the "imaginative" fiction texts, which are most closely modelled on speech, the construction is as infrequent as it is in the spoken language.

PRACTICE — Unit 5

Further reading

These are the two authoritative reference grammars of present-day English which you as students will typically consult first:

Quirk, Randolph, and Sidney Greenbaum. 1990. *A student's grammar of the English language.* Harlow: Longman. (Accompanying exercises: Sylvia Chalker. 1992. *A Student's English grammar workbook.* Harlow: Longman.)

Huddleston, Rodney, and Geoffrey Pullum. 2005. *A student's introduction to English grammar.* Cambridge: CUP. (Includes exercises.)

Both works are based on their much larger parent volumes, viz.:

Huddleston, Rodney, and Geoffrey Pullum. 2002. *The Cambridge grammar of the English language.* Cambridge: CUP.

Quirk, Randolph, Sidney Greenbaum, Geoffrey Leech, and Jan Svartvik. 1985. *A comprehensive grammar of the English language.* Harlow: Longman.

For further references, consult Unit 4.

Practice

5.4

1. Most of our standard grammatical terminology – for example terms such as subject, gerund, conjunction – was first developed in the analysis of Latin and then transferred to the description of other languages, which of course created the occasional problem of "fit."

   Look up the definition of the category *preposition* in two current reference grammars of English, namely Quirk/Greenbaum's 1990 *Student's grammar of the English language* and Huddleston/Pullum's 2005 *Student's introduction to English grammar*. What differences do you note, and what are the results of these differences for the description of English grammar? Which definition would you prefer for a foreign-language teaching and learning context?

2. Has English got a possessive pronoun? Consider the following evidence:

   > I didn't get this book from George but from **his** friend.
   > It seems George has no friends **of his** own.
   > I didn't get this book from George but from a friend **of his**.
   > If you want the recorder you must ask George. It's **his**.
   >
   > Sally left **her** car in the garage.
   > I have my passport on me but Sally left **hers** in her hotel-room.

3. Check three reference grammars of your choice to find out whether they make use of the part-of-speech category *determiner*. If they do, find out what precisely is subsumed under this category in each case. Is there agreement between your sources?

85

4 Indicate which constructional patterns the verbs listed occur in. Do not rely on your intuition only but also use reference works such as monolingual learners' dictionaries. Make notes of rare, idiomatic or otherwise restricted usages such as *the cat wants out* or *I had me a good time*, which might be difficult to analyse in the given framework:

	SP	SPO	SPC$_S$	SPA	SPOO	SPOC$_O$	SPOA
be							
have							
do							
get							
want							
come							
go							
give							
take							
make							
put							
keep							

5 All of the following sentences are structurally ambiguous. Paraphrase the alternative meanings in each case and assign the correct grammatical analysis to each.

I found this book about the women's question in Ireland.
Visiting relatives can be a nuisance.
You can meet all sorts of people hanging around here.

6 Which of the structures in bold italics are subject clauses?

Whether we will get our money back *is still in doubt.*
Almost everything that he has said in his defence *is completely unconvincing.*
What you need *is a good rest.*
Old people living alone and dying of hypothermia *is a bloody shame.*
Old people living alone *are the group most at risk.*
To give up now *would be to accept defeat.*
*It is heartening **that so many people have agreed to help**.*

7 Analyse the syntactic function of constituent(s) in bold italics and argue for your analysis.

*She used to make a living **giving English lessons**.*
*I'm looking for a book **to consult on weak-stress forms in English**.*
*We're all waiting **for the crew to open the door**.*

Coming home, we found the kids **playing in front of the running television**.
This won't prevent you **falling asleep in his classes**.
... several measures that **failed to** *keep the system running ...*
Who would want **there** *to be another war?*
That was the **wrong** *solution to advocate.*

8 Compare the following English and German sentences and comment on causes of the ungrammaticality of * *I have read*.

I have been reading.	Ich habe gelesen.
* I have read.	Ich habe gelesen.
I have read several books on the subject.	Ich habe mehrere Bücher zum Thema gelesen.

9 The following two sentences illustrate a surface sequence of NP + VP + NP + VP (infinitive) + NP.

They persuaded the parents to sell their house.
They wanted the parents to sell their house.

Test which passives are possible in each case and interpret the results in terms of what they indicate about the grammatical function of the noun phrase *the parents* in either case.

Unit 6

Semantics and lexicology – the meaning of words

Orientation | 6.1

The major function of language in communication is the expression of meaning. Issues of meaning therefore play an important indirect role at all levels of linguistic description. For example, meaning contrasts were crucial in the definition of the phoneme in Unit 2, in which we defined phonemes as speech sounds capable of distinguishing meaning in minimal pairs. Similarly, contrasts between grammatical choices (e.g. past or present perfect, singular or plural, variation between competing patterns of complementation of verbs, etc.) usually imply contrasts of meaning.

The pervasive role of meaning in language and linguistic description

Semantics (a term derived from *semantikos*, the Ancient Greek word for "meaningful"), by contrast, is the subdiscipline of linguistics which devotes itself directly and exclusively to the systematic study of meaning. In that, semantics is chiefly concerned with meaning at the level of the linguistic system, that is de-contextualised or potential meaning, rather than the contextually enriched meaning which arises in actual language use and which will be treated in the next Unit under the heading of "Pragmatics."

Semantics – meaning in focus in linguistic analysis

To illustrate the difference in the way meaning is approached in semantics and pragmatics, consider the following conversational exchange which allegedly took place between a giant of 1960s beat music and a hostile interviewer:

Semantics vs. pragmatics – abstract/ general vs. contextual meaning

> Q: And what do you think of Mozart?
> A: I love his paintings.

Here a command of English grammar and a knowledge of the meaning of the words (i.e. their semantics) is only a first step towards an understanding of what is going on. All we can observe at that level is a well-formed request for information ("what do you think of …"), followed by an equally well-formed answer ("I love his paintings"). Indeed, the exchange is no different from:

> Q: And what do you think of Hemingway?
> A: I really love *The Old Man and the Sea*.

Why then is it that we recognise the hostile intention behind the question and appreciate the elegant way in which the answer parries it? This is due to complex context-bound processes of reasoning which extend far beyond semantics and into the realm of pragmatics, the study of language in context or language in use. Then as now, educated contemporaries are supposed to know

Semantics – meaning of propositions

that Mozart was a famous composer and not a painter and to esteem his work highly. A further assumption underlying the question, which was probably more wide-spread in the 1960s than it is now, is that pop music is barbaric and thus self-evidently inferior to Mozart. Given this context, an innocent-looking question turns out to be a hidden act of aggression.

In his answer, the rock musician uses an ironical strategy. He pretends a level of ignorance in cultural matters that is so enormous as to be unbelievable even in a rock musician and thereby puts the questioner in his place. The way from semantics to pragmatics is the way from a proposition (the abstract, de-contextualised logical content of a sentence) to an utterance situated in a discourse context, or from what is said to what is meant. What the semantic analysis of meaning describes is the abstract meaning that the words in a proposition, and the proposition as a whole, have out of context. The full, contextually enriched meaning of the utterance is analysed in pragmatics. Experience shows that in most acts of communication more is meant or implied in context than what is expressed at the propositional level, so that the way from what is said to what is meant can be a long and complicated one at times.

Lexical semantics – meaning of words

Words, lexemes, lemmas

Within semantics, the central area of interest is **lexical semantics**, the study of the meaning of individual words. Strictly speaking, the unit of semantic description is the **lexeme**, the abstract entity subsuming the various inflectional forms of a word. The lexeme *go* thus comprises the word forms *go*, *goes*, *going*, *went*, *gone*. In spite of their contrasting grammatical potential, all these forms share the same meaning. In lexicography, the lexeme is often present as the **lemma**, i. e. the headword of an entry. Thus, we would not expect a dictionary to have a separate entry for the plural *boys* in addition to the singular *boy*, and if a grammatical variant of a word is included as an entry – for example – because it is irregular and therefore a learning problem, the reference would be to the main entry: the user looking up *went* would be referred to the entry for *go*.

Propositional or "sentence" semantics

Lexicology and lexicography

The focus on lexical semantics does not mean that there are not semantic problems which must be addressed at the level of the clause or sentence (for example negation), but the lexicalisation of concepts as words is clearly the key to an understanding of how speakers "make sense" of the world around them in language. Word meaning is a central concern in two other sub-fields of linguistics, which partly overlap with semantics but are characterised by their own additional agenda, namely **lexicology and lexicography**. Lexicology covers aspects of lexical semantics, but in addition studies the morphological form and structural status of words. Lexicography, in its turn, could be said to be an applied branch of lexicology, as it is chiefly concerned with appropriate ways of representing meaning in dictionaries for various types of users. In that sense, it is a branch of applied linguistics.

Structural and cognitive semantics

Currently, two partly incompatible theoretical approaches dominate the field of lexical semantics – a structural one and a cognitive one. The aim of the structural approach is to describe meaning as part of linguistic structure, whereas the cognitive approach is additionally concerned with the way meanings are perceived and processed by the human mind, as part of the human cognitive capacity.

The structural approach tends to handle complex lexical meanings by breaking them down into simpler **components** or **features**. Such features are conceived of as binary. That is their presence or absence can be determined easily, as in the following example:

Semantic features and the componential analysis of meaning

boy	[+ human], [– female], [– adult]
girl	[+ human], [+ female], [– adult]
people	[+ human], [+ plural]
person	[+ human], [+ adult]
woman	[+ human], [+ female], [+ adult]

Table 6.1
Componential analysis

This analysis claims that the difference between *person* and *woman* just resides in the presence of one such "atom" of meaning in the latter word and its absence in the former. If we add the feature [+ female] to the meaning of "person," we get the more complex and specific meaning "woman," whereas if we take out the feature [+ female] from "woman," we're left with "person." (For [+ female], [– male] could of course be used, or vice versa.)

Semantic features are supposed to be general building blocks of the semantic universe of a language, so that they are useful for the semantic analysis of large numbers of individual words. For example, the features [male] and [female] help us in the analysis of many terms used to denote higher animals, such as *bull* and *cow*, or *stallion* and *mare*.

One limitation of the feature-based approach to meaning is that it forces binary decisions where ordinary life-experience would argue for gradual transitions or flexible and context-sensitive case-by-case judgments. On a binary analysis, for example, children and adolescents are summarily ruled out of the category "person" by assigning it the feature [+ adult]. The question is whether this is justified. Corpus data suggest that it may well be. These are the two relevant instances of the use of *person* from the British National Corpus:

Limitations of a feature-based approach to word meaning

1	A10 321	For example, a 70 **year old person** living alone would have their income made up to £53.40 a week.
2	INE 129	Right, the reason that er an officer would still stay <pause> er with an eleven year old child, a three year old child, or <pause> t-- to get to the realms of fantasy a ninety **year old person** is that person can still be at risk <pause> not necessarily from the police officers, but from anybody else in that building and therefore they've got to remain er in that room until such time as I'm satisfied that everything is clear.

Fig. 6.1
The use of *person*, two instances from the BNCweb

Where the word *person* is used in conjunction with an attribute giving the age, it is clear that we are dealing with adults. We would not expect sentences such as the following:

? A three-year old person was observed scrawling paint all over the stair-case.

The definition of persons as [+ adult] thus seems robust and well justified, and the fact that we may occasionally waver in applying the designation to sixteen-year-olds is not a strong argument against the feature-based approach.

There are, however, cases for which such a feature-based semantic analysis does not merely run into the occasional minor problem but is impossible from the very start. A textbook example is the class of English words denoting containers for liquids (*cup, mug, vase, bowl, jug, pot, ...*) – an example first discussed in Labov 1973. Typical "features" which might be invoked in distinguishing cups, mugs and bowls might be:

Fig. 6.2 | Cup

1) size: cups are small, while mugs are bigger
2) shape: cups are short and round while mugs are tall and elongated in shape, with a rectangular profile
3) saucers: cups come with saucers but mugs don't
4) handles: both cups and mugs have handles while bowls don't

On this theory, confronted with the object represented in Fig. 6.2, we would recognise the feature combination "[+ small] [+ round profile] [+ short] [+ saucer] [+ handle]" and use the word *cup*. Fig. 6.3, on the other hand, shows a "mug," because the features are combined differently.

However, it is easy to see that this approach will take us only so far. For one thing, the first two "features" – size and shape – are not binary but gradient. What would be the appropriate name for the following object, for example?

If it stood five inches tall, we would probably refer to it as a mug,

Fig. 6.3 | Mug

even if the shape reminded us of a cup. We would probably continue to do so even if the object came with a saucer. If on the other hand it stood two inches tall and came filled with espresso, it would be a cup even without a saucer.

Fig. 6.4
Cup or mug?

The other two criteria – presence or absence of saucers and handles – are binary features, as handles and saucers are either present or not. Again, though, we note a difference to the feature-semantic analysis of *woman* as [+ human], [+ female], [+ adult]. If we removed the feature [+ female] from this series, we would end up with a different meaning, namely *adult* or, possibly, *person*. If, on the other hand, we thought of a cup or mug without handles, we would not automatically re-label these objects as bowls or vases but continue to consider them as less typical examples of the category of cups and mugs.

The way our semantic categorisation seems to work here is not through decomposition of complex meanings and categories into constituent features. Rather, we have an ideal representative, a perfect example, of a category in mind – or to use the technical term: a *prototype* – and match existing exemplars with this prototype. A category such as "cup," for example, will thus have a clear centre, comprising all those exemplars which match the ideal prototype very closely, and a fuzzy periphery which might even partly overlap with neighbouring categories, so that speakers, depending on the context or their preferences, might actually legitimately use two terms for one and the same object. It is easy to see that such wavering is less likely to occur in deciding whether a particular human being is a boy or a girl, or a man or a woman.

Semantic prototypes – psychologically realistic categorisation

Over-all, "binary" constellations of the "man-woman" type are more difficult to find in natural languages than prototypical or fuzzy ones of the "cup-mug" type. Holistic classification on the basis of prototypes is more realistic psychologically than analysis into semantic features. Therefore, the prototype approach has come to be associated with cognitive semantics.

It should be added, though, that given the current state of research, it would be too early to endorse one of the two competing models whole-heartedly and dismiss the other one as irrelevant or outdated. In spite of the obvious advantages of the prototype approach to lexical meaning, semantic features continue to play a role, for example in the description of lexical fields or in formal descriptions of the interface between semantics and grammar. Thus, the feature [+ human] neatly accounts for the fact that certain types of antecedents in English relative clauses need to be referred to by *who* rather than *which*.

I know **an expert** [+ human] **who** can help you.
I know **a book** [– human] **which** will help you.

6.2 | Demonstration/discussion

Meaning, reference, sense

In everyday usage, the term *meaning* is frequently ambiguous, covering the notion of **reference** or **denotation** (i.e. the relation between a linguistic expression and the entity it refers to in the real world) and the notion of **sense** (i.e. de-contextualised or abstract linguistic meaning). To illustrate the distinction with an example: all of the following expressions have the same **referent**, namely the political leader of the UK at the time of the writing of this book:

> British Prime Minister Gordon Brown
> Scottish Labour politician Gordon Brown
> Tony Blair's successor as Prime Minister

Their **sense**, however, is different in each case, highlighting different properties of the person in question. Strictly speaking, it is only the sense of an expression which is in the proper domain of linguistic semantics.

Polysemy – one word-form with two or more related meanings

The distinction between sense and reference is fundamental because most words in a language tend to be **polysemous**, i.e. they will have more than one sense. The word *party*, for example, has two senses: (1) an organised political group or (2) a festivity or celebration of some kind. These two meanings are not very close, but if we consider other uses such as a *working party*, we can discern a third, more general sense, namely "people united around a common cause or purpose." It is this sense which provides the missing link, so to speak, and which was in actual fact the historical root of both. This polysemy is not a problem in practical communication, though, because in any referential expression only one of the several senses of a word is usually activated.

Homonymy – one word-form with two or more unrelated meanings

There are other cases in which a word has more than one sense but where these senses are not related in any way. Thus, English *grave* has a sense "tomb" (e.g. *from the cradle to the grave*), etymologically related to German *Grab*, and a sense "serious" (as in *a matter of grave concern*), ultimately deriving from the Latin adjective *gravis* via Old French. Here, two originally different words were collapsed into one sound shape owing to the accidents of the phonetic history of English. Linguists generally refer to such cases as **homonymy** rather than **polysemy**. The distinction is clear in principle but difficult to uphold in practice because a decision between the two occasionally requires profound knowledge of complex language-historical processes.

Semantic relations between words and semantic structures in the vocabulary

In practice, the most important challenge faced in semantic analysis is to move beyond the description of the meaning of individual lexical items in isolation. A first step is to study relations holding between two words. These can be of the following types.

1) Synonymy

Two words are considered **synonyms** if they mean the same thing or, to give the precise technical description, if they are fully interchangeable in all contexts of use. Such full synonymy is a luxury that natural languages generally don't afford, so that in practice the study of synonyms is concerned with determining the extent of the overlap in meaning between two or more words. Typical constellations include the following.

Two words have broadly the same **denotation** (i.e. potential reference) but one of them expresses an additional positive or negative emotional **connotation** as part of its sense. The words *youngster(s)* and *youth(s)* are near synonyms in this sense. They both refer to (male) adolescents, but as the following typical examples from the British National Corpus (BNC) show, the contexts of use for *youth(s)* tend to be overwhelmingly negative, whereas those for *youngsters* are neutral or even positive.

Semantic relations holding between two words

Synonyms

Same denotation, but different connotation

20	KRM 1793	Two policemen were hurt when 40 **youths** fought in the centre of Wallingford.
21	KRM 2622	Three **youths** from the Forest of Dean have appeared before Hereford magistrates, charged in connection with an incident in which two policemen were beaten up near Ross-on-Wye.
22	KRT 2989	It follows an incident last month when police reinforcements were needed to quell troubles involving around four hundred **youths** near the Ale House in Castle Street in the city.
23	KRT 4024	There were a number of incidents where **youths** blocked roads with burning tyres, and started hurling stones at passing cars.
24	KRT 4953	In recent incidents, [...] **youths** stamped on a W P C's head as she tried to arrest them, and earlier this week an officer was injured when he and a colleague were attacked by a gang.
25	KRU 74	The demonstrations soon turned into confrontations with Israeli police and army units, a number of **youths** were killed and hundreds of people injured.
20	FLR 198	telling **youngsters**, when they can't actually understand the concept of having sex.
21	FXT 222	Erm we've er we you'll be looking at education, our biggest service, and a service which we should which is going through some very profound changes at the moment where we're trying to er increase the resources that are within individual schools so that they can make their own decisions erm about er how they best meet the needs of their **youngsters**.
22	FXT 377	And the government's so called mum's army proposals for teaching **youngsters** are expected to come under fire at a meeting in Nottingham later today.
23	FXT 594	**Youngsters** at a Nottingham school have become video directors to combat joyriding.

Fig. 6.5
The use of *youth(s)* and *youngster(s)*, some examples from the BNC

24	FXT 675	Aid agencies are claiming that increasing homelessness in Nottingham is forcing more and more **youngsters** to turn to begging or even prostitution.
25	FXT 678	She says many **youngsters** who've been brought up in care are often incapable of looking after themselves when they leave.

Same sense but different stylistic level

Another common constellation in present-day English is the co-existence of a usually Germanic or Anglo-Saxon word in spoken use and a stylistically more elevated synonym of Latin or French origin (which usually remains confined to written and formal styles):

to buy	–	to purchase
to begin	–	to commence
to fight	–	to combat
to hide	–	to conceal
to feed	–	to nourish

Words such as *buy, begin, fight, hide* and *feed* would be common in corpora of written and spoken English, whereas you would have to consult corpora of written and formal English if you were looking for instances of *purchase, commence, combat, conceal* and *nourish*.

2) Antonymy

Antonyms

This sense relation is well illustrated by adjective pairs such as:

tall	–	short
expensive	–	cheap
hot	–	cold
clever	–	stupid

Each of the two members of the pairs defines points at opposite ends of a scale, with transitions in between. For example, "warm," "tepid" or "lukewarm" water has temperatures in between hot and cold; "reasonable" prices are somewhere in between expensive and cheap, and so on.

Markedness

In addition, one member of each pair is the **unmarked** option, carrying with it no presupposition of any kind, whereas the other is the **marked** option. In the pair *clever – stupid*, for example, *clever* is the unmarked member. The question *but how clever are your opponents?* is a neutral one, leaving open whether the opponents are clever or stupid. The question *but how stupid are your opponents?*, which contains the marked choice, on the other hand, comes with a previous assumption that they are more stupid than average.

In a looser sense, the term **antonym** can also be used to cover a number of other contrasting relationships between words. Consider, for example:

alive – dead
married – unmarried

At least in the literal senses of the relevant words, there are no gradual transitions here. Whereas in the case of gradable antonyms such as *clever* and *stupid* the assertion that you are not clever does not automatically imply the opposite, namely that you are stupid, here the negation of one term fully implies the other. If you are not alive, you're dead, and if you're not married, you're unmarried (i. e. single, widowed, divorced, or cohabiting).

Contrasting or opposing sense relations are not confined to the adjectival domain, but are also found in many verbs and nouns. Note that most of these relations are not normally referred to as antonymic in the linguistic literature:

to buy – to sell
to increase – to decrease
master – servant
wealth – poverty

In an even looser sense, a word such as *brother* stands in opposition to *sister*, and *North* stands in opposition to *South*. Note, however, that *brother* can never function as the negation or opposite of *sister* in the way that *poverty* is the negation of *wealth*. Rather, these words occupy contrasting positions in some predetermined relational framework such as a kinship system or the directions of the compass.

3) Hyperonymy, hyponymy

Whereas synonyms and antonyms are not subordinate or superordinate to one another, such hierarchical relationships are found in the following cases:

Hyperonyms and hyponyms

dungbeetle – insect
robin – bird
to strangle – to kill

A *robin* is a kind of bird, along with many other kinds, such as *sparrows*, *doves*, *eagles*, *ostriches*, *chickens*, etc.; therefore *bird* functions as the superordinate term or **hyperonym**, and the other terms are **hyponyms** subordinated under the major category.

A special case of subordination is part-whole relations of the following kind, which are sometimes referred to as meronymy. One term refers to a constituent part of another:

Meronyms

sleeve – shirt
nose – face
finger – hand

Semantics and Lexicology – The Meaning of Words

Semantic relations between larger numbers of words

The lexical field

So far, we have focussed on semantic relationships obtaining between two words. Clearly, it would be nice if we were able to find larger ordered sub-structures within the vocabulary of a language. One promising candidate for such a sub-structure is the **lexical field**, i.e. the structured description of a semantically coherent portion of the lexicon.

There seems to be a negative tendency in natural languages which usually results in more words being available to express negative concepts than positive ones. It would be interesting to speculate on the psychological motivation for this tendency. Whatever the reasons for the trend, it accounts for the following depressingly long but by no means complete list of verbs available in English to specify the act of human beings putting each other and other living creatures to death. At the centre of the field is the most general term, *kill*, and there are at least six axes along which specifications can be added.

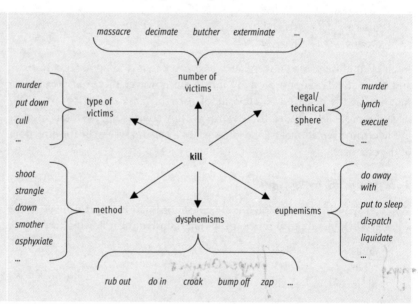

Fig. 6.6 Lexical field "kill"

One axis shows that English speakers wish to make distinctions based on the victim of the killing. Whereas the general verb *to kill* can be used for any kind of victim (people, pets, other animals), *to murder* is reserved for human victims exclusively, and additionally conveys that the killing was the result of malicious intention. In tragic circumstances, people can be killed by mistake, but we would not usually say that someone was murdered by mistake. *To put down*, on the other hand, is used for pets, is carried out intentionally but not maliciously: *our old dog was so weak and sick he had to be put down*. We would not normally use this verb with objects denoting human beings and wild animals. The third verb in the list – *to cull* – is different again. It means "(systematically) select and kill in order to improve the stock, reduce the population or prevent the spread of a contagious disease." As such it can be used both for badgers living in the wild (and suspected of spreading tubercolosis) and for turkeys threatened by avian flu.

All the semantic relations between words which we have discussed in this section have been demonstrated here purely on the level of the linguistic system. Practically all of them, however, are also relevant psychologically – in the "mental lexicon." Confronted with a particular lexical trigger in an association test, speakers often think of synonyms or antonyms. Foreign-language teachers who present new words not as individual items but in sense groups are likely to achieve better learning outcomes than others.

The mental lexicon

Problems and challenges

| 6.3

Collocations – the unknown territory between syntax and semantics

It seems reasonable to assume that the only limits on the combination of words in a clause are that (1) a particular combination makes sense from a semantic point of view and (2) that the combination follows the rules of the grammar of the language in question. Thus, an * *iron paper-cup* is wrong because the combination is nonsensical (violating constraint (1)), and * *this paper-cups* is wrong because the singular demonstrative is combined with the plural noun (violating constraint (2)).

Unfortunately, though, as any advanced learner of a foreign language will know from experience, this is not the way natural languages work, and there is a long way from what is merely correct or logical to what is fully natural and idiomatic.

Much more problematical are the arbitrary restrictions on the combination of words which are generally subsumed under the heading of **collocations**. Collocations are (more or less) fixed expressions in which the over-all meaning remains compositional but the combination is unpredictable in other ways.

As a first illustration, consider the following sentence frames, in which the gaps could all be filled in principle by the verb *to become*:

    the country's oil wells are beginning to _____ dry
    then I _____ ill
    he _____ mad
    Granny _____ 90 last year
    may all your dreams _____ true
    the dusty old classic _____ alive in the film version
    she _____ pale on hearing the story
    as time wore on, her hair _____ pale
    the milk _____ sour in the heat

Become may be an appropriate choice grammatically and semantically, but nevertheless it is not the most natural one in most cases. These are the synonyms of *become* which native speakers would in all likelihood prefer. They are sometimes extremely specific, and their distribution is rather arbitrary and only very partly systematic.

>the country's oil wells are beginning to **run** dry
>then I **fell** ill
>he **went** mad
>Granny **turned** 90 last year
>may all your dreams **come** true
>the dusty old classic **came** alive in the film version
>she **turned/went** pale on hearing the story
>as time wore on, her hair **turned** pale
>the milk **went** sour in the heat

We could argue – on the basis of *the milk going sour* and *people going mad* – that *go* replaces *become* in cases in which the transition is fairly rapid, drastic and has a negative direction. But this "regularity" would be rather limited in scope. Even if we were faced with runaway inflation we would not say * *everything went horribly expensive* overnight. *Turn*, by contrast, seems to denote a gradual process in a more or less expected direction (witness the example involving *hair turning grey*), but again this "generalisation" does not even carry over to the example with the dry oil-well, which – as shown – will *run dry* and not *turn dry*.

Collocations raise an extremely important theoretical-linguistic issue. What linguists have to account for is the huge expressive potential of human languages, the millions and millions of different utterances produced by speakers and writers. How is this achieved?

If we regard the grammar as the driving force, the answer is simple. There is a limited number of phonemes, which combine into several thousand different morphemes, which in turn combine into the several tens of thousands of words found in a typical language. These words are then made into clauses in conformity with a limited number of very general grammatical rules. This model has been dubbed the "slot and filler" model by the famous British corpus-linguist John Sinclair (1933–2007): there is a grammatical structure or pattern, and the words are filled into the empty slots provided by this pattern in accordance with the grammatical rules. On this view, collocational restrictions are irksome exceptions.

If, on the other hand, we take into account the fact that collocational restrictions are pervasive in natural language-use, we will arrive at another conclusion. The deepest foundation of our ability to speak a language is a tremendous feat of memory. We have mastered tens of thousands of more or less fixed building blocks, sentence fragments, chunks of language.

Deciding between these two opposing views (or rather integrating them in a working model of linguistic competence) is a task which requires corpus-based analysis. The study of collocations has been one of the mainstays of corpus-based research since its inception.

Consider, for example, the following pair-wise combinations between two verbs and two possible objects:

	goal(s)	aim(s)
reach	reach (the/a) goal(s)	reach (the/an) aim(s)
achieve	achieve (the/a) goal(s)	achieve (the/an) aim(s)

Table 6.2
Combinations between verbs and objects

All four possible combinations make sense and might therefore be attested. However, corpus-based exploration will soon establish the fact that *reach a goal* and *achieve an aim* are normal usage, and so is *achieve a goal*. *Reach an aim*, however, is not. The BNC, for example, has 220 instances of *achieve* combining with *aim(s)*, but only one [!] such case involving *reach*. As most corpus-search software allows users to compute the statistical likelihood of co-occurrence patterns, it is easy to extend the scope of the analysis to cover further object noun phrases. In the BNC, the following noun phrases collocate with *achieve* and *reach* respectively (listing in descending order of collocational strength):

object collocates of *achieve*	object collocates of *reach*
objectives	agreement
goals	conclusion
success	peak
objective	stage
results	point
goal	age
independence	climax
aim	decision
aims	end
balance	top
ends	level
status	conclusions
result	heights
fame	destination
target	semi-finals

Table 6.3
Collocations between verbs and objects

Note that there is practically no overlap between the two lists. The meanings of the two verbs *achieve* and *reach* thus turn out to differ in subtle ways. In most uses involving *achieve*, there is an idea that an effort to meet some set target has been successful; with *reach*, there is a more literal, spatial underlying idea: a situation develops towards some conclusion or climax through certain stages. However, this vague generalisation cannot explain all the observations exhaustively. The answer to the question why some end-points are achieved, while others are reached is to an extent arbitrary and language-specific.

This leads over to the practical implications of collocational restrictions for foreign language teaching and learning. Something which is arbitrary and language specific is by definition difficult-to-learn, and indeed the example of *achieve* and *reach* nicely serves to make this point. The German verb *erreichen* collocates with objects found with both *achieve* and *reach* in English. In comparison to English, German makes fewer differentiations in this area, and mistakes such as the following, from the "German" sub-section of the International Corpus of Learner English (ICLE), are commonplace even in the English of advanced students.

This is the so-called positive discrimination policy; giving preference to certain 'groups' (e.g. women) in order *to reach a stage of balance* between this group and one or more others.

[…] whether or not *the gradual change* towards a society free from Apartheid *can be reached* without bloodshed.

He or she is faced with a problem, struggles to cope with it, and *reaches a different, more objective view of him-* or herself and his or her relation to community.

Fig. 6.7 | Bram Stoker (1847–1912)

One prominent witness to the plight of the foreign learner is a literary figure and has a Romanian rather than a German native-language background – Count Dracula, from Bram Stoker's 1897 novel of the same title. An extract from *Dracula* is therefore a fitting conclusion to the present discussion.

Text 6.1 | Bram Stoker, *Dracula*, ch. 2

What the writers say

"But, Count," I said, "You know and speak English thoroughly!" He bowed gravely.

"I thank you, my friend, for your all too-flattering estimate, but yet I fear that I am but a little way on the road I would travel. True, I know the grammar and the words, but yet I know not how to speak them."

"Indeed," I said, "You speak excellently."

"Not so," he answered. "Well, I know that, did I move and speak in your London, none there are who would not know me for a stranger. That is not enough for me. Here I am noble. I am a Boyar. The common people know me, and I am master. But a stranger in a strange land, he is no one. Men know him not, and to know not is to care not for. I am content if I am like the rest, so that no man stops if he sees me, or pauses in his speaking if he hears my words, 'Ha, ha! A stranger!' I have been so long master that I would be master still, or at least

PROBLEMS AND CHALLENGES   Unit 6

that none other should be master of me. You come to me not alone as agent of my friend Peter Hawkins, of Exeter, to tell me all about my new estate in London. You shall, I trust, rest here with me a while, so that by our talking I may learn the English intonation. And I would that you tell me when I make error, even of the smallest, in my speaking. I am sorry that I had to be away so long today, but you will, I know forgive one who has so many important affairs in hand."

Of course I said all I could about being willing, and asked if I might come into that room when I chose. He answered, "Yes, certainly," and added.

"You may go anywhere you wish in the castle, except where the doors are locked, where of course you will not wish to go. There is reason that all things are as they are, and did you see with my eyes and know with my knowledge, you would perhaps better understand." I said I was sure of this, and then he went on.

A final, but more trivial problem for semantic description is **idioms**, that is fixed expressions whose meaning is not compositional, that is cannot be added up from the meanings of the individual words contributing to the fixed expressions. Basically, idioms look like syntactic phrases but function as words semantically.   Idioms

Thus, the expression *to spill the beans* means "to tell a secret;" as such, it can be put into various tenses and conjugated throughout the first, second and third persons in the singular and plural:

   Nobody knew until he spilled the beans.
   Don't you dare to spill the beans again.

However, the phrase being an idiom, it is not possible to add adjectives to *bean* or to passivise the phrase, as this would immediately force an entirely absurd literal reading:

   * He spilled some more stale old beans which did not really interest anyone much.
   * Why don't you spill your dirty little beans?
   * Sooner or later most beans were spilled.

Further reading

Culicover, Peter W. 2004. "Review article on *The Cambridge Grammar of the English Language*, by Rodney Huddleston and Geoffrey K. Pullum." *Language* 80: 127–41.
Evans, Vyvyan, and Melanie Green. 2006. *Cognitive linguistics: An introduction*. Edinburgh: Edinburgh University Press.

Labov, William. 1973. "The boundaries of words and their meanings." In: Charles-James N. Bailey & Roger W. Shuy (eds.). *New ways of analyzing variation in English*. Washington DC: Georgetown University Press. 340–373.
Lakoff, George, and Mark Johnson. 1980. *Metaphors we live by*. Chicago IL: University of Chicago Press.
Löbner, Sebastian. 2002. *Understanding semantics*. London: Arnold.
Lyons, John. 1995. *Linguistic semantics: An introduction*. Cambridge: CUP.
Taylor, John R. 2003. *Linguistic categorization: Prototypes in linguistic theory*. 3rd ed. Oxford: Clarendon Press.

6.4 | Practice

1. Propose a semantic analysis of the following words based on the decomposition of word meanings into features.

   horse(s), stallion, mare, colt, filly, foal
   cattle, bull, cow, calf
   sheep, ram, ewe, lamb
   frog

   Which problems do you note?

2. A feature-based componential analysis of the word *mother* might take the following shape:

   mother [+ human, + female, + adult, + "has given birth to at least one child"]

   Is this analysis suitable to capture the many established metaphorical uses of the word *mother* in actual discourse, such as *Mother Earth*, *Mother Nature*, *mother tongue*, *mother land*, *motherboard*?

3. Consult the OED to find out whether the following words are homonyms or polysemous.

   lock, school, grade, lie

4. Search for instances of the words *loneliness* and *solitude* in a corpus of your choice. In which ways do these two words differ in meaning?

   The following is a short extract from a story by American writer Edgar Allan Poe (1809–1849) which uses a lot of synonyms (which I have italicised).

What the writers say

For my own part, I soon found a *dislike* to it [= the cat] arising within me. This was just the reverse of what I had anticipated; but – I know not how or why it was – its evident fondness for myself rather *disgusted* and *annoyed* me. By slow degrees, these feelings of *disgust* and *annoyance* rose into the *bitterness of hatred* [...] gradually – very gradually – I came to look upon it with unutterable *loathing* [...].

Suggest ways of making explicit where the various synonyms differ in meaning.

5 The following table gives one linguist's intuitions about the type of verb + adjective "resultative" constructions discussed above.

Acceptability of V + Adj resultative constructions: a native speaking linguist's intuitions (Culicover 2004)

	become	get	fall	come	go	turn	grow
asleep			Y				
awake	Y			Y			
aware	Y						Y
dead		(Y)	Y		Y		Y
alive	Y			Y			
nasty	Y	Y				Y	Y
nice	Y	Y				Y	Y
tall		Y					Y
short		Y	Y				Y
happy	Y	Y					Y
sad	Y	Y	Y			Y	Y
sharp	Y	Y				Y	Y
flat	Y	Y	Y		Y	Y	Y
smooth	Y	Y				Y	Y
sick	Y	Y	Y				Y
true	Y			Y			
mad	Y	Y			Y	Y	Y
nuts	Y	Y			Y		(Y)
silent	Y	Y	Y		Y	Y	Y
loud	Y	Y					Y
loose	Y	Y		Y			

Text 6.2
Edgar Allan Poe,
"The Black Cat,"
1845

Fig. 6.8
Edgar Allan Poe
(1809–1849)

open		Y	Y	Y			
closed		Y	Y				
red	Y	Y				Y	Y
sour	Y	Y			Y	Y	Y

Now consult a corpus of your choice and find out which of the collocations assumed to be possible are actually attested in your material. Does your material contain any combinations **not** considered possible by Culicover?

V + Adj resultative constructions in [name the corpus of your choice]

	become	get	fall	come	go	turn	grow
asleep							
awake							
aware							
dead							
alive							
nasty							
nice							
tall							
short							
happy							
sad							
sharp							
flat							
smooth							
sick							
true							
mad							
nuts							
silent							
loud							
loose							
open							
closed							
red							
sour							

6 Dictionaries

Dictionaries come in many kinds:

- monolingual, designed for native speakers
- monolingual, designed for foreign learners
- bilingual
- historical

etc.

Consult various dictionaries to find out whether they help you in finding an English equivalent for the German idiomatic collocations *schwacher Trost* und *fauler Kompromiss*.

Which of the dictionaries give you grammatical in addition to semantic information – for example so that you can avoid common learner errors such as writing * *I suggested to have a break* (instead of correct *I suggested having a break*) or * *no possibility to do something* (instead of correct *no possibility of doing something*)?

7

Metaphors we live by is the title of a classic of cognitive semantics written by George Lakoff and Mark Johnson (1980). In this book the authors point out that metaphors, or verbal imagery, are not just an ornamental luxury but an essential feature of language. One of the more obvious conceptual metaphors which are said to be almost universally productive is "TIME is SPACE." German and English instances of this guiding metaphor are *long time*, *lange Zeit*, *die Vergangenheit hinter sich lassen und der Zukunft [!] ins Angesicht sehen* or *life is short*. Somewhat more striking is the "IDEAS are FOOD"-complex, which, however, is also attested cross-linguistically: *unausgegorene Ideen*, *half-baked ideas*; *ein Buch verschlingen*, *devour the book*; *that's food for thought*, *das muss ich erst verdauen*.

Would such ideas be at all useful to explicate the use of metaphor in the following text by Canadian writer Margaret Atwood (b. 1939)?

What the writers say

Giving Birth. But who gives it? And to whom is it given? Certainly it doesn't feel like giving, which implies a flow, a gentle handing over, no coercion. But there is scant gentleness here; it's too strenuous, the belly like a knotted fist, squeezing, the heavy trudge of the heart, every muscle in the body tight and moving, as in a slow-motion of a high-jump [...]

   No one ever says *giving death*, although they are in some ways the same, events, not things. And delivering, that act the doctor is generally believed to perform: who delivers what? Is it the mother who is delivered, like a prisoner

|Text 6.3
Margaret Atwood,
"Giving Birth," in
*Dancing Girls
and other Stories*,
London, 1982, 225

Fig. 6.9
Margaret Atwood
(b. 1939)

being released. Surely not; nor is the child delivered to the mother like a letter through a slot. How can you be both the sender and the receiver at once? Was someone in bondage, is someone made free? Thus language, muttering in its archaic tongues of something, yet one more thing, that needs to be re-named.

It won't be by me, though. These are the only words I have, I'm stuck with them, stuck in them.

Unit 7

Pragmatics and discourse analysis

Orientation

Pragmatics – a word ultimately derived from an ancient Greek verb meaning "to do" – is defined as the study of language in use. In phonology, morphology and syntax the focus is on the study of the formal elements of linguistic structures and the linguistic system. These structures and the linguistic system as a whole are studied in separation from possible contexts of use. As was shown in the preceding Unit, the communicative context and language use do not play a central role even in semantics, the linguistic sub-discipline devoted to the study of meaning. What is in focus in semantics is the propositional content (that is the semantic potential of a clause or sentence), not its actual meaning in a specific context of use. In other words, we can study phonology, morphology, syntax and semantics without really paying any systematic attention to the intentions of speakers or writers, the context of the utterance or text, or the effects they produce on listeners and readers. This is different in pragmatics. Here the focus is on the **utterance** in its specific **communicative context**, and on its relation to the intentions of the speaker and the responses of the listener.

Utterances usually do not occur in isolation but as parts of larger amounts of language in use – conversations, radio interviews, news broadcasts, letters, e-mail messages, newspaper articles, chapters in books, poems, and many more. Such larger units, especially when written, have traditionally been referred to as **texts**. **Textlinguistics**, the study of textual structures and the relation of texts to their context, is a research tradition which therefore overlaps with pragmatics in important respects. One focus of textlinguistic research which every student of English should know about is the study of **coherence** and **cohesion** in texts. While coherence refers to the unity of a text in terms of its subject matter or content (and is thus largely outside the realm of linguistics), cohesion refers to the ways in which links are established between sentences – for example through pronouns, coordinating and subordinating conjunctions, or cohesive adverbials such as *as a result* or *by contrast*. Just take a moment to think about the weaknesses in the use of cohesive devices in the writing even of advanced foreign-language learners, and you will realise how relevant this topic might be for you. A more inclusive term than *text* is **discourse**. It is thus the term preferred by linguists who in addition to the linguistic element also wish to focus on visual or gestural components of the communicative message. Like textlinguistics, **discourse analysis** shares many concerns with pragmatics.

| 7.1

Language as an abstract de-contextualised system vs. language in use

Texts and discourse

Coherence and cohesion

In this introduction, discourse analysis will be represented by the analysis of a stretch of authentic conversation given in Section 7.3 below.

It is fascinating to study language use: how people make public their inner feelings, use language (rather than brute force) to influence others or describe the world around them in words. On such an analysis even a mundane object of study such as an informal and routine conversation turns out to involve a surprising amount of skills. Participants in a conversation signal their continued attention when listening, indicate when they have finished their contribution, or – if they disagree with their interlocutors – are able to express such disagreement in very finely tuned nuances.

Pragmatics is interdisciplinary

It is obvious that in studying language use in context we are pushing the limits of linguistic analysis. In pragmatics more so than in any other subfield, research is interdisciplinary, combining the concerns of linguistics with those of the philosophy of language, cognitive science, psychology, anthropology and sociology. This is reflected by the fact that the scholars who contributed to the development of linguistic pragmatics were very often people from outside the field of linguistics, one example being the prominent psychologist Karl Bühler, whose contribution will be discussed in the next paragraph.

Models of communication

Any kind of pragmatic investigation presupposes a **model of communication** as a basic frame of orientation. One of the earliest such models is the "organon"-model proposed by Karl Bühler (1879–1963). "Organon" is the Ancient Greek word for "tool." Indeed, this captures well the foundational insight of pragmatics that language should not primarily be analysed as a self-sufficient structure but as a tool which speakers and writers use to achieve certain communicative ends. After a long and distinguished academic career in Germany and Austria, Bühler was forced to emigrate to the United States by the Nazis.

Bühler's "organon" model

Expressive, directive and representational functions of language

As can be seen in Fig. 7.1, the model provides for a **sender**, a **receiver**, and a **context**. The linguistic sign ("S") performs three possible **functions** – as symptom, signal and symbol. With regard to the sender, it is a **symptom** and has an **expressive** or **emotive function** (through making public the sender's inner state). With regard to the **receiver**, it is a **signal** and has an **appellative, directive** or **conative function** (by influencing his/her behaviour through appeals, orders, requests or persuasion). With regard to the context, finally, it is a **symbol** and has a **representational** or **referential function** (by putting into words information about the world). As a psychologist interested in child language, Bühler was keenly aware that the expressive and appellative functions emerge much earlier than the representational function in the human infant, and that they remain important in the everyday conversational activity of adults. This is a welcome corrective to a frequently held naïve belief (shared by some traditions in philosophy) that human language chiefly serves to express information.

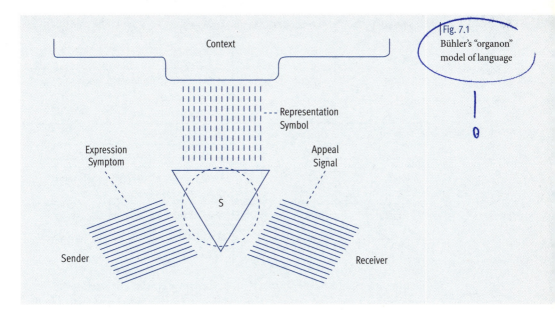

Fig. 7.1
Bühler's "organon" model of language

Bühler's model was eventually refined by Roman Jakobson (1896–1982), who took over the three constituents of the communicative process found in Bühler (**sender**, **receiver**, and **context**), but added three more, namely the **message**, the **channel**, and the **code**. He did so in order to make explicit assumptions which are taken for granted in Bühler's model. Sender and receiver can only communicate if they share a common **code**: A Russian utterance is lost on someone who does not speak this language, and an illiterate cannot make sense of a written text in any language. The utterance is a message which is by definition constructed according to the rules of a given code. Of course, if we wish, we can also critically reflect on the code we are using and challenge some of its rules and conventions (the type of "metalinguistic" activity discussed below). Before we communicate, therefore we usually test the **channel**, i.e. we try to make a first contact to establish whether we share a code that makes communication possible. Finally, Jakobson wishes to emphasise that the **message** itself is worth closer attention. Linguistic structures are complex, and speakers or writers can therefore often choose between alternative ways of performing a communicative task.

Jakobson's model of communication

As in Bühler's model, each of the six constituents of the communicative process is associated with one communicative function. The tabular overview below names them and gives an illustrative example each.

Table 7.1 The six communicative functions in Jakobson's model of communication

Constituent of the communicative process	Associated function	Example
1) sender	expressive/emotive	[A: And then I lost my manners, got up, said "you fool" and left!] B: **You didn't!**
2) receiver	conative	Put that cigarette out!
3) context	referential	Napoleon was banished to St. Helena in 1815.
4) code	metalinguistic	A verb such as *purchase* is not used in spoken English. Replace it by *buy*.
5) message	poetic	When the going gets tough, the tough get going.
6) channel	phatic	[A to B, in nasty weather]: Pretty rainy today, isn't it.

B's utterance in the first example is predominantly emotive because it expresses the speaker's surprise (rather than contributing new information to the discourse). The utterance in (2) is intended to influence the addressee's behaviour, while (3) has a clear information orientation. These are the three functions of language which are also accounted for in Bühler's model.

Metalinguistic, poetic and phatic functions

Utterance (4), however, brings in a new aspect. It is referential in a different sense from (3), as it refers to the language or code used in communication rather than to some aspect of the context. In advising the listener about a stylistic point in the use of the verbs *purchase* and *buy*, it introduces a **metalinguistic** dimension (where the term *metalinguistic* can loosely be glossed as "talk about language"). Example (5) catches the listener's attention not only through its referential content but also through its formal structure, which illustrates the rhetorical figure of "chiasmus." The first and the second half of the statement show inverted order of elements – AB + BA. In spite of what the name "**poetic**" suggests, such playful excess and enjoyment of linguistic form for its own sake is not restricted to literature, but found in proverbs, advertising, word-play and children's language. The "**phatic**" utterance in (6), finally, does not contribute anything new in the specific context. The obvious and uncontroversial topic is merely chosen by A to check whether B might be able and willing to start up a conversation – a clear example of channel-testing.

Pragmatics and the philosophy of language

Ludwig Wittgenstein

Further impulses for the development of linguistic pragmatics came from philosophy, where thinkers such as Ludwig Wittgenstein (1889–1951) had inaugurated a linguistic turn. That the meaning of a word is determined by its uses – a central idea in Wittgenstein's later thinking – is an idea whose appeal to people working in linguistic pragmatics should be obvious. The same is true for another notion of Wittgenstein's – the "Sprachspiel" or "language game," which can be described as a conventional communicative routine constituting some aspect of our social reality. John Austin (1911–1960) and John Searle (b. 1932), two other prominent philosophers of language, are generally considered to be the founding fathers of the **theory of speech acts**, which – as the name and the title of Austin's classic *How to do things with words* (1962) suggest – systematically analyses language as communicative activity. Austin distinguished the **locution** – i.e. the utterance itself – from the **illocution**, i.e. the speaker's intention in uttering it, and the **perlocution**, the effect of the utterance on the listener. This is a framework which is particularly suitable in capturing indirect messages of the following type:

> A: Dad doesn't know about it, either.
> B: Would you like me to phone and tell Mum?

Here we have rather a wide gap to bridge between what is said and what is meant. On the face of it, A makes a referential statement, and B asks an unrelated question. This constellation is thus not much different from the following one:

> A: Dad doesn't read novels.
> B: Would you like me to go to Oslo?

Nevertheless, we would typically make sense of the first exchange through a reasoning process taking us through a number of stages. What we need is an assumption that in a well-run family all members have a right to know about family affairs, which is plausible, and a further assumption, that in this particular family communication with Dad is through Mum, which is not too implausible, either.

To use the technical vocabulary of speech-act theory: the first utterance, or locution ("Dad doesn't know about it, either."), reveals itself to be a declarative sentence only in form. The illocution is that of a request ("as he doesn't know and you and I believe that he should, could you please tell him"). In this case, B recognises the illocution, and the perlocutionary effect is thus as desired. It is not self-evident why speakers should so often choose to express their intentions indirectly – by formulating an order as a question or by phrasing a question as a statement –, but in most cases an indirect expression comes across as more polite because it gives the addressee options that he or she would not otherwise have.

Another focus of speech-act theory are **performative utterances**, i.e. utterances in which the speech act is achieved by the very fact of saying the utterance. Typical examples would be the following:

> I apologise.
> I hereby declare our annual meeting open.

John Austin and John Searle – speech acts

Fig. 7.2
John Rogers Searle (b. 1932) © John Searle

Indirect speech acts

Indirectness as a politeness strategy

Performative utterances

113

By uttering these statements in the first person singular and the present simple tense we perform the speech acts in question – an apology and a ceremonial opening respectively. Note that if we changed the verb form, for example into the present progressive or the simple past, or if we changed the grammatical person, for example from first to third, the performative quality of the utterance would be lost:

> I am apologising.
> I apologised.
> He apologises.

I am apologising merely presents the speaker describing his or her own activity. It is not a sincere apology.

Grice's "co-operative principle" and the maxims of conversation

Another philosopher of language who had a profound impact on linguistic pragmatics was Herbert Paul Grice (1913–1988). He noted that communication among people, especially in spontaneous conversation, was generally successful and surprisingly free from misunderstandings. To account for this observation, he assumed a **cooperative principle**. This principle was spelled out in four maxims of conversation.

1) The **maxim of quality** enjoins participants in a conversation to tell the truth and not to make claims for which there is insufficient evidence.
2) The **maxim of quantity** enjoins participants in a conversation to make their contributions no more and no less informative than is required for the purpose at issue.
3) The **maxim of relation** encourages relevant contributions.
4) The **maxim of manner**, finally, encourages speakers to phrase their contributions in a clear, unambiguous and orderly manner and not to use an undue amount of words.

All this, admittedly, sounds rather trivial. To use the maxim of quantity as an example, we would not answer the question *what's the time?* with *It is now five minutes, 20 seconds and 23 hundredths of a second past nine o'clock in the morning*, although *five minutes, 20 seconds and 23 hundredths* might be a plausible answer to the question *how long do you take to run a mile?* Also, it is easy to think of instances in which any of the maxims can be flouted. Polite utterances, for example, generally flout maxims (1) and (4), because (a) they are often not true and (b) they are usually much more verbose than is warranted. Finally, all except the maxim of quality are highly culture-specific and historically variable. What is considered relevant in one discourse tradition may be regarded as an irrelevant digression in the other (maxim of relation), and even in the history of English periods in which a plain style was cultivated alternated with periods which favoured more ornate diction (maxim of manner).

However, the maxims do capture what a listener seems to assume when interpreting an utterance, and thus they do explain why we end up with satisfactory interpretations even of utterances which appear bizarre at first sight. Consider, for example, the following hypothetical exchange, which is composed of two indirect speech acts in succession:

> A: Let's meet Saturday at three then, o.k.?
> B: Mill Wall are playing.
> A: I see. Not Mile End tube station then.

By the cooperative principle, A trusts that B follows the maxims of conversation, and will therefore try to make sense of B's apparently incongruous answer. This inferencing process might take the following form. Mill Wall is a football club whose followers have a reputation for violence. At the envisaged time, Mill Wall fans might swarm Mile End tube station, and therefore this might not be an ideal place to meet. A correctly interprets B's statement as a polite request to change the appointment. Grice's term for such unstated or implicit meaning is **conversational implicature**. The logic of conversation is, of course, not as rigorous as mathematical or philosophical logic, but where speakers, as is the case here, share common background assumptions, it will work in practical terms.

Conversational implicatures

The logic of natural language is not identical with mathematical or philosophical logic

Compare the implicature in the above example with a proper logical **implication**. In the first of the two sentences below, the use of the verb *manage* carries an implication that the activity expressed in the following verb was actually carried out. Following the statement with a negative is impossible. The second sentence, with *try*, carries no such implication and can therefore be negated:

Implicatures and implications

> I managed to phone him in time. *But I didn't succeed.
> I tried to phone him in time. But I didn't succeed.

The implication connected with the use of *manage* cannot be cancelled at will by a speaker in a particular context, and there is no way in which such an implication can be attached to *try*. The implicature underlying B's statement, by contrast, will be accepted by the listener in the normal case (as it represents a shared assumption), but it can easily be questioned and cancelled on a specific occasion:

> A: Let's meet Saturday at three then, o.k.?
> B: Mill Wall are playing.
> A: Come on, they're nothing like their old reputation. Mile End tube station then.

Note that most implicatures are conversational: They are context-bound and hold for a particular conversational context only. Sometimes, however, repeated conversational implicatures solidify into **conventional implicatures**,

Conventional implicatures

which may eventually be absorbed into the semantics of a form. Over time, the English conjunction *while* (much like its German counterpart *während*) has thus come to express contrast in addition to pure simultaneity.

> I went on reading while they were getting ready. (simultaneity)
> While most Labour MPs supported Tony Blair over Iraq, he didn't. (contrast)

The need for authentic language data in pragmatics

One criticism which has been levelled against approaches in linguistic pragmatics which have been inspired by philosophers of language such as Wittgenstein, Austin, Searle or Grice is that the analyses are very often based not on authentic language data but on constructed fragments of conversation. There is a research tradition in pragmatics which addresses precisely this deficit, namely **conversation analysis** or the study of **talk-in-interaction**.

Conversation analysis/ talk-in-interaction Ethnomethodology

This approach was pioneered in sociology, where it is known as **ethnomethodology** – a term which roughly translates as the study of folk methods. The insight motivating the approach is that a sociologist should not necessarily project the analytical categories of his own theory onto a situation, but might profit by paying attention to the ways in which people themselves make sense of their social relations.

Turn-taking

Thus, a linguist analysing transcribed conversations might start by studying the **turn-taking mechanism**, that is the system of cues which are used to signal that a speaker has finished his contribution or "turn," that a listener wishes to take the floor, and so on. A look at interruptions will show that they potentially serve many different functions – from asserting dominance to expressing sympathy and agreement (by volunteering to finish the other's sentence, as it were). Such an inquiry into the dynamics of real-life conversations could then effortlessly move on to investigate how turn-taking differs in different social milieus. In this way, close attention to linguistic detail will eventually lead to a fresh understanding of how macro-sociological categories such as gender, class or ethnicity are enacted and perpetuated in conversation.

The Prague School – functional sentence perspective

Within linguistics, an important contribution to pragmatics and discourse analysis comes from the work of the Prague School, an international circle of linguists centred in the Czechoslovak capital especially in the years between c. 1930 and c. 1950. These scholars' approach could be described as "bottom up" rather than "top down," with the starting point of the investigation being the question of which relations manifested themselves across the individual sentences of a text. This research revealed systematic interrelations between grammatical structure (at the clause and sentence level) and information structure (at the utterance, text or discourse levels) – a phenomenon which was studied under the heading of **functional sentence perspective.**

Theme and rheme – the distribution of given and new information

In terms of information structure, the normal progression is for the sentence "**theme**" (or **given information**, or information **presupposed** as known to the listener/reader) to precede the "**rheme**" (or **new information**). The sentences of a coherent text passage are thematically linked, for example in arrangements in which the "rheme" of the preceding sentence becomes the "theme" of the following. This is an extract from a newspaper article included in the British National Corpus:

> MORE than anything else, this week's Labour Party conference should kill off **a ritual that** has been acted out over the years in a hundred radio and television studios. **The ritual** went like this: Whenever Labour made news – at a conference, during a policy dispute, before a tense meeting of the National Executive Committee – politicians and commentators would be sat in front of a microphone and asked: "Will the left defeat the leadership?"

| Text 7.1
Peter Kellner,
"The week Labour's left was routed",
BNCweb

The first sentence of the article builds up from a theme – *this week's Labour Party conference*, which presumably was a known fact to the newspaper reading public at the time – to the "rheme," a type of ritual not mentioned before. Note that the information status of these two elements is coded in the language. The party conference is introduced by the modifying genitive *this week's*, which necessarily refers to contextually given or specific information, whereas the rhematic noun *ritual* bears the indefinite article, which signals that it is not contextually established yet. In the second sentence the ritual, introduced in the preceding one, is now the theme, appropriately introduced with the definite article *the*, and the sentence progresses toward a new "rheme." In all, a balanced distribution of given and new information across sentences thus ensures a high degree of textual cohesion.

In other models, different terms have been introduced to capture the facts of information distribution in utterances and texts. Many grammarians use the concept of **focus** to explain aspects of word order within the sentence. There is a principle of "end focus," which usually leads to important information being placed at the end of a sentence rather than at its beginning. A related principle of "end weight" provides for long and complex constituents to appear at the end. Of the following two arrangements, for example, the first is rare, while the second is normal.

1) That even more damaging evidence will come to light in further investigations is likely.
2) It is likely that even more damaging evidence will come to light in further investigations.

In (2) the subject clause is extraposed, which is in line with the principles of end-focus and end-weight. The distribution of information in (1) is less than optimal in most contexts. If a speaker or writer decides to use it anyway, there are usually either strong reasons for doing so in the preceding context, or specific rhetorical effects are intended.

3) The probes undertaken so far have confronted the mayor with a considerable amount of potentially incriminating suspicions. That even more damaging evidence will come to light in further investigations is likely.

Another way of "improving" example (1) is to increase the complexity and informational prominence of the subject complement *likely*.

4) That even more damaging evidence will come to light in further investigations is now not merely very likely but one-hundred per cent certain.

Correlations between syntax, semantics and pragmatics

For pedagogical reasons it is of course useful to separate the analytical levels of syntax, semantics and pragmatis in an undergraduate introduction. In actual language use, however, there is constant interaction and mutual influence between the three. František Daneš has conveniently summarised common correlations between syntax, semantics and information structure.

Table 7.2
A three-level-approach to syntax (Daneš 1964)

	preverbal NP	postverbal NP
grammar	subject	object
meaning/semantics	agent	patient
information structure/pragmatics	given/definite	new/indefinite

The typical subject in a text is an agent semantically and represents given information pragmatically. This is a strong tendency. It explains, for example, why so many subjects are personal pronouns in transcribed spoken language (as can be ascertained from the example text from the Santa Barbara Corpus discussed below). Pronouns such as *I, you, we, he* or *she* denote human beings and hence potential agents, and their referents are always given in the context. The typical object, on the other hand, is a patient semantically and offers new information. As such, object noun phrases are usually longer than subject noun phrases, and they are more likely to bear an indefinite article. Where, as in the following example, there is a clear mismatch between syntactic and pragmatic functions, it is tempting to use the passive to bring the utterance in line with preferences.

> ? The minute I got out of the car, a nasty hornet-like insect stung me.
> The minute I got out of the car, I was stung by a nasty hornet-like insect.

However, the correspondences between the three analytical levels posited by Daneš are tendencies but not iron-clad rules. Speakers and writers retain a high degree of flexibility and stylistic freedom. In the analysis of a stretch of live conversation below (Section 7.3), you will have ample opportunity to appreciate this yourself.

Demonstration/discussion

Since pragmatics is the study of language use in context, one of the chief objects of inquiry have always been the linguistic devices which help us anchor utterances in their context – both the extra-linguistic context of situation and the linguistic context, i.e. the preceding and following portions of the discourse. The cover term for all these devices is **deixis** (from the Greek verb for "show"), and the components of this system are referred to as **deictic** elements.

As was pointed out by Karl Bühler, the deictic centre of an utterance is usually the "here and now" of the first person singular, the speaker. The most important deictic devices are the personal pronouns (*I/we* vs. *you, he/she/it* and *they*). In addition, demonstrative pronouns and a number of adverbs with spatial or temporal meaning further specify the communicative space defined by the personal pronouns. *I don't want this one* indicates that the object is perceived as close to the speaker, whereas *I don't want that one* indicates that it is seen as further away. *I work here* indicates that the speaker is in his place of work, while *I work there* means that the place of work is elsewhere. In the domain of time, *now* similarly contrasts with *then*. *Now* refers to a time broadly coinciding with the time of speaking, as in *I am talking to you now*. *Then*, by contrast refers to a moment "not now" either in the future or in the past, as in *I'll talk to you then* or *I talked to him then*.

The last few examples illustrating deictic adverbs have shown, incidentally, that in addition to its grammatical and semantic functions the tense and aspect system performs an important deictic one. The present progressive establishes the temporal frame for *now*, whereas the past and future tenses correlate with *then*.

Being anchored to specific situational contexts, the meaning of deictic elements is extremely flexible, and therefore difficult to define. In de-contextualised semantic terms, the meaning of the adverb *here*, for example, is "place near or around the speaker." No further specification is possible at this level. What the concrete extension of the intended space is in a given context is the result of pragmatic inferencing processes. In *I work here*, the word will be understood to refer to a room close to the speaker, if the speaker points to it. If, on the other hand, speaker and listener are in a building, the meaning of *here* will be constructed according to the Gricean maxims. If the building is owned by the company the speaker works for, it will be the whole building. If the company rents part of a larger building, it will be precisely this part. If the building is not owned by the company, *here* may even refer to the entire city.

A good practical testing ground for the study of deixis is the problem of reported speech. In reported speech, deictic devices anchoring the utterance in the original context need to be replaced to reflect the context in which the utterance is reported. Consider the following utterance, which is reported by someone else in a different place at a different time.

| 7.2

Deixis – anchoring linguistic utterances in their context

Deixis illustrated – deictic shifts in reported speech

"I'm living here and won't leave this place voluntarily."

He/she said that he/she was living there and would not leave the [or that] place voluntarily.

The pronouns shift from the first to the third person. (Note that in English this raises an interesting problem of gender choice.) The local deixis (*here*, *this*) shifts from "close to the speaker" to "remote" (*there*) or neutral (*the place*), i.e. an expression which is not deictic at all. The tense shifts from the present and future to the past/future in the past. In most grammar books and practical language-learning materials, these changes are presented as a grammatical rule.

However, if we think about the rationale for the changes, we recognise the problem as an exclusively pragmatic one. For example, if the utterance were reported at a different time by a different speaker, but in the same place as the original utterance, *here* and *this place* would remain unchanged:

He said that he was living here and would not leave this place voluntarily.

If the speaker reported his own original utterance in a different place and at a different time, the appropriate form would be:

I said that I was living there and would not leave the [or that] place voluntarily.

Deixis – minor contrasts between English and German

While the general principles of deixis are similar in English and German, there are a number of complications on points of detail. Unlike their German counterparts *kommen* und *bringen*, the English verbs *come* and *bring* are deictic, expressing an orientation towards the speaker. This means that utterances such as *bringt ihn ins Krankenhaus* or *schreib mir eine Karte, wenn Du nach New York kommst* could be made anywhere, whereas the corresponding English forms *bring him to the hospital* and *write me a postcard when you come to New York* make sense only when the speaker is in the hospital or in New York. In all other cases the required forms would be *take him to the hospital* and *write me a postcard when you arrive in New York*.

Anaphors and cataphors – deictic references to preceding and following portions of the text

As has been pointed out, deictic devices need not necessarily point directly to some referent in the context of situation. In the following newspaper article contained in the British National Corpus the forms *this* and *these* are used **anaphorically**, to refer to previously mentioned material within the text.

Text 7.2
Newspaper article from the BNC

Two AI delegates attended a conference in Colombo from 11 to 16 March on trades union and human rights in South Asia as guest speakers. While there, they also met government officials and discussed possibilities for future access by AI to Sri Lanka. Amnesty was last permitted access to the country in 1982. The government subsequently announced that "a research visit to Sri Lanka would be considered favourably if a formal request were made".

PROBLEMS AND CHALLENGES   Unit 7

This pattern of greater flexibility toward outside investigation of human rights abuses is also shown by the Sri Lankan government's acceptance of visits by both the UN Rapporteur on Extra-Judicial Executions and the UN Working Group on Disappearances. **These** are now due to occur in 1991, having been postponed on several occasions over the past few years.

Such developments, along with the continuing work of the International Committee of the Red Cross within the country, are welcome in themselves and also give some evidence that the Sri Lankan Government is responsive to criticism from outside the country.

Unfortunately, **even these modest advances** apply only to the south of Sri Lanka, the primary focus of Amnesty's campaign last autumn. While the situation in the south remains a major concern, greater violations of human rights are now occurring in the North and Eastern provinces of the island, where government security forces are engaged in a full-scale civil war with elements of the Tamil-minority population. The main opposition group in this region is the armed Liberation Tigers of Tamil Eelam (LTTE) whose political aim is a separate Tamil homeland (Eeelam) in North-East Sri Lanka.

References to material following in the text are called **cataphoric**, e. g. *those are the virtues most in demand: competence, industry and honesty.*

Problems and challenges

In the exposition above, I hinted that much work on speech acts and Gricean maxims relies on constructed data. This is justified in a first approach to the problems or as a pedagogical simplification. We need to be aware, however, that authentic conversational data are usually much more complex. Also, as students of English, we may be more interested in the specific contrasts between conversational strategies prevalent in Britain or the United States, men and women, older and younger people, or native-speakers and foreign-language learners, rather than in the properties of conversation in general. For such detailed investigations, we could not construct the data.

The following is a transcribed extract (slightly "cleaned up") from a genuine conversation contained in the Santa Barbara Corpus, a reference corpus of spoken American English. "Sharon," a Californian schoolteacher, recounts her experiences with difficult pupils. Eventually, her narrative develops into a conversation with her friends Kathy and Carolyn.

In the collection of the data for this corpus, the original conversation was tape-recorded and then transcribed. In theory, the transcribers could have used the IPA phonetic alphabet, but this would have been extremely laborious. So the transcription provided is basically orthographic, that is the spoken utterances are rendered in standard English spelling. In this simplified version

|7.3

Analysis of a transcribed extract from an authentic American English conversation

Reducing speech to writing – issues of transcription

of the original transcription, no prosodic transcription is provided. Overlapping speech is indicated by square brackets ([]), while unintelligible passages are put between angle brackets and marked by an X (<X X>). The @-symbol indicates laughter. As we can't get more out of a transcription than was put in, these conventions define the range of phenomena which we could research on its basis. We could not use this transcription for a study of rising intonation in turn-final position, but it would be suitable for the study of constructional breaks in the grammar of spoken American English:

Text 7.3 | Conversation from the Santa Barbara Corpus

SHARON: First they're like, first I only had fifteen kids, right? And the, legally you have to have eighteen. HISD rules has it that you have to have at least eighteen, right? So I'm the only permanent sub. I'm the only teacher who's not experienced, who's not certified, who @just @started @teaching. All these other teachers are old hands, I mean they've all been at it for at-, Well Chris is the least experienced besides me, but still he's, **you know**, he's had his certification, and he's had a year and stuff, he's real good at it.

So, they do shit like, first they tell me, like I find out accidentally, from the other teachers. The principal doesn't even tell me. First she hires me n- like, the Friday before school starts. And expects me to get my room ready, and then, and then I find out on Thursday, in the first week of school, that I might lose my job.

KATHY: Yeah you told me.
SHARON: Come Friday. Yeah. and, and then, th- ... so I come into class, and they've put like, all these third-grade students in there. Did I tell you about that?
KATHY: No.
SHARON: It's really annoying. what they've done, to meet the l- – the
KATHY: They [split <X it X> third] and fourth.
SHARON: [little] technicality that they have to meet, Yeah. <X They just s[plit the whole thing X>].
KATHY: [Challenging].Yeah.
SHARON: it's, well, [it's something],
KATHY: [It's twice] as [much work for you].
SHARON: [it's something for] experienced teachers. It's not ... for me. **You know**, it's like really hard for me. Because, **you know**, [and then –
KATHY: [You have to n- –
SHARON: and then],
KATHY: That's what I was] doing when I was student teaching, I had split fifth sixth.
SHARON: Well they didn't even give me any texts, Coop, I mean I was the only ... teacher, in the whole school, who did not have textbooks. [**You know**],

KATHY:	[<X Mhm X>].
SHARON:	because they were fucking me around so hard. So then on the- -- on Friday I have eigh[teen] kids,
X:	[(SNIFF)]
SHARON:	I'm like great. **You know**. And all these teachers are coming in and saying, Well, <Q my child is on your roll, but I'm gonna keep him in my class Q>. **You know**.
CAROLYN:	[mm].
SHARON:	And I have these three third-graders. **You know**, but the shitty thing is, that they ... pick, what the teachers do, is they go, oh, well this, this kid is bad behaved, I mean he's -- He's really stupid, I'll just send him over to the new instructor.
KATHY:	[Of course].
SHARON:	So they s- -- So the[se are,
KATHY:	[Of course].
SHARON:	th]e kids that I receive, are the three ... third-graders, of the lowest [... e]ducation.
KATHY:	[that nobody wants].
SHARON:	and the worst conduct. Right. And so th- --
CAROLYN:	(SNORT)
SHARON:	Meanwhile in the pri[ncipal]'s o[ffice they're telling me],
KATHY:	[@]
CAROLYN:	[@@ Sorry], I just got a [visual,
KATHY:	[@@@@@]
CAROLYN:	Sharon standing in front of the class] going, (SCREAM)[
SHARON:	[Aw. Sometimes I'm like that].
CAROLYN:	While these little kids kinda], [<L senorita Flinn L>]?
SHARON:	[Hee hee hee hee hee].
KATHY:	[@@]@@@
SHARON:	[Oh, <<THUMP>>] <Q Miss Flinn, Miss Flinn, Mi[ss Flinn Q>],
KATHY:	[@@@@@]
SHARON:	**You know**, towards the last couple of days I'm like, I put up a list of rules. And all day lo[ng,
CAROLYN:	[@
SHARON:	I went back to the rules.
CAROLYN:	<VOX Do not pull on] my [clothes VOX>].
SHARON:	[And they get] up out of [the chair,
KATHY:	[@@@]
SHARON:	and they come up] to me, <Q Miss Flinn, Miss Flinn Q>, and I'd walk over by the rules, and I'd point to number two. And [I'd just look at] them.
KATHY:	[@@] @@

SHARON:	And they knew what number two was. Don't get [out of your] seat without permission.
KATHY:	
SHARON:	You know? So [they'd look at me and they'd] go,
CAROLYN:	[@God].
KATHY:	@@@@@[@]
SHARON:	[they'd go] back to their [chairs].

So what can we learn from this about the nature of American English conversations? The first thing we realise is that both the initial narrative and the subsequent dialogue are full of linguistic detail which is absent from the constructed communicative exchanges found in the literature on speech acts. For example, it is interesting to note how Carolyn and Kathy signal their continuing attention to Sharon, both by linguistic (cf., e.g., the use of *of course*) and non-linguistic means (e.g. laughter). The conversation also illustrates the conventions of turn-taking, that is the strategies the participants in the conversation employ to signal that they have finished their current contribution, that they wish to start speaking, and so on.

Discourse markers

Here, I would like to focus on the role of **discourse markers**, i.e. words or conventional expressions used to mark the boundaries of speech units or give structuring signals to the listener. Note the use of the phrase *you know*, for example, which occurs nine times in this relatively short extract. It never conveys its literal meaning ("you are aware of something"), but always functions as a fixed expression, a discourse marker which helps structure the conversation in ways which the *The Longman Dictionary of Contemporary English* (4th ed., 2005) specifies as follows:

a) to emphasise a statement,
b) to make sure that someone understands what you are saying,
c) to keep someone's attention,
d) used when you are explaining or describing something and want to give more information.

Another recurrently used discourse marker in the extract is, of course, the word *well*, which – like *you know* – never occurs in its literal use (adverb of manner corresponding to *good*).

The grammar of spoken English

Note also that the grammatical structure of spoken English is different from the written language. Constructional breaks and repetitions are tolerated (and repaired) to a considerable extent (as is made clear even by Sharon's very first utterance). Narrative passages are not consistently told in the past tense but also in the present. Together with the frequent direct quotation of the narrator's own and other people's utterances this creates a more dramatic and vivid effect. Grammatical structures which help to focus or highlight material which the speaker thinks important are used liberally, for example *That's what I was doing when I was student* or *what they've done to meet the little technicality that they have to meet, they just split the whole thing.*

References and further reading

Austin, John L. 1962. *How to do things with words: the William James lectures delivered at Harvard University in 1955.* Cambridge MA: Harvard University Press.
Blakemore, Diane. 1992. *Understanding utterances: An introduction to pragmatics.* Oxford: Blackwell.
Bublitz, Wolfram. 2001. *Englische Pragmatik: Eine Einführung.* Berlin: Schmidt.
Bühler, Karl. 1934. *Sprachtheorie. Die Darstellungsfunktion der Sprache.* Jena: Fischer.
Daneš, František. 1964. "A three-level approach to syntax." *Travaux Linguistiques de Prague* 1: 225–40.
Grice, Paul. 1957. "Meaning," *The Philosophical Review* 64: 377–388.
Horn, Laurence R., and Gregory Ward, eds. 2004. *The handbook of pragmatics.* Malden MA: Blackwell.
House, Juliane. 1996. "Contrastive discourse analysis and misunderstanding: the case of German and English." In Marlis Hellinger and Ulrich Ammon, eds. *Contrastive sociolinguistics.* Berlin: Mouton de Gruyter. 345–361.
Jakobson, Roman. 1960. "Closing statement: linguistics and poetics." In Thomas A. Sebeok, ed. *Style in language.* Cambridge MA: M.I.T. Press. 350–377.
Searle, John. 1969. *Speech acts: An essay in the philosophy of language.* Cambridge: Cambridge University Press.
Verschueren, Jef. 1999. *Understanding pragmatics.* London: Arnold.

Practice

| 7.4

1 Analyse the following exchange between an adult and a young child, using Grice's cooperative principle and maxims. The adult asks her question a few days before the child's third birthday:

   Adult: And when are you going to be three years old?
   Child: On my third birthday.

   What has gone wrong?

2 Study the use of *like* in the extract from the Santa Barbara corpus given above. What functions does this form perform in context? Are these usages recorded in your learner's dictionary?

3 Arrange the following commands in descending order of politeness. Which qualify as indirect speech acts? Which linguistic devices add to the politeness of the utterance?

> Get out of this room!
> You'll get out of this room.
> Could you get out of this room?
> Couldn't you get out of this room?
> Get out of this room, could you please?
> So you're staying, are you?

4 Comment on the relationship between syntactic structure and discourse context on the basis of the following examples of reported speech.

> Betty said: "I won't come back here tomorrow."
> Betty said that she wouldn't go back there tomorrow.
> Betty said that she won't go back there tomorrow.
> * Betty said that she won't go back here tomorrow.

Find one further acceptable example of indirect speech, and one further unacceptable one.

5 In a study of contrasting pragmatic conventions in German and English conversations, Juliane House (1996: 347) has suggested that expectations differ along the following five dimensions:

German		English
Directness	↔	Indirectness
Orientation towards Self	↔	Orientation towards Other
Orientation towards Content	↔	Orientation towards Addressees
Explicitness	↔	Implicitness
Ad-hoc formulation	↔	Verbal routines

A typical native speaker of German would express himself or herself directly, display an orientation towards the content of the message and the speaker, make his message explicit and use creative ad-hoc formulations in doing so. The typical speaker of English, by contrast, would value indirectness/implicitness, have a different orientation and tend to use prefabricated set expressions such *as if you know what I mean* or *I wonder if you could help me*.

In the same paper, she relates the following illustrative anecdote – from an American student's diary documenting her stay in Germany:

> When I said something (in English) to my (German) boyfriend like 'Would you like to go to the cinema tonight?', which means to me 'I want to go to the cinema tonight and you're taking me' – and it's got much more force than it sounds as though it has – he would just say 'No, not really'. (House 1996: 351)

Using House's theoretical framework, make explicit what has gone wrong in this particular exchange (if not the relationship). Suggest ways of raising German learners' awareness of such contrastive-pragmatic issues.

Unit 8

Applied linguistics, language teaching and translation studies

Orientation

Unlike **theoretical linguistics**, which investigates language structure and language use for their own sake, **applied linguistics** emphasises the contribution that linguistic descriptions, methods and theories can make to the solution of language-related problems in individual and social life.

Such potential applications of linguistics are manifold. There are many kinds of language and speech disorders, from relatively common and mild impairments such as stuttering to severe conditions such as the various types of aphasia (language loss) which result from specific types of damage to the brain. These are the focus of **clinical linguistics** – a field in which linguists work together with doctors and speech therapists. Another branch of applied linguistics is **forensic linguistics**, which is concerned with the assessment of linguistic evidence in criminal and civil law cases. A court might want to know, for example, whether an asylum seeker's linguistic repertoire is consistent with his or her story or whether the slang term *to jook* is more likely to mean "punch" or "stab" when evaluating a surreptitiously recorded telephone conversation. In **computational linguistics**, the aim is to process natural language on and for the computer, for example in order to develop computer-based information systems which can adequately respond to people. Linguists are also called on for advice on questions of **language planning** and **language standardisation**. As shown by the recent debate about spelling reform in the German-speaking countries, such issues tend to arouse considerable emotions – even if the measures taken are limited. By comparison, the scope and need for language planning and standardisation is vast in many developing countries, which are usually highly multi-lingual and need to re-define the role of their former colonial languages.

All these fields are interesting and important but of course also so complicated that a full treatment is beyond the scope of this introduction. The two areas of applied linguistics that we shall focus on below are therefore linguistics and the **teaching and learning of foreign languages** and linguistics and **translation** – two issues which are also likely to be of personal concern to many readers of this book.

|8.1

Theoretical and applied linguistics

Sub-branches of applied linguistics

8.2 | Demonstration/discussion

Contrastive linguistics in the teaching and learning of foreign languages

Transfer and interference

One of the oldest branches of applied linguistics is **contrastive linguistics**, the systematic comparison of two languages undertaken in order to understand learner errors and improve teaching materials and methods. In **applied contrastive linguistics**, the term **transfer** is used to indicate that patterns and rules of the mother tongue are used in the foreign language. Obviously, such transfer is harmless or even useful in cases in which the mother tongue and the foreign language are structured identically. For example, it is a rule of both German and English that attribute adjectives are generally positioned before the noun they modify, and even the relative order in which several such adjectives are placed is the same:

    ein schmutziges grünes Hemd   –   a soiled green shirt
    * ein grünes schmutziges Hemd –   * a green soiled shirt

Adjectives denoting permanent qualities of an object such as its colour follow those which denote temporary attributes (denoting state of cleanliness, for example) or subjective evaluations (such as "beautiful" or "ugly"). A German learner of English can thus transfer this knowledge into English without any problems. A German learner of French or Italian, on the other hand, where there are complicated rules governing the placement of adjectives before or after the noun they modify, could not.

Where transfer leads to errors, we speak of **interference** (and of **interference-caused errors** in the foreign language). A foreign accent can thus be described as the result of interference between the sound systems of the mother tongue and the foreign language (see Unit 2). In the following extract from American realist writer William Dean Howells' 1890 novel *A Hazard of New Fortunes*, for example, one character, Lindau, distinguishes himself from his American partners not only through his sympathies for the trade union movement but also through a fairly broad German accent:

Fig. 8.1 |
William Dean Howells (1837–1920)

Phonetic interference – a foreign accent

Text 8.1 |
William Dean Howells, *A Hazard of New Fortunes* (1890)

"The fact is, those fellows [i.e. the working classes] have the game in their own hands already. A strike of the whole body of the Brotherhood of Engineers alone would starve out the entire Atlantic seaboard in a week; labor insurrection could make head at a dozen given points, and your government couldn't move a man over the roads without the help of the engineers."

"That is so," said Kendrick, struck by the dramatic character of the conjecture. He imagined a fiction dealing with the situation as something already accomplished.

"Why don't some fellow do the Battle of Dorking act with that thing?" said Fulkerson. "It would be a card."

"Exactly what I was thinking, Mr. Fulkerson," said Kendricks.

Fulkerson laughed. "Telepathy – clear case of mind transference. Better see March, here, about it. I'd like to have it in 'Every Other Week.' It would make talk."

"Perhaps it might set your people to thinking as well as talking," said the colonel.

"Well, sir," said Dryfoos, setting his lips so tightly together that his imperial stuck straight outward, "if I had my way, there wouldn't be any Brotherhood of Engineers, nor any other kind of labor union in the whole country." "What!" shouted Lindau. "You would sobbress the unionss of the voarking-men?" "Yes, I would."

"And what would you do with the unionss of the gabidalists – the drosts – and gompines, and boolss? Would you dake the righdt from one and gif it to the odder?"

"Yes, sir, I would," said Dryfoos, with a wicked look at him. Lindau was about to roar back at him with some furious protest, but March put his hand on his shoulder imploringly, and Lindau turned to him to say in German: "But it is infamous – infamous! What kind of man is this? Who is he? He has the heart of a tyrant."

Note that – within the confines of standard English orthography – the novelist renders the expected features of a German accent – chiefly the substitution of phonemes such as [ð], which do not exist in German, by sounds that do (*other* → *odder*) and the pervasive tendency towards the devoicing of syllable-final consonants (*unions* → *unionss*, *give* → *gif*). The passage contains no example of interference on levels other than the phonetic one. Many cases of interference at the lexical and grammatical levels, however, emerge from the following (sadly, authentic) translation of a German newspaper article into English by a German-speaking student:

Interference-caused errors in grammar and vocabulary

After the critic on America's solo-tour in Iraq by many US partners, George W. Bush tries harder to settle the deep cracks. Not only because of massive difficulties in Iraq, Bush is promoting for international support to rebuild the country. During the next days he therefore gets several occasions.

In the very first line, we have a classic example of a "false friend," that is a pair of lexical items – in this case *Kritik* and *critic* – which are formally similar in English and German but nevertheless differ considerably in meaning and use. The meaning of German *Kritik* is usually rendered by the English word *criticism* (or – in some specific instances – by *critique*), whereas *critic* means "Kritiker." Somebody who is not familiar with German ("Nach der Kritik an Amerikas Alleingang im Irak …") will have trouble understanding what the sentence means. For an example of a grammatical error possibly caused by interference from German, consider the final sentence of the brief passage, where the present is used with future reference. This is normal and common in German, but very rare in English – restricted basically to cases in which we deal with precisely scheduled arrangements (e.g. *The boat leaves at 9 a.m. tomorrow morning*). As this does not apply in the present instance, we would

"False friends"

e.g.
kritik – critic

expect some other verb form, such as – for example – *for that, he will get several opportunities over the next few days* or *for that, he is going to get several opportunities over the next few days.*

Interference and over-/under-representation of structures

Sometimes, interference does not lead to a straightforward error in the target language but merely to an **over-representation** of target-language forms which are backed up by the learner's mother tongue – at the expense of alternative and potentially more suitable constructions which are not (and which might therefore be said to be under-represented). Consider, for example, English relative clauses, which come in a great variety of structural types:

> students who wish to take the exam are expected to register by 1 May
> students that wish to take the exam are expected to register by 1 May
> students wishing to take the exam are expected to register by 1 May
>
> he's the professor with whom you should speak if you are interested in New Zealand
> he's the professor who you should speak with if you are interested in New Zealand
> he's the professor that you should speak with if you are interested in New Zealand
> he's the professor you should speak with if you are interested in New Zealand
> he's the professor to speak with if you are interested in New Zealand

In each case the first example is the one which is closest to the corresponding German structure. In each case, this also happens to be the most ponderous and formal way of putting the idea. Nevertheless German learners of English may prefer these forms to their more natural and informal alternatives. The result is a style which is not appropriate to the situation, or language which shows a highly restricted stylistic range if compared to native-speaker usage.

Hyper-correction and avoidance

Finally, there are two interesting indirect effects of transfer and interference which should be mentioned. The first is **hyper-correction**, which occurs whenever a learner over-uses new forms and constructions which he or she has recognised as typical of the foreign language. Beginning learners of German, for example, may substitute the English phoneme /w/ by /v/ (cf. Unit 2, p. 32) and produce:

> * [veri vel]

– a straightforward case of interference. Rather than move on to the correct target [veri wel], however, advanced learners will often pronounce:

> * [weri wel]

– in particular in those cases in which the two sounds /w/ and /v/ occur in close proximity. The second indirect effect of transfer is **avoidance**. Expressions or constructions which are perfectly possible in the target language are not used by sophisticated advanced learners, who have come to distrust similarities between the source and target language as possible error. Thus, somebody who has learnt to their cost that some German idioms have no English equivalents at all and that others – like *zwei Fliegen mit einer Klappe schlagen* – come in a different guise (*kill two birds with one stone*) may hesitate to use the perfectly ordinary and acceptable *to drink someone under the table*.

Quite clearly, an awareness of the structural differences between **source language** (which for the sake of brevity is often referred to as **L1** in the literature) and **target language** and an understanding of the varied effects of transfer and interference are helpful for language teachers. In addition to transfer and interference, however, there are many other factors which promote or hinder progress in foreign language learning. Not surprisingly, therefore, assessing the extent and importance of "L1 influence" in foreign-language learning, and determining the role of the L1 in the classroom, has remained one of the major controversial issues in applied linguistics and language teaching and learning research (on which see Section 8.3 below).

In a contemporary applied-linguistic approach to foreign-language teaching and learning, contrastive linguistics is just one piece in a complex inter-disciplinary mosaic of approaches. Empirical error analysis shows that there are many learner errors which are not due to L1 influence – such as, for example, the over-generalisation of foreign-language rules. Learners often produce forms such as *childs* or *knowed* instead of *children* and *knew*, which are also used by English-speaking children during mother-tongue acquisition. Such errors raise the cognitive-psychological issue of possible parallels between first- and foreign-language learning. Many causes of success or failure in foreign-language learning are beyond the scope of purely linguistic analysis. Factors such as motivation, attitudes towards the foreign language and the culture of its speakers, the institutional context of language education all have a deep impact, and they need to be studied from a psychological or sociological perspective.

In spite of many controversies in applied linguistics, there is general consensus that learner language is not just a corrupt version of the target-language but a semi-autonomous system which develops in a force-field created by three factors – input from the target-language norm, influence from the L1 and, last but not least, its own internal dynamic. One widely used term to capture this transitional and evolving competence is **inter-language**. Among the concepts developed in inter-language studies which are immediately useful to language teachers is the distinction between **mistakes** and **errors**. Mistakes are due to lapses in concentration or other factors external to the learning process, whereas errors are systematic and recurrent deviations from the target-language norms characteristic of a particular stage in the development of target-language competence and thus need systematic attention. In general, familiarity with research in foreign-language teaching and learning helps raise

The limits of the contrastive approach to the teaching and learning of foreign languages

The interlanguage model

Mistakes vs. errors

an awareness that life in the classroom is rarely as simple as is suggested by binary oppositions bandied about in many quarters: grammatical correctness versus communicative competence, teacher authority versus learner autonomy, and so on. For example, the question of whether the explicit teaching of grammatical rules is useful or not should never be answered wholesale. The answer depends on the way grammar is defined and grammatical rules are formulated, on the type of learner who is taught and the type of skills to be developed in the limited time available – to mention just three important factors. Similarly, grammatical correctness is a pre-condition for communicative competence in many domains, and thus not in opposition to it.

Applied linguistics and translation

Like foreign language teaching and learning, **translation** is an activity which was successfully carried out for millennia without the benefit of advice from (applied) linguists. Nevertheless, the insights of applied contrastive linguistics are of potential use for translators in several ways. For example, it is a well-known fact (also discussed in Section 5.3 of the present book) that, in comparison to German, English has a greater variety of non-finite (= infinitival, gerundial and participial) clauses. This is a statement about two grammatical systems, and its implications for the translator's text-based activity are not immediately obvious. After all, translators work with language in use.

Translation strategies

However, the contrast between the grammatical systems has direct and regular consequences in language use, as is illustrated by the following two "translation strategies" which are suggested in a well-known textbook (Friederich 1969). Strategy V, "Deutsche Adverbien, englisch verbal ausgedrückt," for instance, can be illustrated by the following examples:

German adverbs translated as verbs in English

Table 8.1
Translation strategy according to Friederich (1969)

used to + VERB	VERB + früher
keep VERB -ing	VERB + ständig
continue VERB-ing	VERB + weiter
fail to + VERB	VERB + nicht
cease VERB -ing	VERB + nicht mehr
like to + VERB	VERB + gerne
tend to + VERB	VERB + leicht/gerne

The claim is that the right translation for English *I used to play tennis* or *I kept talking* is not *ich pflegte Tennis zu spielen* or *ich fuhr fort, zu reden* (which copy the grammatical structure of the English originals), but freer translations involving verb-adverb combinations such as *ich habe früher Tennis gespielt* or *ich redete weiter*. This list, which could easily be extended, makes clear why "*Ich liebe es, im Garten herumzuwerken*" is not a very good German translation of English *I like pottering about in the garden*. Conversely, in translation from German to English, we might think of replacing adverbial expressions such as *formerly* (or even less idiomatically, *in former times*), *in the old days* or *in those days* with *used to*, the English semi-auxiliary which succinctly conveys the notion of a habit in the past. And indeed, *in former times*, one of those lexical chunks which is extremely common in German learner's English, occurs just 17 times in the whole of the British National Corpus.

Strategy XIV, "Der Infinitiv als syntaktisches Bindeglied," alerts us to the following recurring correspondences:

> she longed **to see** her children/ ... sehnte sich nach ihren Kindern
> we waited **to see** what would happen/ ... warteten auf das, was kommen würde
> she bought a small camera **to take** snapshots/eine kleine Kamera für Schnappschüsse
> she wept **to see** him go away/ ... weinte bei seinem Abgang
>
> we want **to see** the economy turning around/ ... wollen eine wirtschaftliche Wende
>
> what have we done **to offend** you?/was haben wir dir angetan?
> you won't live **to see** the day/du wirst den Tag nicht mehr erleben.

English infinitives used as syntactic linking devices

Having digested these examples, we understand why the translation of "Rooney verwandelte den Elfmeter zum 3 : 3" is not "Rooney converted the penalty into a three-all," but "Rooney converted the penalty to make it three all." Conversely, "Ich hasse es zu sehen, wie die Abendsonne untergeht" is not a very good translation of *I hate to see that evening sun go down*, the classic opening line of the "Kansas City Blues."

Other strategies could be illustrated. Like the two examples discussed, they would show that contrastive analysis becomes productive for translation whenever we take the step from grammar as an abstract structural system to grammar-in-text or grammar-in-use.

Translations, translations, translations ...

BASQUE

1. atala

Gizon-emakume guztiak aske jaiotzen dira, duintasun eta eskubide berberak dituztela; eta ezaguera eta kontzientzia dutenez gero, elkarren artean senide legez jokatu beharra dute.

GERMAN

Artikel 1

Alle Menschen sind frei und gleich an Würde und Rechten geboren. Sie sind mit Vernunft und Gewissen begabt und sollen einander im Geist der Brüderlichkeit begegnen.

ESPERANTO [an artificial language, constructed in 1887 by Polish doctor Ludwik Zamenhof to promote international peace and understanding]

Text 8.2
"Universal Declaration of Human Rights" – the most widely translated document in the world; five out of 335 versions (source: http://www.unhchr.ch/udhr/index.htm)

> **Artikolo 1**
>
> Ĉiuj homoj estas denaske liberaj kaj egalaj laŭ digno kaj rajtoj. Ili posedas racion kaj konsciencon, kaj devus konduti unu al alia en spirito de frateco.
>
> **BISLAMA [an English-based pidgin language of the Pacific region]**
> **Atikol 1**
>
> Evri man mo woman i bon fri mo ikwol long respek mo ol raet. Oli gat risen mo tingting mo oli mas tritim wanwan long olgeta olsem ol brata mo sista.
>
> **ENGLISH**
> **Article 1**
>
> All human beings are born free and equal in dignity and rights. They are endowed with reason and conscience and should act towards one another in a spirit of brotherhood.
>
> **KRIO [an English-based creole language of Sierra Leone]**
> **Atikul Wan**
>
> ɛvribɔdi bɔn fri ɛn gɛt in yon rayt, nɔn wan nɔ pas in kɔmpin. Wi ɔl ebul fɔ tink ɛn fɛnɔt wetin rayt ɛn rɔfj pantap dat wi fɔ sabi aw fɔ liv lɛk wan big famili.

8.3 | Problems and challenges

Beyond the contrastive hypothesis in foreign-language teaching and learning

In applied linguistics, curriculum design and language teaching methodology – areas which, it must be said, are unfortunately given to rather rapid changes of fashion – there was a time (about half a century ago) when contrastive linguistics was seen as the key to efficient foreign-language teaching and learning. This is Robert Lado's classic formulation of the "contrastive hypothesis," i. e. the assumption that the learner's first language is the major obstacle to the acquisition of a native-like competence in the foreign language and the most important source of errors in learner performance:

> […] we can predict and describe the patterns that will cause difficulty in learning, and those that will not cause difficulty, by comparing systematically the language and culture to be learned with the native language and culture of the student. In our view, the preparation of up-to-date pedagogical and experimental materials must be based on this kind of comparison. (Lado 1957: preface, n. p.)

Today, we tend to see such far-reaching claims with a lot of caution. First, some of the errors supposedly "predicted" by structural differences are not made. For example, English-speaking learners of German make the expected error of substituting [k] for the German fricatives in words such as *Technik* or *Bach*, but they are not tempted at all to produce voiced consonants at the end of a syllable in the wrong places, in spite of the fact that word-final voiced consonants are extremely common in their language. To give a simple illustrative example: an English learner of German will have a relatively easy time learning that

German *Fahrrad* is pronounced with a final /t/ in spite of its spelling; German learners, by contrast, usually find it difficult to get used to articulating /d/ in words such as *bid*, *red* or *grad* (not to mention the even more difficult voiced clusters, such as *bids*, *reds* or *grads*).

This observation cannot be explained within the narrow framework provided by the "contrastive hypothesis" but requires a different approach. The key concept needed to understand what is going on is **markedness**. A linguistic form is **unmarked** if it is structurally simple, occurs frequently in texts and is common across the languages of the world (to mention just three factors out of several more important ones); it is **marked** if it is structurally complex, rarely used in texts and uncommon among the languages of the world. In that sense, syllables consisting of one consonant followed by one vowel are unmarked, whereas syllables containing complicated consonantal clusters are marked (remember the illustrative examples given in Unit 2, p. 29). Returning to the issue of word-final voiced stops and fricatives, we observe a clear markedness differential between English and German. There are a few languages in the world which do not have a phonemic distinction between voiced stops and fricatives anywhere in the word (either initially, medially or finally). There are many languages which are similar to German, in that they have such a distinction initially and medially, but not finally; and – at the other end of this gradient – there are a few languages like English, which have the opposition in all positions. With regard to this particular variable English thus represents a marked pattern, which will be difficult to learn for foreigners. English-speaking learners of German, by contrast, face no such obstacles as they have to master a situation which is simpler than the one they are used to. In this connection, it is interesting to note that young children learning English as a mother tongue usually go through a stage where they display word-final devoicing before they conform to the adult norm – which provides nice additional support for the "markedness differential hypothesis" from a language-internal, psycholinguistic perspective.

In a book which has generally emphasised the role of corpora in linguistic research it is probably a good idea to conclude with a brief glimpse at a new resource for the study of learner English, namely the *International Corpus of Learner English* (ICLE), which assembles student writing by learners from many different L1 backgrounds. The material is made up of argumentative essays written by advanced learners (= university students) of English from diverse language backgrounds (Bulgarian, Czech, Dutch, Finnish, French, German, Italian, Japanese, Norwegian, Polish, Russian, Spanish, Swedish, with several more sub-corpora being compiled) and a corpus of British and American undergraduate essays, which serves as a native-speaker reference corpus. This, for example, is a number of correct examples involving the construction *possibility of doing something* from the ICLE material produced by German learners:

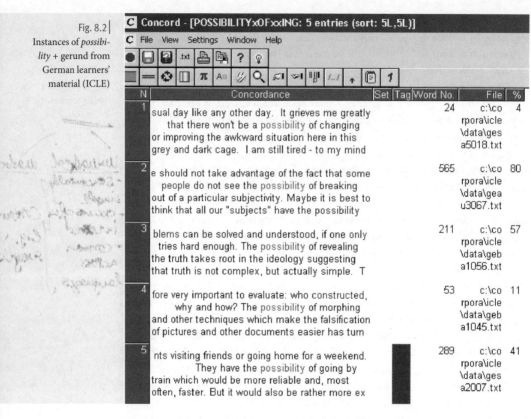

Fig. 8.2 | Instances of *possibility* + gerund from German learners' material (ICLE)

N	Concordance	Set	Tag	Word No.	File	%
1	sual day like any other day. It grieves me greatly that there won't be a possibility of changing or improving the awkward situation here in this grey and dark cage. I am still tired - to my mind			24	c:\corpora\icle\data\gesa5018.txt	4
2	e should not take advantage of the fact that some people do not see the possibility of breaking out of a particular subjectivity. Maybe it is best to think that all our "subjects" have the possibility			565	c:\corpora\icle\data\geau3067.txt	80
3	blems can be solved and understood, if one only tries hard enough. The possibility of revealing the truth takes root in the ideology suggesting that truth is not complex, but actually simple. T			211	c:\corpora\icle\data\geba1056.txt	57
4	fore very important to evaluate: who constructed, why and how? The possibility of morphing and other techniques which make the falsification of pictures and other documents easier has turn			53	c:\corpora\icle\data\geba1045.txt	11
5	nts visiting friends or going home for a weekend. They have the possibility of going by train which would be more reliable and, most often, faster. But it would also be rather more ex			289	c:\corpora\icle\data\gesa2007.txt	41

This is good news, showing that learners produce correct English. Note, however, that a wrong construction, namely *possibility **to do** something*, occurs even more often in the same material:

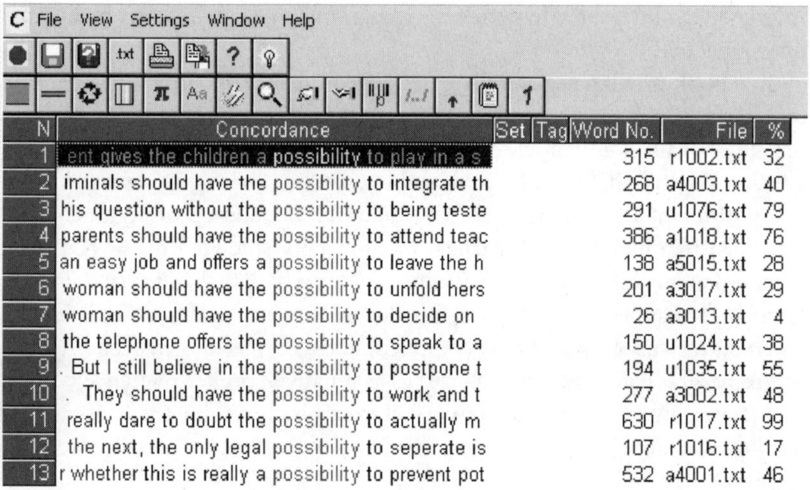

Fig. 8.3 | Instances of *possibility* + infinitive from German learners' material (ICLE)

N	Concordance	Set	Tag	Word No.	File	%
1	ent gives the children a possibility to play in a s			315	r1002.txt	32
2	iminals should have the possibility to integrate th			268	a4003.txt	40
3	his question without the possibility to being teste			291	u1076.txt	79
4	parents should have the possibility to attend teac			386	a1018.txt	76
5	an easy job and offers a possibility to leave the h			138	a5015.txt	28
6	woman should have the possibility to unfold hers			201	a3017.txt	29
7	woman should have the possibility to decide on			26	a3013.txt	4
8	the telephone offers the possibility to speak to a			150	u1024.txt	38
9	. But I still believe in the possibility to postpone t			194	u1035.txt	55
10	. They should have the possibility to work and t			277	a3002.txt	48
11	really dare to doubt the possibility to actually m			630	r1017.txt	99
12	the next, the only legal possibility to seperate is			107	r1016.txt	17
13	r whether this is really a possibility to prevent pot			532	a4001.txt	46

As we are talking about essays written by very advanced learners of English, namely students, this is bad news, and raises two obvious questions. The immediate one to ask yourself is whether you would have made the same mistake. The scholarly and academic question relates to the cause of this particular error, which is probably to be found in interference from German *eine Möglichkeit, etwas zu tun*.

The ICLE material is available in convenient digitised format and opens up new horizons for systematic cross-linguistic research on important issues in foreign-language teaching and learning research, such as interference.

For example, if there are certain types of error which are found only in one ICLE sub-corpus, an explanation in terms of mother-tongue interference is rather likely. If, however, a type of errors recurs in a large number of sub-corpora representing typologically diverse L1 background, interference cannot be the sole factor, and others, such as typological markedness, come into play.

Corpus-based studies of interference

Beyond the issue of interference, learner corpora are extremely useful for the study of all those aspects of learner language in which statistics play a role and which have been very difficult to investigate in traditional error analysis. For example, in assessing learner competence it certainly makes a difference whether a group of learners gets the target form right 80 per cent of the time or just 20 per cent of the time. Corpora are also useful to document how learners systematically over-represent or under-represent certain forms in their English.

Corpora and the statistical profiling of learner language

Finally, as ICLE is made up of the English of very advanced learners of English on their way to becoming English-language professionals, it is also the ideal resource to focus on the problems facing learners like you. For advanced learners, who get their basic grammar right and have a rich and differentiated vocabulary, it is often frustrating to realise that what they've written may not contain a large number of mistakes but somehow still doesn't sound natural. Not surprisingly, one of the biggest obstacles in the path from "mere" correctness to stylistically natural English writing is collocations (studied in Unit 6, p. 99–103). Indeed, one recent study on ICLE data (Nesselhauf 2003) has revealed a striking discrepancy between native speakers and German learners in the use of verb-noun collocations (such as *make a decision* or *do one's homework*). Of course, by now you have had it drilled into you that it is *do your homework* and not **make your homeworks* (on the pattern of German *deine Hausaufgaben machen*). But what about *discuss about a topic*? Would you have recognised this construction as incorrect, which it is? Would you even have used it yourself?

From correctness to naturalness – a near-native command of the foreign language

The statistical side of Nesselhauf's work need not concern us here – except the rather depressing over-all message that even in the English of very advanced German learners almost a quarter of all verb-noun collocations used are still faulty in one way or another. However, her data are very interesting because they show how interference combines and interacts with other factors in accounting for the various errors made. Some of the collocational errors noted by Nesselhauf are straightforward examples of interference: *ride on a bike* (for

Interference and other causes of error in the use of English collocations

"auf dem Fahrrad fahren," Engl. *ride a bike*), *undertake a step* (for "einen Schritt unternehmen," Engl. *take a step*). Others are due to over-generalisation, such as when the multi-purpose verb *get* is used in *get out of fashion*, instead of the correct *go out of fashion*.

References and further reading

Davies, Alan, ed. 2005. *The handbook of applied linguistics*. Malden MA: Blackwell.
De Cock, Sylvie. 2000. "Repetitive phrasal chunkiness and advanced EFL speech and writing," in: Christian Mair & Marianne Hundt (eds). *Corpus linguistics and linguistic theory. Papers from the Twentieth International Conference on English Language Research on Computerized Corpora (ICAME 20), Freiburg im Breisgau 1999*. Amsterdam: Rodopi. 51–68.
Friederich, Wolf. 1969. *Technik des Übersetzens: englisch und deutsch. Eine systematische Anleitung für das Übersetzen ins Englische und ins Deutsche für Unterricht und Selbststudium*. München: Hueber.
Granger, Sylviane, ed. 2002. *Computer learner corpora, second language acquisition and foreign language teaching*. Amsterdam: Benjamins.
Lado, Robert. 1957. *Linguistics across cultures: applied linguistics for language teachers*. Ann Arbor: University of Michigan Press.
Nesselhauf, Nadja. 2003. "The use of collocations by advanced learners of English and some implications for teaching," *Applied Linguistics* 24 (2): 223–242.
Seidlhofer, Barbara, ed. 2003. *Controversies in applied linguistics*. Oxford: OUP.

8.4 | Practice

1 Consult various web resources on forensic linguistics and identify two high-profile cases in which linguistic evidence has played a role. What type of evidence was involved, and how important was the role of the linguistic expert in sentencing or acquitting the defendant? Discuss some ethical issues which you see arising for linguists working in this field.

2 Analyse all the non-standard spellings in Lindau's utterances in the extract from Howells' novel (Text 8.1). Which features of a German accent in English are they supposed to represent, and are they successful in doing so?

3 The extract from the student's translation discussed above is repeated here for convenience:

> After the critic on America's solo-tour in Iraq by many US partners, George W. Bush tries harder to settle the deep cracks. Not only because of massive difficulties in Iraq, Bush is promoting for international support to rebuild the country. During the next days he therefore gets several occasions.

Which errors do you note in addition to the two already discussed above? Which of them are very likely due to interference from German, and which of them are more complicated to account for?

4. Consult German and English dictionaries for the meaning and grammatical constructions of the words *Möglichkeit* and *possibility* and then try to account for the following two learner's errors:

> * Immigrants are often attracted by economic possibilities.
> * What makes mothers go for part-time employment is the possibility to combine children and a career.

5. As a final example of interference-caused errors consider the following warning printed on millions of railway tickets sold by *Deutsche Bahn*:

> Applications for refund on unused tickets submitted after the first day of validity, or in respect of partially used tickets, must be addressed in writing, within a period of six months from the expiry dates of the tickets, to the issuing office or to one of **the transport undertakings** involved in the journey.

Monitor translations on documents or in public places and collect further examples of institutions or corporations going public with flawed English.

6. Transcribe the following statement phonetically, using the IPA alphabet, first in a native-speaker pronunciation, then in a German accent showing maximal interference, then in a German accent showing maximal hyper-correction:

> the verbal wit in Goldsmith's Vicar of Wakefield *works very well*

Discuss the following sentence from a term paper written by a student. In your view, is the wrong verbal form of the predicate due to hyper-correction? Or are there other, more plausible explanations for this error?

> * Words from the Continental period are showing early borrowing by corresponding forms in other Germanic dialects, or by their phonological form.

7. A few years ago Helmut Bonheim published a short article ("Problems of English in German letters of recommendation," *Anglistik* 9 (1998): 120, 121), in which he deplored the linguistic standards in letters of recommendation issued to students by their (German-speaking) university teachers. Sadly, some of his examples even seem to emanate from English departments:

> In particular he has already in school successfully participated in abroad programs and more recently toured Spain and England on his bike.
> This is especially remarkable as he studies three (instead of our customary two) subjects.

> N. N. has taken my "Introduction to the Study of English" a year ago.
> One can tell that she has set herself a goal and firmly intends to reach it all the way.
> Ms. N. was participant in one of my language courses last semester.

Identify the errors and comment on interference from German as a possible cause.

8 While the errors in the examples in task 7 are largely grammatical, the question arises whether there are language-specific or nationally specific textual (= stylistic or pragmatic) norms which should be known to somebody writing a recommendation in English. Find out reliable sources which might help you answer this question.

9 Friederich's translation strategy III, "'Eins durch zwei' oder Hendiadyoin," is illustrated by the following examples, among others:

beauty and magic	zauberhafte Schönheit
buildings of individuality and charm	Gebäude von eigenem Reiz
sanity and reason	gesunder Menschenverstand
care and attention	sorgfältige Beachtung

Consult German and English textual material, including – if possible – digital language corpora to find out whether this piece of advice to translators is based on a solid generalisation.

10 Below you find one German original and two English translations:

> In Verbindung mit einer zunehmenden Nachfragesättigung im Bereich der Massengüter löste der Verdrängungswettbewerb der sogenannten Billiglohnländer vor allem in den altindustriellen Branchen des verarbeitenden Gewerbes tiefgreifende Strukturkrisen aus, die schwere Beschäftigungskrisen nach sich zogen.

> **Version A:** Linked with an increasing saturation of demand in the area of mass-produced goods, the competitive pressure from so-called low-wage countries led particularly in the old industrial branches of the manufacturing sector to profound structural crises, which drew serious employment crises in their wake.

> **Version B:** The new competition from so-called low-wage countries coincided with increasingly saturated demand for mass-produced goods. This led to profound structural crises – and hence severe employment crises – particularly in old, established sectors such as manufacturing.
> (source: Salkie, *THES*, 31 March 1989)

Which of the two translations is the better one in your view, and why? Give the two translations to fellow students who do not know the original text and ask them to translate the English texts into German. Comment on the results of this "translating back" exercise.

Unit 9

A pluricentric language – standard Englishes around the world

Orientation

The present Unit and the following two will deal with language variation and, as regards the English language, with **varieties of English**. A variety of a language is defined as a regionally, socially, situationally or otherwise specific sub-type of the language. The identifying features of such a sub-type can be orthographic (if we are dealing with the written language), phonetic, grammatical, lexical-semantic or pragmatic.

While in principle we could compare any variety of English to any other one, the more usual perspective is to describe a particular variety with regard to how it differs from the **standard**. Like other European languages with a long writing tradition, English has developed a norm or **standard** of usage which is used almost exclusively in writing and commonly also in spoken communication on formal and public occasions. This standard is taught in schools, both to native speakers and foreign learners, and it is described in numerous dictionaries and grammar books. It is socially prestigious and has the authority of the education system, the publishing and media business and other institutions behind it. People therefore tend to regard it as superior to other varieties of a language, which are therefore often referred to as "sub-standard." As this term is liable to misunderstanding and goes against the descriptive orientation in linguistics, varieties outside the standard are usually subsumed under the label "**non-standard**" in linguistic work.

English developed its first standard version at the end of the Old English period, in the 10th and 11th centuries. It was based on the West Saxon dialect spoken around Winchester, which was an important centre of culture and learning at the time. When the Normans conquered England in 1066, writing in English was largely discontinued. For almost three centuries most writing in England was in Latin or French, and the old standard therefore fell out of use. A new standard, the direct historical pre-cursor of our own, began to emerge in the late 14th and 15th centuries, when people started to use English in writing more and more. This time the standard variety was based on the usage of the court and government in London. In the late 15th century, printing was introduced to Britain, and this rapidly led to the emergence of a fairly homogeneous written standard which was used throughout the English-speaking world, including the colonies. This explains why differences between, say, British and American standard English are relatively insignificant in writing but considerable in speech. The standardisation of spoken English did not get seriously

9.1 Varieties of English

Standard English

Standard and non-standard varieties of English

Standard English – a brief history

141

under way in Britain until the 19th century and gathered force in the early 20th century, when the standard pronunciation was spread by the media. The origin of an American national pronunciation standard (which is essentially based on an inland Northern/Midwestern accent) is even more recent, going back to the mid 20th century.

Standardisation as suppression of optional variability

Assuming that the natural state of languages is to be variable, the process of standardisation can be described as the suppression of optional variability. In technologically advanced societies, in which opportunities for travel and long-distance communication abound, some standardisation of linguistic usage is useful and, indeed inevitable. For example, while it made sense to copy a manuscript into the local dialect by hand, printing thousands of copies of a book in a local dialect is a waste of time. Similarly, TV programmes which are broadcast nationwide should use pronunciations which are intelligible to the majority of the viewing public. Beyond what is functionally necessary, though, standardisation is also driven ideologically. Particular linguistic usages are singled out fairly arbitrarily as markers of desirable group membership, while others are discriminated against. Consider, in this connection, the fact that "non-rhotic" pronunciations are considered standard and/or educated in Britain, whereas they are considered regional or dialectal, i. e. non-standard, in the United States.

Major determinants of variation in standard and non-standard varieties of English

Regional variation

Most people are aware of specific instances of linguistic variation. There is, for example, regional variation, as in the following contrasts between British (BrE) and American English (AmE):

BrE:	AmE:
a five-pound note	a five-dollar bill
waiter, could I have the bill, please?	waiter, could I have the check please?

The words *note*, *bill* and *check* (British spelling *cheque*) exist both in British and in American English. They share many of their meanings. For example, the meaning "*note* = written reminder," as in *I left a note for him on the table*, is shared. So is, at least in the majority of cases, the meaning "request for payment" for *bill* – as in *the bill for the repairs amounted to 500 pounds/1,000 dollars*. However, both the words *note* and *bill* cover additional senses in British English which are not current in American English, namely "paper money" (for *note*) and "list of items consumed in restaurants" (which is a specific kind of "bill" that, for whatever reason, is not covered by the term in American usage). Note that this example illustrates variation between standard varieties of English, showing that not even standard English is an invariable monolith. It would, of course, be even easier to identify instances of regional variation among non-standard varieties of English.

Social variation

There is variation between English which is considered educated and socially acceptable and English which is considered uneducated or vulgar:

> I didn't tell anything about it to anyone.
> I never told nobody nothing about it.

Even though both sentences mean the same thing, only the first is likely to be uttered by educated speakers or on a formal or public occasion. There is nothing wrong with multiple negation in principle. In fact, it was quite common in English texts written before the 18th century. Since then, however, its use has been actively and successfully discouraged in standard English by generations of language teachers and linguistic authorities. In non-standard usage, it has, of course, lived on.

In the English-speaking world, in addition to multiple negation, there are a number of non-standard grammatical constructions which are not regionally specific but rather indicate that the speakers belong to the lower classes and/or have had little access to formal education. They include:

- *ain't* for *am not, aren't, isn't, haven't, hasn't*:
  you ain't seen nothing yet, it ain't easy

- replacement of *doesn't* by *don't*:
  after a while, nothing don't matter no more

- *them* used instead of the plural demonstrative *those*:
  I don't want my kids mixing with all them people

The traditional approach to the study of social variation in language was through social class, distinguishing upper-class and middle-class from lower or working-class usage. More recently, ethnicity and gender have been added to the range of determinants of variation which are studied extensively in sociolinguistics (on which see Unit 11).

The most obvious example of situation-dependent variation in language use is stylistic variation, as in the following contrast between a formal and an informal statement:

> What are you purchasing?
> What're you buying?

Situational variation

Again, the two sentences mean the same thing. Both, moreover, qualify as standard English. However, the use of the verb *to purchase* (instead of *to buy*) is enough to create a formal atmosphere. Situation-dependent varieties of a language are commonly referred to as *registers*.

To give a systematic survey of such variation is a task of vast complexity, and we will approach it in steps – after introducing and defining a few more important terms. As we have seen above, there is regional variability even in the standard, and – of course – even more so in non-standard varieties of English, in which case we speak of *dialects* of a language. Note in this connection that the term *dialect* in everyday language is used somewhat more loosely than

Dialects of English

143

in linguistics. For example, many people refer as dialects to languages without a writing system (as in "the many local dialects which are spoken in Nigeria …"), in spite of the fact that these "dialects" may not even be mutually intelligible. This usage is obviously derogatory and therefore avoided in linguistics.

Dialect vs. regional accent

At the other extreme, the term *dialect* is often loosely used to describe a variety of language which does not differ from the standard in anything but pronunciation, such as when a speaker from Scotland reads a text in his or her regional pronunciation. Linguists would refer to this as "(standard) English with a Scottish accent," and not as "Scottish dialect of English." In linguistics, the term *dialect* refers to a variety of a language which differs from the standard or from other varieties of the same language not only in its pronunciation, but also in its vocabulary, and in its grammar.

As an example, consider the following sentence, which is Standard English in its grammatical structure and in its vocabulary:

> Students find it difficult to register for their exams before the end of the term.

Calling up an acoustic image of this sentence before your inner eye, you probably imagine it being read in a British R. P. accent or in the standard American "network" pronunciation, because these happen to be the dominant pronunciation standards used in teaching English as a foreign language. Clearly, however, we can think of many other accents in which this sentence could be read, including, of course, a Scottish one, and the result would be, as hinted above, "standard English with a Scottish accent." For a true example of Scottish dialect, we would need more: not only phonetic but also lexical and grammatical characteristics, as in:

> The bairn isnae greeting cause he's hungry, ken.
> [the child isn't crying because he's hungry, you know]

This is instantly recognisable as non-standard English. It is not possible to read this sentence in another accent than a Scottish one, and in addition to the local pronunciation, there are several lexical and grammatical features which mark the sentence as belonging to a specific regional dialect, Scots. For example, the word *bairn*, a Scandinavian loan word, is used for "child," and *greet* means "cry." The grammatical morpheme indicating negation takes a different shape from other varieties of English (*isn't* – *isnae*), and the verb *ken* "know," also unknown in most other varieties of English, serves as a tag or discourse marker.

Languages vs. dialects – socio-historical and ideological considerations

The analysis of Scots as a dialect of English proposed above is historically well founded but would be resented by Scottish nationalists, including several well-known linguists, who prefer to regard Scots as a language in its own right. Such a view is not absurd, and its proponents are able to cite a number of good reasons for it, most importantly the fact that Scotland had its own written standard in the later Middle Ages and only gave it up after the Scottish Stuart kings succeeded to the English throne and moved to London. Whether you regard Scots as a dialect of English or an independent language threatened by Anglicisation thus ultimately depends on your political orientation and the corresponding view of Scottish history.

Once you start looking, you will find many more such cases which show that objective linguistic criteria are not sufficient to distinguish between languages and dialects. Afrikaans, a West Germanic language spoken in South Africa, used to be considered a dialect of Dutch ("Cape Dutch"). More recently, Letzebuergsch, historically a dialect of German, was officially designated a national language in the principality of Luxembourg. Further afield, the North Germanic varieties spoken in continental Scandinavia are very close to each other structurally but are today regarded as languages – Norwegian, Swedish, Danish –, presumably because this corresponds to current national boundaries. The "dialects" of Chinese, by contrast, are much more heterogeneous linguistically but are nevertheless considered as instances of one and the same language because of a shared cultural tradition and a shared writing system.

As is indicated by the morphologically somewhat daring plural form *Englishes* in the title of the present Unit, there are now several co-existing standard forms of English. Starting with British and American English, the present Unit will describe the most important ones among them. The vast field of non-standard usage will be approached in the subsequent Units 10 and 11.

Demonstration/discussion

Today, English is a pluricentric language, with several standards coexisting side by side. Of course, this pluricentricity is not an easy democracy of voices. As we shall see in Section 9.3 below, all standards apart from British and American English are historically recent. Some are still emerging. Some have low prestige internationally, and quite a few are not even fully endorsed by their own speakers, who very often still look to British or American English norms for guidance. This section will therefore focus on a comparison of British and American standard English, the only standard varieties which have a truly global reach.

At the outset of such a comparison we should note that, outside the areas of spelling and pronunciation, there are very few general and systematic contrasts between the two standards. In contrast to a widespread popular perception (reflected, for example, in numerous linguistic jokes such as the one presented in Fig. 9.1), standard British and American English are very similar.

A pluricentric language

9.2
Many standard varieties – two standards with a global reach

British and American standard English – a comparison

Fig. 9.1 | Post office **clerk** – Mr. Ralph E. Smith Sr., first African American to work in US Post Office in Mattoon IL (© Board of Trustees, Eastern Illinois University)

Fig. 9.2 | Post office **clock**, Allendale NJ, USA (source: www.allendale.org)

American: And what do you do for a living?
Englishman: I'm a clerk – at the post office.
American: What, they pay you for going "tic-toc" all day long?

The following is a list of the salient **spelling** contrasts between British and American English:

Table 9.1 | Systematic contrasts in spelling between British and American English

1)	*-re* vs. *-er*: Words such as *centre* or *theatre* (BrE) are consistently spelled as *center* and *theater* in American English.
2)	*-our* vs. *-or*: British English prefers *-our*-spellings in words such as *harbour* or *favour*, American English spellings in *-or* (*harbor*, *favor*). Note that British English is rather inconsistent in this regard as many agent nouns such as *donor*, *dictator* and *governor*, though interestingly not *saviour* are spelled the "American" way.
3)	double consonants: Most spelling rules for the doubling of consonants operate the same way in British and American English (cf. *set* → *setting*, *occur* → *occurred*). However, there are minor differences in the treatment of ‹l› following unstressed vowels. British English prefers double spellings in words such as *travelling* and *traveller*, whereas American English usually has one ‹l› only (*traveler*, *traveling*), as in the root *travel*.
4)	further isolated contrasts: In addition to the systematic contrasts mentioned above, there are a number of additional differences restricted to the spelling of specific words or small groups of words. In general, American English prefers the simpler spellings in such cases. The word *plough* (BrE), for example, tends to be *plow* in American English; *dialogue* (BrE) is *dialog* (AmE), and *programme* (BrE) is *program* (AmE). (Note that *program* in the sense of "computer instruction" is spelled in this way also in British English.)

DEMONSTRATION/DISCUSSION   Unit 9

Sometimes spellings cut across national boundaries. For example, while *-ize* spellings for words such as *organize, digitize* and *realize* are universal, the corresponding *-ise* spellings (*organise, digitise, realise*) are largely restricted to Britain. Similarly, "simplified" spellings such as *encyclopedia* or *gynecology* are found all over the English-speaking world, whereas the etymologically correct ones (*encyclopaedia, gynaecology*) are mainly restricted to BrE.

The major contrasts in **pronunciation** between British and American English are the following:

1) "rhoticity" (from the Greek name "rho" for the letter ⟨r⟩):
   In British English, ⟨r⟩ following a vowel (= "post-vocalic" ⟨r⟩) is silent. In American English, by contrast, it is pronounced. Thus, we do not hear an /r/ in the words *water* and *hard* in British English Received Pronunciation, but we do hear it in standard American. Note that this holds if the words are pronounced in isolation. In connected speech, the /r/ in *water* is heard also in British English when the following syllable starts in a vowel: *water and food*.

2) /t/:
   This voiceless stop is pronounced as a "flap" ([ɾ]) between vowels or following /r/ and preceding a vowel. Following /n/ and preceding a vowel, the /t/ tends to disappear. This phenomenon can be observed in the typically American pronunciations of words such as *writer, dirty* or *center*. Note that this rule applies only if the stress is on the first syllable preceding the /t/. Thus, the /t/ in *atom* is flapped (['æɾəm] – so that, interestingly, the word comes to sound like *Adam*), whereas in *atomic* it is pronounced as a voiceless plosive [t] ([æ'tamɪk]). This simple rule explains complex facts – for example the fact that the /t/ may be silent in *quantum physics* (['kwɔnəm], that both /t/-s can be reduced in *quantity* (['kwɔnɪɾɪ], but only the first and the third in *quantitative* (['kwɔnɪˌteɪɾɪv], because here the third syllable bears a secondary stress.

3) vowel contrasts:
   The absence of the short back vowel phoneme of British R. P. (/ɒ/) from the American inventory is the most salient phonological contrast between the two standard accents in the field of vowels. In a standard American pronunciation, the vowel in words such as *hot, stop, lock, John* or *horror* is long (/ɔ:/ or /a:/ depending on the phonetic context or dialect).

   Another high-profile contrast is the pronunciation of /ɑ:/ (BrE) as /æ/ (AmE) in words such as *dance, demand, rather* or *staff*. Note, however, that this contrast is not carried through systematically, but restricted to about 80 words. For example, while the word *pass* is pronounced as expected in R. P. (/pɑ:s/), the word *standard* has /æ/. The word *mass* has /æ/ when meaning "a lot of," but varies between /ɑ:/ and /æ/ in the meaning "religious service." In American English, the obvious pronunciation in these cases is, of course, /æ/.

   Finally, where there is variation between /ju:/ and /u:/, British English generally prefers the former, whereas American English prefers the latter (e. g. *new* or *duty*: [nju:] vs. [nu:] and [dju:tɪ] vs. [du:ɾɪ]).

Table 9.2
Systematic, comprehensive and salient contrasts in pronunciation

4) **word stress:**
There is a general tendency for American English to preserve more secondary stresses in polysyllabic words such as *dictionary*, *necessary* or *secretary* than British English R. P. Thus, a two-syllable pronunciation of the word *secretary* (as [sektrɪ]) is just about plausible in rapid speech in British English, but not in American English, where [ˈsɛkrəˌtɛrɪ] would be preferred.

5) **further isolated contrasts:**
In addition to the differences described, there are further isolated contrasts in the pronunciation of individual words or morphemes. For example, *tomato* has a monophthong in British English (/ɑː/), but a diphthong (/ɛɪ/) in American. *Neither* and *either* have /iː/ in American English, but /aɪ/ in BrE. The syllable ‹-ile› in *fertile*, *missile* etc. tends to be pronounced as [aɪl] in British English, but as [l̩] in AmE.

BrE and AmE pronunciation – stable contrasts and further divergence

Note that historically most of the typically British pronunciation features, such as the loss of post-vocalic /r/ and the pronunciation of /ɑː/ in words such as *dance* are innovations. Moreover, with the exception of the move from /juː/ to /uː/, where there are signs that British pronunciation preferences follow American ones, most contrasts are stable, and there is no sizable influence of American norms on British usage (which – as we shall see – is rather different from what we can observe in the vocabulary).

British and American lexical differences – overlap and convergence

In the **vocabulary**, the relationship between the two standards is a very dynamic one. First of all, American words tend to be borrowed into other standard varieties very easily, so that all comparative lists have a relatively short validity. Secondly, lists of lexical contrasts suggesting that there is exclusive use of one or the other form on either side of the Atlantic are usually grossly simplistic. For example, the claim that *shop* is British and *store* American is at best a weak statistical generalisation, hiding a lot of complex usage facts. Both words are in use in both standards, and the difference is one of markedness. Thus, in British English, *book-shop* is the unmarked term, and use of *book-store* suggests that the establishment is of greater than average size. In American English, *book-store* is unmarked, and *book-shop* suggests a small establishment with a cosy atmosphere of personalised service.

British and American lexical differences – some areas of stable contrast

That having been said, there are certain domains, particularly of institutional life, where there are fairly stable and distinct national terminologies in British and American English. The first member of each pair in the following list gives the British term, the second the American one.

DEMONSTRATION/DISCUSSION   Unit 9

a)	**business and finance:** *bank guaranteed cheque – certified check, bill – check, building society – thrift bank, current account – checking account, deposit account – savings account, hire purchase – installment plan*
b)	**education:** *class/form – grade, primary school – grade school, public school – private school, state school – public school, secondary school – high school, 1st-2nd-3rd-4th-year student – freshman-sophomore-junior-senior, staff – faculty, curriculum vitae – resume* [but *CV* in both varieties], *postgraduate – graduate, maths – math*
c)	**clothing:** *anorak – parka, braces – suspenders, dinner jacket – tuxedo, dressing gown – bathrobe, handbag – purse, press stud – snap, purse – change purse, pyjamas – pajamas, suspenders – garters, tights – pantyhose, trousers – pants/slacks, vest – undershirt, waistcoat – vest*
d)	**food and drink:** *aubergine – eggplant, biscuit – cookie, chips – French fries, crisps – chips, grill – broil, jam – jelly, jelly – jello, kipper – smoked herring, mince – ground/hamburger meat, neat – straight (whisky), soft drink* [an Americanism in the 1930s!] *– soda/pop, sultanas – raisins*
e)	**household and accommodation:** *lodger – roomer, semi-detached – duplex, flat – apartment* [if rented]*-condo(minium), cloakroom* [restaurant] *– checkroom, public convenience/toilet* [originally an Americanism replacing *lavatory*]*/loo – restroom/washroom*
f)	**car and travel:** *articulated lorry – trailer truck, bonnet – hood, boot – trunk, book a holiday – make a reservation, caravan – trailer, car park – parking lot, central reservation – median strip-divider, junction – intersection, lay-by – pull-off, motorway/dual carriageway – freeway/ superhighway/expressway, subway – underpass, tube/underground – subway*

Table 9.3
Distinct national terminologies in British and American English

In addition to these lexical contrasts, there are also some differences at the level of **pragmatics, style** or **idiom**, which may occasionally give rise to misunderstandings. An obvious example is the abbreviated reference to dates, where British usage has the order "day – month – year," whereas American has "month – day – year." This contrasting preference has recently been highlighted in the customary reference to the terrorist attacks on the World Trade Center in New York City on 11 September 2001, which, following American usage, is *nine-eleven*:

British and American contrasts in idioms, collocations, and style

   11 September 2001:   11-9-01 (BrE), 9-11-01 (AmE)

Similar potential for confusion is inherent in abbreviated time references such as "half ten," which is colloquial British for "ten thirty" or "half past ten," or in the way floors of a building are counted in Britain or the United States (with Britain usually following continental European practice and distinguishing a "ground floor" and a "first floor" and the US counting the entry-level floor as the "first floor"). As the following snippet from a newspaper shows, this difference became a matter of life and death in the following sad circumstances:

The front door of 118 Whitfield St. in Dorchester [...] does not provide access to first-floor apartments. Police who mistakenly stormed into the second-floor apartment of a retired minister – who died during the raid – say their informant considered the first landing that had apartments to be the first floor, much the same way floors are numbered in Europe and elsewhere. When he told police the apartment housing drug dealers was on the second floor, he was referring to what most North Americans would call the third floor, police said. (*The Boston Globe*, 29 March 1994)

British and American grammatical differences – small in number, statistical rather than absolute

In comparison to the contrasts between British and American English discussed so far, the following differences in **grammar, morphology** and **syntax** are relatively insignificant – first because they are usually not categorial but merely concern variety-specific statistical preferences in those areas of the grammar in which present-day English allows its speakers choices and secondly because very often the synchronic contrasts to be observed are transitory, representing different stages of development in processes of historical evolution which are taking both varieties in the same direction and towards the same ultimate end-point.

This is true, for example, for processes of morphological and syntactic regularisation, which are generally more advanced in American English than in British English. For example, irregular past-tense forms such as *learnt*, *spoilt* and *dreamt* still have some foothold in British English (where they are used alongside their regular alternatives *learned*, *spoiled*, *dreamed*), whereas they have almost disappeared completely from American English. Similarly, the verbs *need*, *dare* and *have* are more commonly used in main-verb syntax in American English. Thus the forms on the right-hand side of the following table are internationally current, whereas those on the left-hand side are frequent only in British English:

Table 9.4 | British English and internationally current forms

I haven't a clue who did it	I don't have a clue who did it
Have you (got) no sense of shame at all?	Don't you have any sense of shame at all?
Need I say more?	Do I need to say more?
This is a challenge that as a politician he dare not shirk	This is a challenge that as a politician he does not dare to shirk

There is no generalisation about varieties which has not got its exceptions, and in a small number of cases it is American English which displays more irregularity, for example in the past-tense for the verb *to dive*, where – alongside regular *dived* – it also has *dove*. American English also preserves the special form of the past participle of the verb *to get*, *gotten*, which disappeared from British English in the course of the 19th century and thus has a subtle contrast between:

Who's got the letter? ("Who has it in his/her possession?")
Who's gotten the letter? ("Who has received it?")

In "mandative" clauses (i. e. subordinate clauses expressing a wish, a request or an order), present-day English allows the following options:

1) *should* + infinitive: The opposition insists that the report should be published.
2) subjunctive: The opposition insists that the report be published.
3) indicative: The opposition insists that the report is published.

The subjunctive (that is option (2)) is more common in American English than in most other varieties. So is the use of the past tense instead of the present perfect to report events in the recent indefinite past (as in *did you have dinner?* vs. *have you had dinner?*).

Grammatical structures largely restricted to British English, on the other hand, include variable concord with collective nouns (cf. ex. (4) and (5) below) and the use of "pro-predicate *do*" (ex. (6) below):

4) The band is/are preparing for a tour of the US.
5) The audience was/were enthusiastic.
6) Have you learned any foreign language? – Yes, I have done.

In American English, the short response expected would be *Yes, I have* (which is, of course, a possibility in British English).

Problems and challenges   9.3

To accept the fact that English is a pluricentric language with several co-existing standards is one thing; to agree on the varieties which can lay claim to being such a standard is quite another. To tackle this question, it is useful to distinguish between three social-linguistic constellations in which English is used.

1) "**English as a Native Language**" (ENL), in which English is the native language of the majority of the population of a state or community. This is the situation which we find in the UK, the Republic of Ireland, the United States, the greater part of Canada, Australia and New Zealand – to mention the most uncontroversial examples.   *English as a Native Language (ENL)*

2) "**English as a Second Language**" (ESL). Here English is usually not spoken as the native language of the majority of the population, but nevertheless serves important functions in the nation or community – for example as an official language in public administration or as the dominant language in the media and the educational system. ESL countries are commonly found among former colonies of the British Empire such as Nigeria, India or Sin-   *English as a Second Language (ESL)*

gapore or among the rather smaller number of formerly American colonial dependencies, such as the Philippines.

English as a Foreign Language (EFL)

3) **"English as a Foreign Language"** (EFL). This is the situation encountered in countries such as Germany, Brazil or China, where English is an important foreign language but does not serve any central functions in the countries' institutional life. For example, while English is an important subject in German schools, English-medium schools (where English is the medium of instruction used for the teaching of subjects such as history or maths) are still the exception. Similarly, German continues to be the language of Parliament, the law courts and most media.

The rise of an American standard of English – successful linguistic de-colonisation

The history of American English shows us that linguistic standardisation is a long historical process which involves practicalities (such as developing locally produced teaching materials and reference works) and ideological considerations (such as, for example, the desire to identify with or distance oneself from a former colonial power). The US gained its political independence from Britain between 1776 and 1783, and yet it was not until the early 20th century that educated speakers in the United States stopped looking over their shoulders in order to see what norms of good usage were in Britain. Since then, of course, the vast majority of Americans has been aware that there is a British English norm, has accepted this fact but has not allowed it to influence or determine educated usage in the US to any significant extent. What the American experience shows is that there is a time lag between political and cultural and linguistic decolonisation, and that the move from an **exo-normative** situation (in which a community's linguistic norms are taken over from elsewhere) to an **endo-normative** one (in which the norms are defined by a local educated elite) is a slow one. Given that in the English-speaking world political decolonisation is a recent phenomenon, with the significant exception of the US not going back further than the 20th century, we can thus see that new standard varieties of English will mostly be very young or still emerging.

From exo-normative to endo-normative standardisation

Some ENL standards emerging in the 20th century

New standards are most likely to be accepted uncontroversially – both by their own speakers and internationally – if they emanate from ENL communities. Over the past half century, for example, there has been a significant development in which British Received Pronunciation stopped serving as the norm of choice for most educated Australians and a socially neutral Australian accent became the new standard. Similar developments are going on in New Zealand, Ireland and Canada and to an extent even in South Africa, where the situation is, of course, complicated by the fact that the native-speaker community is a minority and English is a second language for most citizens of the country.

Contemporary ENL standards – the major phonetic variables

In our comparison of British and American standard English we were able to observe that, to put it simply, accent divides and syntax and the lexicon unite. This trend is much in evidence when it comes to the new and emerging standards. In the following diagram, which is supposed to represent a stylised map of the world, Peter Trudgill has succinctly summarised the situation for ENL communities.

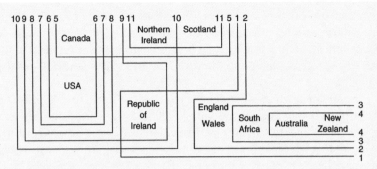

Fig. 9.3
Major phonetic variables distinguishing ENL standards (from Trudgill/Hannah 2002, 5)

Key
1. /ɑː/ rather than /æ/ in *path* etc.
2. absence of non-prevocalic /r/
3. close vowels for /æ/ and /ɛ/, monophthongization of /ai/ and /au/
4. front [aː] for /ɑː/ in *part* etc.
5. absence of contrast of /ɒ/ and /ɔː/ as in *cot* and *caught*
6. /æ/ rather than /ɑː/ in *can't* etc.
7. absence of contrast of /ɒ/ and /ɑː/ as in *bother* and *father*
8. consistent voicing of intervocalic /t/
9. unrounded [ɑ] in *pot*
10. syllabic /r/ in *bird*
11. absence of contrast of /ʊ/ and /uː/ as in *pull* and *pool*

As you can see, the various names are where they belong in a map. Scotland is to the North of England, Ireland to the West. Further West there are Canada and the US, and in the "far East," "down under" you find Australia and New Zealand. The number of lines crossed when moving from one variety to another is a good measure of linguistic distance. Note that there are only minimal contrasts between the British English pronunciation standard (R. P.) and South Africa, Australia and New Zealand, but that five lines need to be crossed on the way from England to Northern Ireland. And this will indeed correspond to your auditory impression when you happen to find yourself confronted with a speaker from Northern Ireland and Australia. In spite of the close regional proximity, the former's accent will be much more different from R. P. than the latter's.

ESL standards – emerging and controversial

In the dispassionate judgment of the investigating linguist, there is no reason **not** to include educated ESL varieties such as Indian English or Nigerian English among the new standards. In India, for example, there is a tradition of almost 200 years of administration and education in English. Since independence in 1947, Indians have learned English not from British native speakers but from Indian teachers trained in India. And use of the language by generations of Indians to talk about Indian affairs has left many marks on the variety of English which has developed. In this sense, Indian English has become an essential strand in the nation's multilingual fabric, and the way the local educated élites use the language has clearly become a *de facto* norm. Nevertheless, non-native speaking users of English find it difficult to accept and endorse their norm as a legitimate standard, which leads to an interesting paradox. Many Indians continue advocating British English as their standard in theory, but would regard a too perfect imitation by an Indian speaker as arrogant or snobbish.

In a situation which is rapidly developing it is difficult to give an exhaustive description of the "English-speaking world" – clearly a pre-requisite if we want to answer the question of how many standard varieties we should distinguish. It is easy to establish a core of countries in which English is spoken as a native language by the majority of the population:

Table 9.5 Countries in which English is spoken as a native language by the majority of the population

1) the ENL core:
United Kingdom, Republic of Ireland, United States, Canada, Australia, New Zealand, Jamaica, Trinidad & Tobago, Guyana, Barbados
[To this might be added a large number of countries and territories in which English is the majority language but which are probably too small to become the focus of endo-normative standardisation – from independent mini-states in the Commonwealth Caribbean, such as St. Kitts and Nevis or Antigua, to the former Empire's last colonies in the Falklands, St. Helena or Tristan da Cunha; an interesting case is South Africa, which has a sizable English native-speaker minority whose influence on the emerging standard is probably out of proportion to their statistical presence.]

2) countries with English as a recognised second or official language:
Botswana, Cameroon, Fiji, Gambia, Ghana, Hong Kong, India, Kiribati, Lesotho, Liberia, Malawi, Maledives, Malta, Marshall Islands, Mauritius, Micronesia, Namibia, Nauru, Nigeria, Pakistan, Papua-New Guinea, Samoa, Seychelles, Sierra Leone, Singapore, Solomon Islands, South Africa, Tonga, Uganda, Vanuatu, Zambia, Zimbabwe

3) countries in which English serves second-language functions informally:
Bahrain, Cyprus, Ethiopia, Indonesia, Jordan, Kenya, Kuwait, Lebanon, Malaysia, Myanmar, Nicaragua, Panama, Philippines, Qatar, Sri Lanka, Sudan, Swaziland, Suriname, Tanzania, United Arab Emirates

The following two maps provide a geographical representation of the "English-speaking world." On top, we have the English-speaking world narrowly defined, as those parts of the world where there is a significant native-speaker presence. Disregarding the smaller communities, this is the British Isles, most of North America, Australia and New Zealand, and – partly – South Africa. The bottom map adds to this the important regions in which English is used as a second or official language: the Asian sub-continent and important parts of

West and East Africa and the Pacific region. Note that the two maps disagree about the status of the Commonwealth Caribbean as an ENL or ESL region, which reflects the borderline situation in the region.

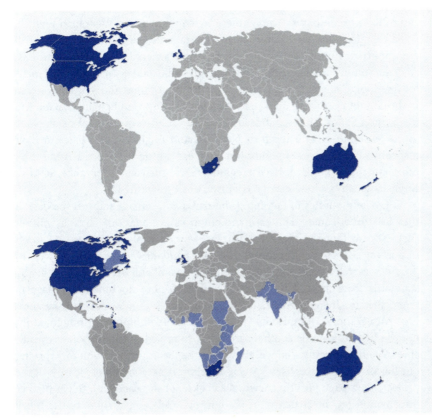

Fig. 9.4
Two maps of the English-speaking world

But even after we have listed the names of countries and shaded regions on a map, we still have a long way to go in order to answer the question of how many important standards of English there are in the world. Closer study usually reveals that the history and present status of English usually differ in important details among the various countries described. In addition, there are vast differences with regard to average levels of proficiency and the proportion of the population who have access to education in the various ESL countries. In that sense, presumable new standards such as Singaporean English, Cameroonian English, "black" South African English, Maltese English or Jamaican English are comparable only in the most general terms.

More important than answering the question of precisely how many standards of English there are in the world today, therefore, is understanding the general principles underlying pluricentric standardisation. Here, the most important insight is that pluricentricity does not imply that all the standards which exist are of equal status and importance. Even today, there are only two standards with an undisputed global reach, namely British and American English. In the second rank, so to speak, is a small number of standards which do not have a global reach but are undoubtedly important beyond the boundaries of their home-bases. Among these we could mention Australian English, Indian English, and Jamaican English. Australian English and Indian English are important points of reference for foreign learners in the Pacific and East African/Southern Asian regions respectively, while Jamaican English is a focus for developing norms in the Commonwealth West Indies and – possibly – also in the vibrant Caribbean diaspora which has developed in Britain, Canada and the United States. Other standards have an exclusively national reach, such as, for example, Irish English or New Zealand English. Their place in their respective home bases is secure but they exert little influence beyond. Still other emerging standards have a regional reach, such as, for instance, Scottish English, which has long had a recognised position in the UK.

International Corpus of English (ICE) – a resource for the study of pluricentric standardisation

Ultimately, studies of emerging standards will remain stabs in the dark if they lack an adequate data base and empirical foundation. Thus, it will not surprise you that the present Unit closes by drawing your attention to an important collection of corpora. The *International Corpus of English* (ICE) provides matching corpora documenting several important ENL and ESL standards from around the world: the sub-corpora documenting usage in Great Britain, Ireland, Australia [restricted access], New Zealand, Jamaica, East Africa, India, Hong Kong, Singapore and the Philippines [though, sadly, not the US] are complete; others are being compiled. If the corpora are available in your university, you will find them the ideal starting point for working out the answers to Exercises 3, 4 and 6 below. If not, you can at least visit the project's web-page (at http://www.ucl.ac.uk/english-usage/ice), to get further information on the structure of the corpora and sample some of the freely downloadable portions, including selected audio-files. Typically, ICE sub-corpora are made up of ca. 600,000 words of orthographically transcribed speech

World English – unity in writing, diversity in speech?

and 400,000 words of written texts covering a wide variety of genres. This is a useful arrangement because it allows you to demonstrate that standard varieties of English are usually very similar in formal writing, but tend to differ from each other most in informal conversation. Or, to summarise the Unit in four words: "Accent divides, grammar unites!"

References and further reading

The most comprehensive compendium documenting standard and non-standard varieties of English is:

Kortmann, Bernd, et al., eds. 2004. *A handbook of varieties of English*, 2 volumes. Berlin and New York: Mouton de Gruyter. [comes with a CD containing interactive maps and sound samples]

A survey focussing on pronunciation is:

Wells, John. 1992. *Accents of English.* 3 vols. Cambridge: CUP.

More compact introductions are:

Bauer, Laurie. 2002. *An introduction to international varieties of English.* Edinburgh: Edinburgh University Press.
Crystal, David. 2003. *English as a global language.* 2nd ed. Cambridge: CUP.
Jenkins, Jennifer. 2003. *World Englishes. A resource book for students.* London and New York: Routledge.
McArthur, Tom. 2002. *The Oxford guide to world English.* Oxford: OUP.
Melchers, Gunnel, and Philip Shaw. 2003. *World Englishes. An introduction.* London: Arnold.
Trudgill, Peter, and Jean Hannah. 2002. *International English: a guide to varieties of standard English.* 4th ed. London: Arnold.

For an authoritative analysis of standards and standardisation, see:

Milroy, James, and Lesley Milroy. 1991. *Authority in language: investigating language prescription and standardisation.* London: Routledge.

Practice   9.4

1 In view of the difficulties involved in distinguishing between "languages" and "dialects" described above, comment on the following wide-spread usage:

   "In Nigeria English continues to be used as an official language because none of the local dialects would be acceptable in this function to the entire population."

   Consult the Summer Institute of Linguistics' Ethnologue Languages of the World database (www version) to find out about the major "dialects" of Nigeria. How many speakers do they have? Do they have standard writing systems?

2 Check the spelling of sensitive words in American top-level web domains such as .us, .gov or .edu and compare your results to those obtained from the British top-level national domain .uk. Do conventions in .ca (Canada), .ie (Ireland), .in (India) or .nz (New Zealand) follow British or American orthographical norms?

3 Consult corpora documenting various national standards of English for occurrences of the following variables:

   – *got* vs. *gotten*
   – *learned* vs. *learnt*, *dreamed* vs. *dreamt*, *dived* vs. *dove*
   – *garbage* vs. *rubbish*

4 In the preceding task you were asked to search for word forms, which is computationally easy. Now devise an intelligent search routine to investigate the use of the mandative subjunctive in the same corpora.

5 Consult reference materials to find out at least one more contrast each between British and American standard English at the level of spelling, grammar and vocabulary.

6 In present-day English there is a choice between the following constructional options after verbs of prevention such as *prevent* or *stop*.

1) *I tried my best, but I was unable to prevent him from leaving the room.*
2) *I tried my best, but I was unable to prevent him leaving the room.*

3) *Good, that should stop them from trying this trick again.*
4) *Good, that should stop them trying this trick again.*

Check reference grammars or corpora of present-day English to find out whether the use of these variants is regionally restricted.

Unit 10

Dialectology – regional variation in English

Orientation

It does not take an expert in linguistics to realise that different varieties of a language are spoken in different regions. As was shown in the preceding Unit, there is some regional variation even within standard English, and among the many topics studied in academic linguistics the study of dialects – unlike, say, phonological theory – certainly belongs to those which tend to arouse interest among the general public. Note, however, that in linguistics the term **dialect** has a somewhat more specific meaning, referring to a regionally specific non-standard variety of a language which differs from the standard and other dialects of the same language in pronunciation, in grammar and in vocabulary. If deviation from the standard is restricted to pronunciation, we speak of regional **accents**.

The results of dialectological research are often published in dialect atlases. These are based on linguistic fieldwork with local informants and offer large numbers of maps. In the production of such maps, the first step is usually to mark the localities investigated for their preferred variants. For example, a few hundred British informants could be asked about whether they pronounce the vowel in *come* as /ʊ/ or /ʌ/. Usually, the responses will not be distributed arbitrarily. There will be regional clusters, around which it is possible to draw lines – **isoglosses** (from the Greek for "same speech"). The more isoglosses run parallel or in close proximity, the sharper the corresponding **dialect boundary** is felt to be. Considering the processes of abstraction involved, dialect boundaries drawn on maps are to some extent simplifications. Especially the border territory will usually be more heterogeneous than is suggested by the graphic representation.

Traditional dialectology focuses on the usage of a **n**on-mobile **o**lder **r**ural **m**ale population – a group of people often facetiously subsumed under the acronym NORM. In a sense, the focus in this type of research is therefore on varieties of English which are vanishing fast or have disappeared already. However, the fact that throughout the English-speaking world traditional rural dialects are disappearing does not mean that the language is necessarily becoming more homogeneous or standard-like as a result. As we shall see in the next Unit, factors such as social class, race or ethnicity lead to the emergence of new varieties in urban and mobile communities.

The study of regional dialectology offers an interesting window on the diachronic evolution of the language. Compared to the standard, some dialects are more conservative in that they preserve linguistic forms of previous

| 10.1

Dialects – language variation in geographical space

Dialect atlases

Isoglosses and dialect boundaries

NORMS as preferred informants

Regional variation and diachronic change

ages. Thus, pronunciations such as /sʊm/ or /mʊnɪ/ (for *some* and *money*), which are characteristic of the North of England today, used to be the general pronunciations of these words all over Britain in the Middle English (c. 1100 – c. 1500) period. In that sense, a trip from London to the North of England or to Scotland and Ireland is also a trip back in time – into the history of English. Of course, dialects may also be more innovative than the standard, thus anticipating usages which are not established in the standard yet although they may be one day. Thus, what is still a long monophthong in British English R. P. in /siː/ (*see*) is pronounced as a diphthong (/səɪ/) in a London regional accent, and this may well be the direction in which developments in the standard are heading (via an intermediate stage in which a barely perceptible glide is inserted before the long /iː/ – /sɪiː/).

10.2 | Demonstration/discussion

Linguistic fieldwork in dialectology

Linguistic dialectology is an empirical discipline based on field-work with informants. The early dialectologist investigators of the 19th and early 20th centuries interviewed their informants and took notes; later sound recording technology became an indispensable aid to dialectologists' work. The most important "classic" dialectological research project in the British Isles has been the *Survey of English Dialects* (SED), started by Harold Orton and the Swiss scholar Eugen Dieth in the 1940s. The publication in 1978 of Orton/Sanderson/Widdowson's *Linguistic Atlas of England* represents a culminating point of the work. Fig. 10.1 shows the map recording the pronunciations of the word *butter*.

The Survey of English Dialects – SED

The situation here is rather tidy. A major isogloss separates the South-East, including East Anglia, and the South-West from the North. There is just one /ʌ/ pocket in the North-West; and there is some messy transition in the region of Bristol. Compare, by contrast, the map for *tongue*, from the same work (Fig. 10.2).

This is a much more confusing picture. The major isogloss extending from the "Wash" (North of East Anglia) to the Bristol region, which figured prominently in the *butter* map, is recognisable here, as well, but in addition there are numerous outlying pockets and transitional forms.

The major dialect regions of England

By repeatedly over-laying such maps, both for this variable and for other ones, we can eventually construct a map which gives us the dialect regions of England. Given the complexity of the input data, any such representation is beset with problems, but can nevertheless serve as a reasonably good approximation. Fig. 10.3 shows a map representing important dialect boundaries in contemporary England (which have of course evolved slightly since the days of the SED fieldwork).

DEMONSTRATION/DISCUSSION **Unit 10**

Fig. 10.1 Orton/Sanderson/Widdowson, *Linguistic Atlas of England*, Map Ph50, *butter*

The Eastern half of "our" isogloss (/ʊ/ vs. /ʌ/) represents the major dividing line between the South Midlands and the East Midlands, whereas the Western part serves as a secondary boundary separating the Upper and Central Southwest. In the South, a largely vertical isogloss separates the South-East, a non-rhotic region, from the South-West, a region in which post-vocalic /r/ is sounded, so that a word such as *arm* would not be pronounced as /ɑːm/, as in R. P., but as /arm/. (At least this would be the pronunciation used among the vanishing group of speakers of traditional rural dialects. Someone getting off the train

DIALECTOLOGY – REGIONAL VARIATION IN ENGLISH

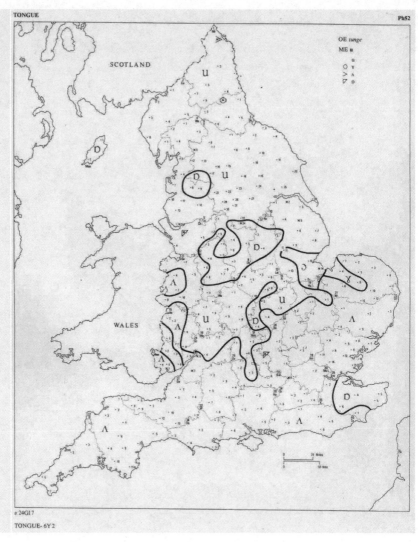

Fig. 10.2 | Orton/Sanderson/Widdowson, *Linguistic Atlas of England*, Map Ph52, *tongue*

Regional variation in American English

or bus at Exeter or some other major urban centre of the Southwest would of course be more likely to hear the non-rhotic Southern British forms.)

Fig. 10.4 takes us across the Atlantic and into the study of lexical regionalisms. It records data provided by a very large number of respondents on a well-known instance of regional variability in the lexicon of American English – namely the use of *pop*, *coke* or *soda* for "fizzy drink."

In this map, each county represents a measuring point, and because there is more than one respondent per locality, some statistical sophistication is possible by indicating preferences as percentages. What we see in this map is a heterogeneous picture. The thinly populated state of Alaska, for example,

DEMONSTRATION/DISCUSSION   **Unit 10**

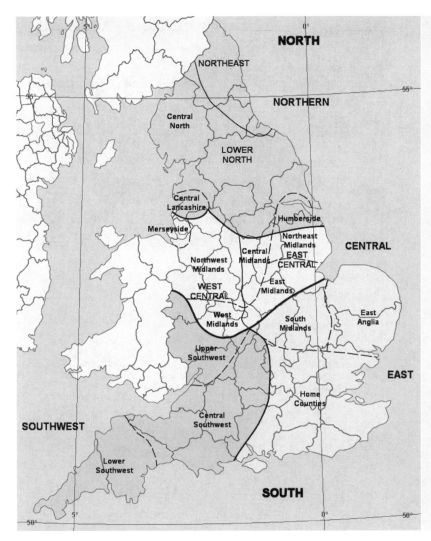

Fig. 10.3 Present-day dialect regions of England (based on Trudgill 1999; source: Jeremy Smith: http://www.peak.org/~jeremy/dictionary/figures/dialectsUK.gif)

records instances of all forms, and there are surprising outliers of Southern usage in places as far apart as Nevada or Indiana. Nevertheless, it is safe to say that most of the Midwest and the Northwest go for *pop*, whereas *coke* is the dominant form in the South, and *soda* dominates in the New England states.

As in the case of England, we will conclude with a representation of the major dialect regions of the US, based on the phonetic investigations carried out by Labov and collaborators in major American cities for the *Atlas of North American English* (s. Fig. 10.5).

Two sizable portions of the country emerge as fairly large and homogenous dialect areas – the South, which has always been a distinct cultural region in the history of the nation, and the West, where settlement came too late to

Major dialect regions of the US

DIALECTOLOGY – REGIONAL VARIATION IN ENGLISH

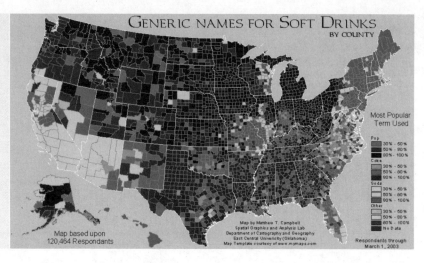

Fig. 10.4 | Preferred generic names for "soft drink" in American English (schematic representation; see accompanying homepage for further details)

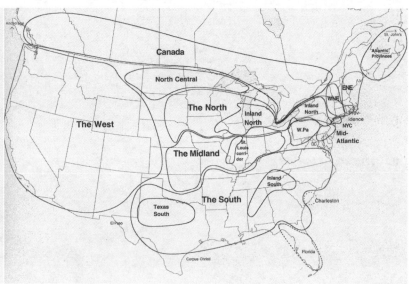

Fig. 10.5 | Dialect survey map of US and Canada; from Labov/Ash/Boberg (2006, 148) – ENE = Eastern New England; WNE = Western New England; W.Pa = Western Pennsylvania

allow significant linguistic diversification. The North (or – to be precise – the North-East) is more complex. There is Eastern New England, the diminishing regional base of a dialect which was once far more wide-spread and even enjoyed national prestige well into the last century. And there is a corridor starting from the mid-Atlantic seaboard and fanning out into the Midwest through Western Pennsylvania. This corridor was historically important for the emergence of the present-day American standard. While the inhabitants of New England and the coastal South, two of the oldest areas of settlement, were sedentary in their majority, many inhabitants of the mid-Atlantic region moved westwards across the Appalachians, spreading out their dialect in a fan-like pattern over much of the territory of the North and Central States.

Problems and challenges

Beginning students are unlikely to engage in linguistic fieldwork of the authentic "dirty-feet" variety. Fortunately, however, modern technology, and in particular the World Wide Web, have provided easy public access to types of non-standard English which would have been very difficult to sample a mere 20 years ago. Anybody beginning the study of English linguistics now should use these opportunities to the maximum. There's nothing to beat the excitement of working with live data. In this spirit, the remainder of the section sketches a few promising routes one might take in the collection of dialect data. In view of the tremendous range of opportunities on offer, the presentation can, of course, be neither systematic nor exhaustive.

If your interest is in variation close to the standard end of the dialect-standard continuum (see Unit 11 for a precise definition of this notion), you can draw data from web-based radio broadcasting. I will assume that students of English regularly tune in to the global English-language broadcasters such as BBC or CNN, anyway. And indeed, if you're lucky, these broadcasters will occasionally supply you with fantastic examples of various types of non-standard English usage. For a more systematic dialect analysis, though, stations with a more local reach are preferable. This is where portal sites such as radiotime.com can be very useful. This particular site guides you to thousands of stations dispersed all over the world. For example, if you are interested in the question of whether contemporary Caribbean broadcasters' talk is influenced more by the traditional colonial British norm or by the currently dominant American one, you will be pleased to note that several promising sources are available.

The screenshot provided in Fig. 10.6 shows that all of the English-speaking West Indies is represented: from Anguilla through Barbados and Jamaica all the way to the Virgin Islands. Some of the stations thus identified can be played straight from the portal site. For others, you can obtain the instructions you need before you can start listening.

Coverage of non-standard varieties is much richer in the *International Dialects of English Archive* (IDEA), hosted by the Department of Theatre and Film at the University of Kansas, Lawrence (http://web.ku.edu/idea/). Table 10.1 lists what is on offer in this archive on the English of Alabama, a state in the "deep South" of the US.

| 10.3

How to obtain data on non-standard varieties of English – the alternatives to field-work

Obtaining audio samples from web-based broadcasting

International Dialects of English Archive – IDEA

Fig. 10.6 Screenshot – www.radiotime.com: Caribbean Islands radio stations

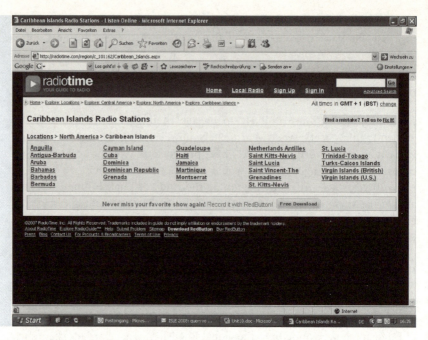

Table 10.1 List of Alabama informants in the *International Dialects of English Archive*

Sound Sample	Basic Information	Text Files
Alabama One	White male, twenties, theatre student, Birmingham, AL	Alabama One
Alabama Two	White female, twenties, theatre student, Birmingham, AL	Alabama Two
Alabama Three	White, female, born 1950, born and raised on a farm in Northeast Alabama, college educated	Alabama Three
Alabama Four	African-American, female, born 1928, born and raised in Chambers County, Alabama, retired office administrator	Alabama Four
Alabama Five	White, male, student, born 1980, born and raised on a farm in Brewton, Alabama	Alabama Five
Alabama Six	White, male, student, born 1981. Raised in Elberta, Alabama	Alabama Six
Alabama Seven	White, male, student, born 1988, Auburn, Alabama	Alabama Seven
Alabama Eight	African-American female, born 1934, Auburn, Alabama, retired, mother of four sons	Alabama Eight
Alabama Nine	African-American female, born 1942 and raised Tuskeegee, Alabama	Alabama Nine
Alabama Ten	White female, born and raised Lanett, Alabama	Alabama Ten Transcription
Alabama Eleven	African-American male, 20, born and raised Montgomery, Alabama	Alabama Eleven

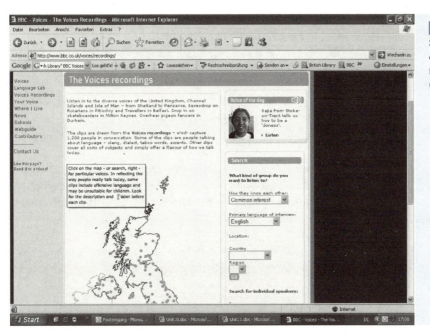

Fig. 10.7
Screenshot – adolescent Asian informant from Stoke-on-Trent (BBC Voices)

Since we started our survey with a mention of the BBC World Service, it is probably fitting to conclude it with another BBC venture, the BBC Voices project (www.bbc.co.uk/voices). If you had been happy to take a lucky dip on 4 December 2007, you could have listened to the "voice of the day," Sajia from Stoke-on-Trent. Alternatively, you could have clicked one of the many dots on the map to take you into the corresponding region or you could have used the search facility.

BBC Voices

References and further reading

Chambers, Jack, and Peter Trudgill. 1998. *Dialectology*. 2nd ed. Cambridge: Cambridge University Press.

Orton, Harold, Stewart Sanderson, and John Widdowson, eds. 1978. *The linguistic atlas of England*. London etc.: Croom Helm.

Labov, William, Sharon Ash, and Charles Boberg. 2006. *The atlas of North American English: phonetics, phonology, and sound change*. Berlin and New York: Mouton de Gruyter.

Trudgill, Peter. 1999. *Dialects of England*. 2nd ed. Oxford: Blackwell.

Practice

10.4

1 Explain the following joke:

> Cockney nurse [to patient]: Cheer up, you're going home to die.

2 Consult your library for a copy of the *Computer-Developed Linguistic Atlas of England* (Viereck et al., 1991 & 1997) or the *Linguistic Atlas of New England* (LANE; Kurath et al., 1939–1943), identify a region of your choice each and draw up profiles listing the phonetic, grammatical and lexical characteristics identifying the local dialect.

3 Visit web sources such as the BBC's "Voices" or the "International Dialects of English Archive (IDEA)" and download one audio-file each illustrating a British and an American regional dialect. Describe the salient characteristics of each of the two varieties.

4 The British Library and the United States' Library of Congress are the two most prominent libraries of the English-speaking world. Check their homepages to see what types of audio and audiovisual holdings they offer. Identify holdings which are of interest to linguists.

5 Consult a reference work such as Peter Trudgill's *Dialects of England* to find out which pronunciation features are represented by those isoglosses in Fig. 10.2 which were not discussed in the text.

6 Somewhat exceptionally for dialects and languages which have not been standardised, there is a long and distinguished tradition of literary writing in Scots. Below you find two typical examples of how writers handled the problem of reducing spoken language to writing at two successive stages in time.

Text 10.1 | Robert Burns, Scots poems & 200 songs contributed to the Scots Musical Museum, including "Auld Lang Syne," and "Scots wha hae" ["Bruce before Bannockburn"]

Literary writing in Scots

Scots, wha hae wi' Wallace bled, "who have" [should be "at has"?]
Scots, wham Bruce has aften led,
Welcome to your gory bed,
Or to victorie.

Now's the day, and now's the hour;
See the front of battle lour;
See approach proud Edward's power –
Chains and slaverie!

Wha will be a traitor's knave?
Wha can fill a coward's grave?
Wha's sae base as be a slave?
Let him turn and flee!

Wha for Scotland's King and Law,
Freedom's sword will strongly draw,
Free-man stand, or free-man fa'?
Let him follow me!

Fig. 10.8 | Robert Burns (1759–1796)

By oppression's woes and pains!
By your sons in servile chains!
We will drain our dearest veins,
But they shall be free!

Lay the proud usurpers low!
Tyrants fall in every foe!
Liberty's in every blow!
Let us do, or die!

this is thi
six a clock
news thi
man said n
thi reason
a talk wia
BBC accent
iz coz yi
widny wahnt
mi ti talk
aboot thi
trooth wia
voice lik
wanna yoo
scruff. if
a toktaboot
thi trooth
lik wanna yoo
scruff yi
widny thingk
it wuz troo.
jist wanna yoo
scruff tokn.
thirza right
way ti spell
ana right way
to tok it. this
is me tokn yir
right way a
spellin. this
is ma trooth.
yooz doant no

Text 10.2
Tom Leonard,
from *Intimate Voices*
(1984)

Fig. 10.9
Tom Leonard
(b. 1944)

> thi trooth
> yirsellz cawz
> yi canny talk
> right. this is
> the six a clock
> nyooz. belt up.

As a starting point for your analysis, re-write the texts in standard English. Which Scots (and Scottish English) features do the three writers attempt to represent? Identify dialect dictionaries and other reference works you might use in those cases in which you do not get the meaning of a passage.

7 In his history play *Henry V,* Shakespeare presents three officers – Fluellen (= Llewellyn), Jamie, and Macmorris –, whose English is distinctly non-standard. Given the context of the play, which varieties might Shakespeare have had in mind?

Text 10.3
William Shakespeare,
Henry V, III, 6; 2

What the writers say

Fluellen: Ay, so please your Majesty. The Duke of Exeter has very gallantly maintained the pridge; the French is gone off, look you, and there is gallant and most prave passages. Marry, th'athversary was have possession of the the pridge, but he is enforced to retire, and the Duke of Exeter is master of the pridge. I can tell your Majesty, the Duke is a prave man.

Fluellen: Captain Jamy is a marvellous falorous gentleman, that is certain, and of great expedition and knowledge in th'ancient wars, upon my particular knowledge of his directions. By Cheshu he will maintain his argument as well as any military man in the world in the disciplines of the pristine wars of the Romans.

Jamy: I say gud-day, Captain Fluellen.

Fluellen: God-den to your worship, good captain James.

Gower: How now, Captain Macmorris, have you quit the mines? Have the pioneers given o'er?

Macmorris: By Chrish la tish ill done; the work ish give over, the trompet sound the retreat. By my hand I swear, and my father's soul, the work ish ill done; it ish give over. I would have blowed up the town, so Chrish save me la, in an hour. O tish ill done, tish ill done; by my hand tish ill done.

Language in the city – social and ethnic variation, multilingualism

Orientation

Historically, the rise of the city led to dialect mixing and language contact on an unprecedented scale. This means that traditional regional dialects have not usually survived urbanisation. However, this certainly does not mean that city-dwellers all speak standard. On the contrary, some of the English-speaking world's most heavily stigmatised varieties are urban dialects such as Cockney (London), Scouse (Liverpool) or the African American dialects of the urban ghettos of the United States.

If we note the decline of traditional dialects in a heavily urban contemporary Britain, we should not forget that there are wide regions of the English-speaking world in which traditional dialects never even took root in the first place. In spite of the huge distances encountered by the settlers, Australian English, for example, has always been remarkably homogeneous from the point of view of regional variation. It seems that the conditions of colonial settlement were such as to foster dialect mixing and dialect levelling rather than differentiation of new dialects in isolation. The same is true for those regions of the United States which were peopled in the 19th and early 20th centuries as part of the great movement towards the West. The end result of modernisation, urbanisation and the recent global spread of English has thus been that there is probably more variability in the language than ever before but that a speaker's regional origin is just one factor out of a whole range of others which influence linguistic usage.

To understand the complexities of linguistic variation in modern cities and the modern world in general, we have to recall that regional distance is no longer the important obstacle to communication that it used to be and that social stratification manifests itself in much more fine-grained and complex ways today than in traditional farming villages. In cities, an important part of the population belongs to a mobile and socially aspiring middle-class, which is strongly influenced by the norms of the educated standard. At least as important as this middle-class, however, is the local working-class, which cultivates its own local **vernacular** (a technical term denoting the informal usage of the common people of a locality). As both groups occupy the same geographical space and, of course, interact with each other, we cannot draw a dialect map of a city with clear isoglosses. Rather, the dialect landscape of the modern

Unit 11

| 11.1

Developing a dialectology for urban spaces

Developing a dialectology for the "new Englishes"

Regional and social variation interacting in city dialects

LANGUAGE IN THE CITY – SOCIAL AND ETHNIC VARIATION, MULTILINGUALISM

The dialect-standard continuum

city is determined by dialect-standard continua which define the norms of local usage. In contemporary London, for example, even speakers of broad Cockney are aware that the educated pronunciation norm in England today is R. P. and will move some way towards this norm at least in formal situations. On the other hand, few middle-class residents of London want to purge their speech of any local trace of an accent. Thus, most residents will cover a span in the middle range of the R. P. – Cockney continuum, and this span is in fact referred to as "popular London pronunciation" by many linguists.

Cities are multilingual spaces

Of course, the standard-dialect continuum is a vast over-simplification in that it suggests that there is only one important language in a modern city. Practically all major cities in the modern English-speaking world, and London more so than many others, are multilingual.

Fig. 11.1 Bengali-English street sign – Brick Lane, London E1

Brick Lane is in the heart of London's working class heartland, the East End, which has been a traditional first port of call for generations of immigrants – from the Yiddish-speaking Eastern European Jews that came in the 19th century to the Bangladeshis who followed in their footsteps after WW II. In the long run, immigrant minorities tend to assimilate linguistically, but this is a process which may take many generations. In the meantime, there will be intensive language contact. The Bengali spoken in London will have some impact on the local English vocabulary. (Of course, the reverse influence – from London English on Bengali – will be even stronger in this situation.) Bengali-speaking immigrants and their children have to choose which language they prefer on which occasion. Mixed and hybrid styles of usage may emerge such as **code-switching**, the variable use of both languages within one and the same conversation or even within one and the same utterance.

In this Unit, we shall explore appropriate ways of handling this type of complexity and at the same time familiarise ourselves with the essentials of **urban dialectology** and **sociolinguistics**.

11.2 | Demonstration/discussion

William Labov and the rise of sociolinguistics

From the 1960s onwards, **sociolinguistics** emerged as a sub-discipline of linguistics which systematically focussed on these complexities which were beyond the scope of traditional regional dialectology. Pioneering work was carried out by William Labov in New York City.

He noted that the traditional regional dialect of the city was non-rhotic, in line with the neighbouring New England dialect region, and that therefore post-vocalic /r/ was not sounded in words such as *arm*. Nevertheless, pronunciations such as /arm/ and /ɑːm/ existed side by side in New York City. In the course of his investigations, Labov was able to show that this variation was neither random nor free, but that there were statistically significant correlations between independent social or situational variables (in this case: the speaker's social class and the formality of the situation in which the recording took place) and the dependent linguistic variable (in this case: the presence or absence of postvocalic /r/).

The sociolinguistic variable – example: postvocalic /r/ in New York City

| Fig. 11.2
William Labov, studying a map from the *Atlas of North American English*

Clearly, it is not possible to represent these regularities in a dialect map of the traditional kind, but the following classic diagram from one of Labov's studies makes it possible for us to find out what types of insight into linguistic variation are possible in urban dialectology of this kind.

Statistical correlations between independent social and situational variables and dependent linguistic variables

The horizontal axis of the chart distinguishes five levels of formality, from casual speech at the informal end to the reading of minimal pairs, which presumably makes informants pay maximal attention to the way they are pronouncing words. The vertical axis charts the percentage of "rhotic" pronunciations of relevant items. Note that in American (though not in British) terms, a rhotic pronunciation represents the national standard, whereas the non-rhotic pronunciation represents the local dialect. The first regularity which emerges

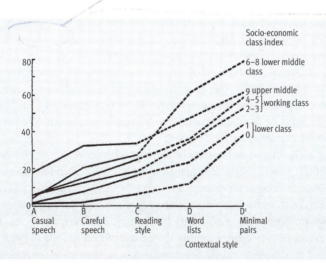

| Fig. 11.3
Post-vocalic /r/ in New York City (source: Labov 1966, see 237–249, 342–355 for table and discussion)

from the results is that for all social classes there is a shared tendency to move closer to the standard as the situation gets more formal. In other words: all New Yorkers are aware of what prestigious (or standard) use is in New York and the United States as a whole, and they all agree that the standard should be used in formal speech. Where the social classes differ is, of course, in their ability to hit the target. For the lowest class, prestige pronunciations (with post-vocalic /r/) do not exceed 40 per cent even in the most formal situation (reading potential minimal pairs such as *balmy* or *barmy*); they are practically absent from the two informal registers. The upper middle class, by contrast, kicks in at about 20 per cent in informal situations and displays around 60 per cent prestige pronunciations for the most formal one.

Hypercorrect usage among the lower middle class

This reveals the second regularity to be observed. Regardless of the situation, there is a consistent layering of speakers determined by their social class – with one exception: the lower middle class, whose behaviour is difficult to account for at first sight. In casual speech, careful speech and reading style, they behave as expected, whereas in the two word-list tasks they overshoot the mark. "Hyper-correction" of this type reveals that these speakers are in a borderline social situation, probably living on a working-class income but sharing upper-middle class aspirations. When they thus concentrate on their own linguistic usage, they consciously attempt to "improve" the impression they are making on their hearers.

Overt vs. covert – two types of linguistic prestige

Note that so far we have used the term *linguistic prestige* only in relation to the standard. Speakers of the standard variety of a language convey the impression that they are rich, well-educated and in a position of power. In sociolinguistic terms this is called open or **overt prestige**. In addition, however, there is also a hidden or **covert prestige** which attaches to non-standard or vernacular varieties and ensures that they survive even in a climate in which they are heavily stigmatised by the social mainstream. Covert prestige of this type relates to factors such as being likable, a trustworthy member of a local community or group solidarity at the neighbourhood or local level. The two contrasting kinds of linguistic prestige are apparent in our diagram, as well. In informal situations, speakers of all classes use relatively greater proportions of stigmatised local forms, because using too many standard variants might make them appear snobbish or arrogant. In formal situations, on the other hand, this covert or "solidarity" prestige is irrelevant, and what counts is the overt prestige conveyed by the standard.

Synchronic sociolinguistic variation and diachronic change

Note, finally, that as in the case of regional dialects such a diagram can be interpreted from a diachronic dimension, as a record of change in progress. Historically, non-rhotic pronunciations were prestigious in the United States in New England and some neighbouring regions and in large parts of the coastal South. Since the mid-twentieth-century, however, there has been a growing trend in the country among the educated and mobile middle classes to conform to standard rhotic pronunciations at least in formal situations.

Seen from this point of view, the diagram is a historical snapshot taken in the 1960s and showing how this change affected middle-class New Yorkers more strongly than working-class and lower-class residents. The direction of the change is clear: the local dialect will be pushed back in favour of the national standard (at least with regard to this particular variable), and the prediction can be made on the basis of the diagram that the change will have proceeded even further now. This is in fact what replications of Labov's 1960s studies carried out in the 1990s found out.

Labov's work inspired numerous studies throughout the English-speaking world and beyond. This impressive body of sociolinguistic research has enabled us to understand the dynamics of linguistic variation among monolingual residents of modern cities. For example, it is easy to see now how traditional regional variation and variation based on social class and education interact. The following diagram, illustrating a number of pronunciations of the word *home* which might be encountered in contemporary Britain, makes this clear.

Systematic interaction of regional and social variation in urban dialects

Social class		Pronunciation of the word *home*				
		Edinburgh	Newcastle	Liverpool	Norwich	London
Upper class/ Upper middle class	RP	[həʊm]	[həʊm]	[həʊm]	[həʊm]	[həʊm]
Lower middle class	Regional standard	[hɔʊm] [ho:m]	[ho:m] [huom]	[hɔʊm] [ho:m]	[hu:m] [hʊm]	[hʌʊm] [ʌʊm]
Working class	Non-standard/ vernacular	[he:m]	[hiem] [jem]	[o:m]	[ʊm]	[æʊm]

Fig. 11.4
Some pronunciations of the word *home* encountered in contemporary Britain, adapted from Dirven 1985: 15

As we can see, there is a national pronunciation standard which holds for England and, less uncontroversially, also for Scotland. It is cultivated by an educated upper-middle class, particularly in formal situations. As is signified by the thin edge of the wedge, only a small portion of the population in Britain can be described as competent and habitual users of this standard. Estimates range from 3 to 5 per cent. As a supra-regional and non-localisable standard, this type of pronunciation is also encountered in formal and official communication in the media, for example in serious news broadcasts. As we go down the social scale in each of the five cities, pronunciations get increasingly specific to the place in question, and increasingly different from each other. The compromise forms in the middle range will probably turn out to be the majority preferences in the long run. For London, for example, /hʌʊm/ lacks the double Cockney stigma of the "dropped aitch" and the /æʊ/-diphthong, and nevertheless retains enough of the local covert prestige to prevent the speaker from sounding distant or "posh." Similar regionally modified versions of the standard accent have emerged elsewhere and have become the majority accent in most regions of contemporary Britain. As the transitions between the various vowel values are smooth, the diagram in fact illustrates not discrete options but dialect continua.

11.3 | Problems and challenges

New departures in sociolinguistics – beyond the Labovian approach

The Labovian approach to the study of social variation in language has been phenomenally successful. Time and again, and in a wide range of locations, researchers have been able to establish statistically significant correlations between independent social variables and dependent linguistic (in practice mostly phonetic) variables. Even exceptional behaviour such as the hyper-correction displayed by the borderline lower-middle class in the New York sample tended to recur in similar circumstances in other locales. This success must not blind us to the fact, however, that there are places in the sociolinguistic landscape where a Labovian approach may not reach.

Qualitative and interaction-based approaches

More recent work in sociolinguistics has therefore explored the potential of qualitative and interaction-based methods. The emphasis is no longer on the question of how speakers' social status (the independent variable assumed as given) is reflected in or even determines their average linguistic behaviour (the dependent variable). Interesting as such group-based statistical correlations may be, they nevertheless disregard the individual speaker's personal identity and linguistic choices in a specific situation. The focus in interaction-based sociolinguistic studies therefore shifts on the individual speaker, who – after all – uses the linguistic resources available to him or her in order to achieve some communicative goal. Seen in this light, the linguistic variable is no longer necessarily dependent but may help to create a speaker's social profile rather than merely reflect it. Speakers using their language(s) keep making "acts of identity" – choices which both signal who they are and, at least to some extent, allow them to project the kind of person that they want to be.

Language and ethnic identity

Such a qualitative perspective makes it easy to incorporate several competing determinants of variation, without prioritising one at the expense of others. Among the determinants of linguistic variation which interact with social class in complex ways are ethnicity, race and gender. To understand the development of /r/ in New York City, for example, it is necessary to keep in mind that /r/ in this particular context "means" two things. Historically, non-rhotic pronunciations recall a New England past. In the present, though, they are probably far more strongly associated with the English spoken by the African-American poor all over the United States. Large numbers of them migrated to New York from the early 20th century, and this certainly upset the linguistic ecology. In a situation characterised by conflicting norms and orientations, there is no guarantee that the black and white working-class (or, for that matter, the black and white middle-class) should handle this variable in precisely the same way.

In the United States, *African-American Vernacular English* (AAVE), the variety of English used by uneducated and poor blacks, was long ignored in linguistic research. From the 1960s onwards, this trend has reversed, and it is now one of the best-researched non-standard varieties of English anywhere in the world. It is an ideal case to demonstrate how regional, social and ethnic factors interact in shaping linguistic variation. Historically, this variety originated in the American South, sharing many features with other Southern dialects of the United States. Today, it has its home base among the black working class and the black poor, who usually inhabit urban ghettoes dispersed all over the United States. Owing to the high degree of residential segregation, it has also become an ethnic marker, in addition to signalling the class status of its speakers. To understand such a complex and politically charged linguistic phenomenon, we need to approach it from several perspectives.

<small>The case of *African-American Vernacular English* (AAVE)</small>

A first necessary step, even preceding the sociolinguistic study of its use, is to identify the salient structural features of AAVE. These are the most important ones:

<small>AAVE – structural features</small>

- AAVE tends to be non-rhotic, carrying the loss of /r/ even further than other non-rhotic varieties by also omitting intervocalic /r/ as in *warrior*.
- AAVE simplifies many word-final consonant clusters, such as, for example [st] (as in *test* or *passed*), or [kt] (as in *fact* or *looked*). As can be seen, this phonetic feature has a profound impact on the grammar of the verb, as regular past-tense endings tend to disappear.
- AAVE tends to omit the unstressed copula verb *to be*: *he sick* (for standard "he is sick" [at the moment]).
- Unlike other non-standard varieties, in which *ain't* replaces negated forms of *be* and *have*, it also functions in the negation of full verbs in AAVE: *I ain't answer the man* ("I didn't answer the man").
- While some of the above features suggest that AAVE is primarily characterised by simplification if compared to other varieties, this is not always so. For example, it has a number of preverbal markers expressing various tense and aspect notions. Invariant *be* signals habituality: *he be sick* (unlike the *he sick* discussed above) thus means that "he is sick regularly = he's in frail health." Note that while the momentary expression is usually negated using *ain't* (*he ain't sick*), the appropriate negation for the habitual statement is *he don't be sick*.

Taking the cue from this structural description, the sociolinguist will have to investigate the frequency and systematic distribution of these features in authentic usage, for example by documenting the same speaker or speakers at various levels of formality, or by comparing lower-class or middle-class speakers. Recent research in the sociolinguistics of African-American Vernacular

<small>AAVE – the sociolinguistic issues</small>

English has particularly focussed on the question of whether "white" or "black" vernaculars are converging or diverging – a question which has obvious relevance for answering the question whether integration has been successful at the grassroots level.

AAVE – the political issues

Other problems, which a sociolinguist can contribute to discussing but not solve, include the question of whether AAVE is a separate language from other varieties of North American English, because it embodies the distinct cultural and historical experience of blacks in the United States, including a submerged "substratal" influence from the ancestral West African languages of the slaves. Advocates of this point of view turn up in the United States with great regularity, and with equal regularity meet with bitter opposition. The stakes in such controversies are high, involving access to educational funds and other material privileges, but also non-material ones, such as the public status and explicit public recognition of a prominent minority's cultural heritage.

The 1996 "Ebonics" controversy

One recent such public controversy was sparked off by a resolution passed by the Oakland (San Francisco Bay area) School Board in 1996 which advocated the teaching of standard American English through the medium of the African American vernacular spoken by many students in the area. The wording of the resolution may have been unfortunate in places, the name "Ebonics" chosen for AAVE misleading. The intention, however, was good: to help those "problem" students which other teaching methods had failed miserably. Amazingly, at least to anyone not aware of the importance of the issue of race in US politics and culture, the ensuing debate did not remain an exchange among experts and the concerned public about the pros and cons of various compet-

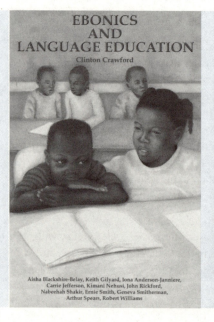
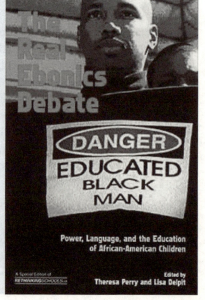

Fig. 11.5 "Ebonics" – two books sparked by the controversy

ing teaching methods. Instead, it erupted into an all-out scandal whose reverberations continue to be felt on the World Wide Web to this day. Completely misunderstanding the context and intention of the resolution, conservative opinion presented it as a vicious and socially divisive attempt to rob young black people of their future in American society: allowing ghetto language into the class room was equated with teaching students to become gangsters. White middle class fellow travellers of rap and hip-hop culture, on the other hand, used the opportunity to publish entertaining "English-Ebonics" glossaries and translation manuals which simplified the linguistic issues in a different way (and certainly added their own bit to the stereotyping of African American language and culture). In the end, the controversy even inspired several books, some of which might actually help prevent similar misunderstandings in future if they found enough readers (cf. Fig. 11.5).

AAVE or (to quote one prominent expert) "Black English – socially marginal, melodious, in-your-face, percussive, marvelous, *to be*-dropping, slangy, gangsta-rapping, exotic Black English" – is a many-faceted phenomenon which needs to be studied from more perspectives than merely a descriptive-linguistic one. However, the linguistic perspective remains indispensable in a climate of debate which is so intensely charged emotionally and ideologically, because it is the only one which makes a basic point very clearly, namely that this stigmatised and publicly controversial variety of American English "is every bit as sophisticated as the prose of Jane Austen" (McWhorter 1998: 129).

<small>Sociolinguistics, literary and cultural studies?</small>

Here at the latest you should begin to see that a good grasp of the sociolinguistic landscape of present-day English can help you enormously even in areas outside the purely linguistic components of your course. In practical terms, it is enough for you to develop a good active command of spoken and written English in one of its standard forms. As for your receptive (listening and reading) skills, however, more is required. Travelling in the English-speaking world, you will have to understand what speakers of non-standard varieties are saying on numerous occasions. Even if you don't venture outside your study, you can't help noticing that numerous non-standard varieties of English are represented in the great works of English literature. If you don't know about the sociolinguistic background of the works in question, all this will be "funny English" to you but not mean much else. If you are aware of the background, though, you will be able to fully appreciate an author's skill in characterisation or to assess the degree of linguistic realism of a work.

As for AAVE, one question which might serve as a promising starting point for such an inter-disciplinary research project integrating linguistics, literature and cultural studies is to ask why rap and hip-hop, forms of verbal-cultural expression with distinctly local roots in the US black urban ghettos, should have become so popular among white middle-class college students, first in the US but subsequently all over the world. One linguistic symptom of this global success of a formerly sub-cultural art-form is the presence of many words and expressions from rap or hip-hop language in general American English and, indeed, in foreign languages such as German or French. Cases in point are *def* or *da bomb* – just two of several more synonyms for *cool* (which incidentally is itself a borrowing from an earlier layer of African-American slang into general English).

Text 11.1 | **What the writers say**
John Dos Passos,
"Preface" to the *In the preface to his trilogy U.S.A. (1938), John Dos Passos (1896–1970) formulates*
U.S.A. trilogy (1938) *a programmatic statement explaining his vision of what it means to be American.*
vi–vii *The vernacular, "the language of the people," emerges as the tie that binds the whole nation together.*

Only the ears busy to catch the speech are not alone; the ears are caught tight, linked tight by the tendrils of phrased words, the turn of a joke, the singsong fade of a story, the gruff fall of a sentence; linking tendrils of speech twine through the city blocks, spread over pavements, grow out along broad parked avenues, speed with the trucks leaving on their long night runs over roaring highways, whisper down sandy byroads past wornout farms, joining up cities and fillingstations, roundhouses, steamboats, planes groping along airways; words call out on mountain pastures, drift slow down rivers widening to the sea and the hushed beaches.

U.S.A. is the slice of a continent. U.S.A. is a group of holding companies, some aggregations of trade unions, a set of laws bound in calf, a radio network, a chain of moving picture theatres [sic], a column of stock quotations rubbed out and written in by a Western Union boy on a blackboard, a publiclibrary full of old newspapers and dogeared history books with protests scrawled on the margins in pencil. U.S.A. is the world's greatest rivervalley fringed with mountains and hills, U.S.A. is a set of bigmouthed officials with too many bankaccounts, U.S.A. is a lot of men buried in their uniforms in Arlington Cemetery. U.S.A. is the letters at the end of an address when you are away from home. But mostly U.S.A. is the speech of the people.

Bilingual speakers, While most sociolinguistic studies focus on linguistic variation within varieties
multilingual com- of one language, we need to remind ourselves that most major contemporary
munities cities, particularly in the English-speaking world, are decidedly multilingual places. New York City, the site of Labov's pioneering research, is an obvious example. In the classic era of mass immigration to the United States in the latter half of the nineteenth and early twentieth centuries, hundreds of thousands of New York residents, for example, spoke German, Yiddish, Italian, Polish or some other European language. Today, in the contemporary era of global migration which started in the 1970s and 1980s and gained in momentum after the collapse of the Soviet bloc, their places (and in fact the literal residential neighbourhoods) have been taken over by Puerto Ricans, speakers of Spanish from other parts of Latin America, Haitians, Koreans and Chinese.

PROBLEMS AND CHALLENGES   **Unit 11**

As in the introduction to this Unit we mentioned London's Bengali speakers as a first example of a multilingual community, we will conclude this section by looking at three London maps of a rather special kind:

Mapping multilingual London

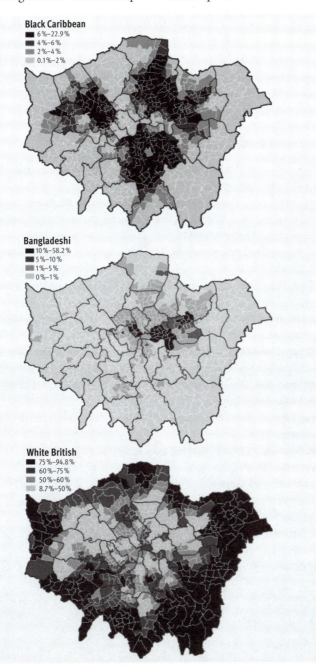

Fig. 11.6
Caribbean, Bengali and "white British" residential patterns in contemporary London (source: www.guardian.co.uk)

The over-all message of the maps is clear. Residential segregation in London is not complete. Londoners of all ethnic and linguistic backgrounds will have occasion to meet and communicate with each other. However, the statistical tendencies in the individual boroughs show that there are residential ethnic communities living within fairly precisely circumscribed geographical locales – the East End (i.e. the traditional home-base of the Cockney dialect) for the Bengalis, Brixton, Brent and Haringey for the Caribbean community, and more or less the entire ring of suburbs for the white population. To find out what this residential distribution means for the future of the London dialect is a problem which you might want to turn to at a later stage in your studies.

References and further reading

Bailey, Richard W., and Manfred Görlach. 1982. *English as a world language.* Ann Arbor MI: University of Michigan Press.

Chambers, Jack C. 2003. *Sociolinguistic theory.* 2nd ed. Oxford: Blackwell.

Cheshire, Jenny, ed. 1991. *English around the world: Sociolinguistic perspectives.* Cambridge: Cambridge University Press.

Coupland, Nikolas, and Adam Jaworski, eds. 1997. *Sociolinguistics: A reader and coursebook.* London: Macmillan.

Dirven, René. 1985. *Die Leistung der Linguistik für den Englischunterricht.* 2nd ed. Tübingen: Niemeyer.

Keefe, Susan, and Amado Padilla. 1987. *Chicano ethnicity.* Albuquerque NM: University of New Mexico Press.

Labov, William, Sharon Ash, and Charles Boberg. 2006. *The atlas of North American English. Phonetics, phonology and sound change.* Berlin and New York: Mouton de Gruyter.

Labov, William. 1966. *The social stratification of English in New York City.* Washington DC: Center for Applied Linguistics.

McWhorter, John. 1998. *The word on the street: fact and fable about American English.* New York: Plenum Press.

Mufwene, Salikoko S., John J. Rickford, John Baugh, and Guy Bailey, eds. 1998. *African-American English. Structure, history and use.* London and New York: Routledge.

Rickford, John R. 1992. "Grammatical variation and divergence in Vernacular Black English." In Gerritsen, Marinel and Dieter Stein (eds.). *Internal and external factors in syntactic change.* Berlin and New York: Mouton de Gruyter. 190–191.

Romaine, Suzanne. 2000. *Language in society: An introduction to sociolinguistics.* 2nd ed. Oxford: OUP.

Sánchez, Rosaura. 1983. *Chicano discourse: socio-historic perspectives.* Rowley MA: Newbury.

Practice

|11.4

1. Classify the following instances of variable or non-standard usage according to (a) their regional spread (specific vs. general) and (b) their degree of linguistic stigmatisation (high or low). A reference work which will prove extremely helpful for this task is Kortmann and Schneider's 2004 *Handbook of Varieties of English*:

   I don't know nothing about that.
   If you're honest, it don't matter whether you are rich or poor.
   I don't know where I've putten the bloody receipt.
   I'll be afraid as long as they haven't caught the bloke what done it.
   Come quick! We need a doctor.
   He's the type that only works good under pressure.
   Read this. That'll stop you asking any more silly questions.
   Is you is my baby or is you ain't?
   He's gonna wanna talk to you again about it, I'm sure.
   Them youngsters had it coming for some time.

2. Consult the *Atlas of North American English* by Labov, Ash and Boberg (2006). What does this atlas tell you about the occurrence of post-vocalic /r/ in present-day American English?

   As a dialect atlas, this work primarily covers regional variation in American English. Which groups of speakers/types of linguistic variation are excluded from coverage?

3. Explain the conflicting pressures of overt and covert linguistic prestige alluded to in the following personalised column from the London *Sunday Times*:

   > Many years ago my then future (now ex) husband used to reduce me to near-hysterics whenever we took a taxi back to his house. As soon as we neared home, he'd lean forward, slide open the glass partition, and tell the cab driver: "There's a li'el slip road just dahn on the right, mate, alrigh? Cheers." Then he'd shut the partition, lean back, adjust the collar on his Prada coat, and, in his normal voice, say something like: "That claret at supper was utterly divine."
   >
   > This happened most nights. He'd laugh, too, but he still continued addressing cabbies in his pretend accent. The husband wasn't – isn't – a braying Hooray of the incurable kind (I know someone who goes to "marse" every Sunday) and, with time, his of-the-people accent became pretty convincing, to the point where he now marches around Hackney, east London, speaking like a native whenever the mood takes him. It works beautifully until some enterprising market stallholder asks him if went to school local.
   >
   > I used to think this was terribly funny until I started doing it myself. Put me on Radio 4 and I speak normally. Stick me in a taxi and my natural accent completely disappears. Take me to a smart restaurant and I'm Lady Bracknell;

   |Text 11.2
   India Knight, "Speak proper? Not likely," *Sunday Times*, 11 Nov. 2001, 5–4

take me down the market and naturally, without thinking twice, I'll ask the stall-holder: "Are you avin' a laugh?" when he tries to overcharge.

Like some schizoid chameleon, I alter my accent to match that of my interlocutor – but only if said interlocutor speaks, for want of a better phrase, like a Kevin. And there's an expression you don't hear very often any more, because political correctness has sprung to the rescue of every single kind of accent. Except mine.

The only accent it is now actively all right to pillory is the so-called "posh" – the clear enunciation that comes from being privately educated or having upper-middle class parents. Mention the amazing ugliness of the Birmingham accent, for instance, and some bien pensant type will reproachfully inform you that it's a wonderful accent, actually, and that it's terribly important to maintain this kind of regional linguistic diversity (which it is). Make a joke about speaking like Tim Nice-but-Dim, on the other hand, and everybody will laugh like drains at the absurdity of public school voices. Why? Why is received pronunciation invalid and every other accent imaginable not so?

Speaking properly – because no matter how unfashionable it is to say it, I speak properly and many of the people I meet do not – has become comical.

4 Explain the conflicting pressures of overt and covert linguistic prestige apparent in the following two statements by African-American informants:

> "It pisses me off when the Oreos – they be trying to correct your language, and I be like, 'Get away from me! Did I ask you to – correct?! No! No! No, I didn't! Nuh-uh!" ("Fabiola", teenager)

> "I do think it's – it makes a difference, because in our day an' time, if you don't use your English as near right, people kinda look at you as if, 'Oh, I don't want her in – on my job, to speaking' dis way or in my kitchen, around' my childrens, you know, so I think it does make a difference how you speak [...]
>
> I have to try, you know, I guess. I – I tries to put the words right, the verbs and things, I try my best to – take my time if I – especially if I'm – speaking' to someone tha's is – uh- educated, you know." ("Penelope Johnson", cleaner, in her fifties)
>
> (quoted from Rickford 1992: 190–191):

Comment on the non-standard linguistic features used by both speakers. How are they related to the image which is being projected?

5 Consider the following three texts, which each in its own way deal with the linguistic situation of the Latino minority in the U.S. The first is from a sociological treatise, the second from the autobiography of a reformed gang-member, and the third is a poem by a New York-based Puerto Rican (= "Nuyorican") writer:

For native-born Mexican Americans, the ethnic community is made up of Mexican Americans who have selectively acculturated and interact with Anglos, as well as other Mexican Americans. However, the content and degree of interethnic interaction is governed by time and place and reflects a situational ethnicity. At times, some of our respondents are Mexican Americans, part of the larger society, knowledgeable about American culture and interacting with the mainstream population. At other times, the same respondents are American Mexicans, carrying on traditional culture, taking pride in their heritage, and tied intimately to others of similar ethnicity. At still other times, they are Chicanos, practicing new and emergent cultural patterns and sustaining an ethnic community set apart from both Anglos and recent immigrant Mexicans.

| Text 11.3
Susan Keefe/Amado Padilla, *Chicano ethnicity*, 1987, 190

But the kicker was when Mrs. Baez returned the newly-typed versions of my writing; I couldn't believe I had anything to do with it. The shape of the words, the forms and fragments of sentences and syllables, seemed alien, as if done by another's hand.

The fact was I didn't know anything about literature. I had fallen through the chasm between two languages. The Spanish had been beaten out of me in the early years of school – and I didn't learn English very well either.

This was the predicament of many Chicanos.

We could almost be called incommunicable, except we remained lucid; we got over what we felt, sensed and understood. Sometimes we rearranged words, created new meanings and structures – even a new vocabulary. Often our everyday talk blazed with poetry.

Our expressive powers were strong and vibrant. If this could be nurtured, if the language skills could be developed on top of this, we could learn to break through any communication barrier. We needed to obtain victories in language, built on an infrastructure of self-worth.

| Text 11.4
Luis Rodriguez, *Always running – La vida loca: gang days in L.A.*, 1993, 219

my NUYORICAN being
      my eagle knife caution
filled mind reads your neon
      signs AQUI YOUR CREDITO ES GOOD
and I feel sad that in school,
we're forced to reach for standards
      do you know what I mean?
      standards like
STANDARD ENGLISH
      STANDARD SPANISH
      but meanwhile your neon
      signs tell the real truth:
you are bilingual Puerto Rico
you are NUYORICAN on

| Text 11.5
Miguel Algarín, "Nuyorican", 1975 (cited in Bailey/Görlach 1982: 224)

your own home soil.
your schools scold me for illiteracy
while your Cuban/American bankers
sell me the island in spanglish.

Unit 12

Language change and the history of English

Orientation

Like most other languages spoken in Europe today (the notable exceptions being Hungarian, Finnish, Turkish, Estonian, Maltese and Basque), English is a member of the Indo-European family of languages. That is to say that its historical roots go back to a common proto-language or *Ursprache* which is believed to have been spoken in the fourth millennium BC, probably in a region north of the Black Sea, and then spread out over large regions of Europe and Southern Asia, dividing into numerous more or less distantly related "daughter" languages. Within this group, English is a member of the Germanic branch and particularly close to members of the "West-Germanic" group, i.e. Frisian, High and Low German, Yiddish, Dutch, Flemish and Afrikaans (the language developed by the Dutch-descended white settlers of present-day South Africa).

12.1 The Indo-European ancestry of most modern European languages

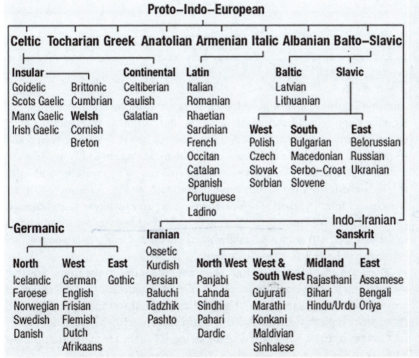

Table 12.1 The major subgroups of the Indo-European family of languages (source: http://www.bbc.co.uk/wales/history/sites/language/images/language_family_tree.gif)

187

English and its relatives

The relationship between English and the North-Germanic languages is a little more distant, but still close. Additionally, it was re-inforced through intensive language contact in historical times, in particular the Old English period (on which see below). While these close relationships are often apparent even to lay observers, the more distant ones, for example those obtaining between English and Pashto (historically a member of the Iranian branch of Indo-European and currently the language of the majority ethnic group of Afghanistan), reveal themselves only to the specialist.

Sound laws

The most important tool for the historical-comparative linguist reconstructing the history of a language family is the **sound-law**. Sound-laws are regular and systematic correspondences between sounds that do not just hold between individual pairs of words in two languages but across entire series of words. Note, for example, the following correspondences between English and German:

Table 12.2 English-German correspondences

English /p/	German /pf, f/
pan	Pfanne
pound	Pfund
path	Pfad
ship	Schiff
ripe	reif
open	offen
weapon	Waffe

Interpreting this evidence in isolation, there are two possible conclusions: (a) At some stage in the history of German, the stop consonant /p/, inherited from Germanic, became /pf/ at the beginning of words before following vowels and /f/ inside the word and word-finally; or (b) at some stage in its history, English collapsed an inherited distinction between /pf/ and /f/ by replacing both with /p/. In context, story (b) is impossible to maintain, and (a) is the incontrovertibly correct interpretation. The development is part of a larger sound change, commonly referred to as "Hochdeutsche Lautverschiebung," which sets apart Old High German from Old English and all other Gemanic languages (see Exercise 8 below for further illustration).

Internal and external evidence used in dating sound changes

There are, of course, numerous apparent exceptions to the sound law that we have just found out. For example, the German equivalents of *pill* and *place* are not *Pfille* and *Pflatz*, as would be predicted by our sound law, but *Pille* and *Platz*. Since both are loanwords (from Latin and French), this need not bother us. On the contrary, it helps us date the change. The shift from /p/ to /pf/ must have taken place **before** these words were taken over into German.

Unit 12

ORIENTATION

In comparison to the other Germanic languages, English has been very innovative. While the Indo-European proto-language is assumed to have been of the synthetic type, most daughter languages have developed toward the analytical end of this typological continuum. Thus, the modern Romance languages are more analytical than Latin, and modern Bulgarian is more analytical than Old Church Slavonic, the oldest attested member of the Slavic branch. To return to the Germanic languages: even modern German is somewhat more analytical than Old High German. In English, however, the trend toward analyticity has been massive. This can be seen, for example, in the inflectional paradigm of the definite article. In Old English, the oldest historically attested form of the language, the article had four (marginally five) cases, three genders and separate forms for the singular and plural:

The shift from synthetic to analytical grammar

	Singular			Plural
	masculine	feminine	neuter	
nominative	se	sēo	þæt	þā
Genitive	þæs	þǣre	þæs	þāra
Dative	þām/þǣm	þǣre	þām	þām/þǣm
Accusative	þone	þā	þæt	þā
(instrumental)	þȳ/þon		þȳ/þon	

Table 12.3
Inflectional paradigm of the definite article in Old English

Taking the noun *stān* (*stone*) as an illustration, we could have distinguished between *se stān* "the stone" in the singular nominative, and *þām stāne* "the stone" in the dative singular, as in *on þām stāne* "on the stone." This complexity was reduced drastically by c. 1100, when all these forms had collapsed into one: *þe*, identical in all but spelling to our present-day *the*. The reason why the levelling of inflectional paradigms proceeded so much faster in English than in most other Germanic languages is probably language and dialect contact. There must have been a lot of dialect mixing as various Germanic tribes started invading and settling England from the fifth century AD. There was further mixing and contact with the North Germanic languages of the Viking invaders who played such an important role in the history of Britain from the 8th to the 12th centuries. In that type of linguistic environment, new generations of speakers are very likely to simplify inflections, for example by generalising endings which are frequent at the expense of rare ones, or by dropping them altogether.

The beginnings of the English language are shrouded in some mystery. We know that various continental Germanic tribes living on the North Sea coast – in particular the Angles, Saxons, Jutes and Frisians – started invading and colonising Britain from the early 5th century onwards. The reason was a

The major periods in the history of English

political power vacuum left by the Romans, who withdrew from Britain at the time. Over time, the various continental dialects which these settlers brought with them melded into a new idiom which was called "English." This designation is derived from the name of one particular settler group, the Angles, but was eventually used more loosely, to cover the language of all settlers of Germanic descent (just as the name *England* (from *Engla land*, "land of the Angles," came to denote the country as a whole). From around 700, we have written evidence of this new language. Conventionally, we distinguish the following major periods in the history of English.

12.1.1 | Old English period (c. 500 – c. 1100)

Old English

Old English, or Anglo-Saxon, was the Germanic vernacular spoken in Britain, co-existing with several Celtic languages, but more profoundly influenced by Latin, the language of Christianity, culture and learning at the time, and by Old Norse, the language of the Vikings. The Vikings arrived as raiders from the end of the 8th century, but eventually settled alongside the local population, providing opportunity for intensive language contact.

In its grammar, Old English was clearly of the synthetic type, with complex inflectional paradigms for the noun, the adjective and the verb. Its vocabulary was largely Germanic, with some loans from Latin which by now are usually fully assimilated phonetically and thus no longer recognisable as such (e.g. *mint*, from Vulgar Latin *munita* = *moneta*; or *street* from *(via) strata*). Culturally, Anglo-Saxon England was an important centre in early Medieval Europe,

Fig. 12.1 |
St. Boniface's baptism and martyrdom, from the 11th century, Fulda Sacramentary

with the influence of English and Irish missionaries and scholars extending over large areas of central Europe. St. Boniface (c. 675–754), the "Apostle of the Germans," for example, grew up as Wynfrith in the Southwest of England and was educated in Exeter before departing to the Continent. One of the most important scholars at the court of Charlemagne, Alcuin (c. 732–804) was also of English origin and obtained his education at York, another early medieval English centre of learning.

By the late 10th century, the West Saxon dialect of Old English had developed a written standard which was in use all over England – an exceptional achievement at a time in which Latin tended to be the preferred choice for writing elsewhere. This tradition of writing in English, however, disappeared soon after the Norman Conquest (1066).

What do the sources that students of Old English deal with actually look like? The illustration below shows an extract from the Old English text of *Beowulf*, a heroic epic encompassing almost 3200 lines. This poem is part of the Germanic oral tradition and was passed on from generation to generation before it was written down, possibly at some stage in the 10th century. It is preserved in exactly one manuscript, which almost went up in flames in a fire about 200 years ago. It is on display in the British Library in London.

Facsimile of Old English manuscript – *Beowulf*

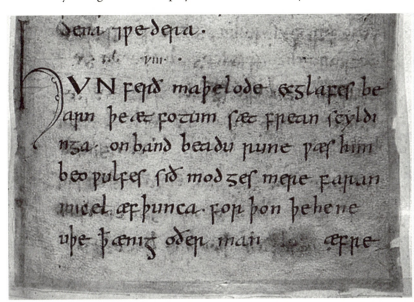

Fig. 12.2
Beowulf, lines 500 ff.
(British Library, MS Cotton Vetellius A. XV)

The text reads "(H)unferð maðelode Ecglāfes bearn þē æt fōtum sæt frēan Scyldinga ...;" or in modern translation, "Unferth spoke, the son of Ecglaf, who sat at the feet of the Scyldings' lord." Note that the usual way in which this is presented in modern editions would be:

Hunferð maðelode,	Ecglāfes bearn,
þē æt fōtum	sæt frēan Scyldinga

This arrangement makes clear the metrical structure of the alliterative "long lines" of the poem to the modern reader (a complicated business which we cannot go into in an introduction to linguistics). Another courtesy of the editors is that they introduce punctuation, almost completely absent in the original, and that they place bars over long vowels such as the <ō> in *fōtum* "feet," so that we can read the text more easily.

Note, by contrast, that the lines just run on without punctuation in the original version, and the line-breaks may occur even inside a word. The language is very far away from Modern English. In fact, there is continuity only between *æt fōtum*, which is the preposition *at* followed by the dative plural of *fōt* "foot," and the following verb *sat*, which was spelled slightly differently from Modern English (*sæt*) but pronounced similarly. The word *bearn* survives in some non-standard Modern English dialects as *bairn* ("child"). The mere writing, however, is not too difficult to decipher. Runic signs are used for the dental fricative "<TH>" phoneme that was not represented in the Roman alphabet; the shapes of some letters are slightly unusual by modern standards; but with a little practice such one-thousand-year-old texts are fairly easy to read.

12.1.2 | Middle English period (c. 1100 – c. 1500)

Middle English

In a dispute over the succession to the English throne in 1066, William Duke of Normandy ("the Conqueror") took his chance and beat the English forces in the famous Battle of Hastings. The Norman invasion of England ushered in a period in which the ruling elites in England were speakers of French or at least bilingual in French and English. English, by contrast, became a language of low prestige, spoken by the mass of the population, particularly the rural peasantry.

While the Norman invasion and the long period of French influence in the later Middle Ages did not have a profound impact on the development of English grammar, it led to the addition of several thousand French loan words to the English vocabulary. This first massive wave of borrowing paved the way for subsequent ones so that present-day English has become a language which easily incorporates words from diverse sources into its vocabulary. Very often, the new words did not entirely replace the old ones, but both live on as near synonyms with some degree of semantic or stylistic differentiation (e.g. *begin – commence, loneliness – solitude*). Grammatically, Middle English resembles present-day English in that it has few inflections and mainly relies on analytical strategies to code grammatical relations.

Towards the end of the Middle English period, English gained in prestige again and started to replace French and Latin in the more prestigious domains of communication, including writing. This gradually led to the emergence of a new written standard, based on the speech of London and the East Midlands, which is the direct historical antecedent of the present-day standard variety.

Facsimile of Middle English manuscript – Geoffrey Chaucer, Canterbury Tales

This is what a Middle English text looks like. The text is from the opening of the General Prologue to Geoffrey Chaucer's *Canterbury Tales*. Chaucer (c. 1343–1400) is the most famous English poet of the later Middle Ages; the *Canterbury Tales* are his most widely read and studied work.

Fig. 12.3
Geoffrey Chaucer, "General Prologue" (from the Hengwrt Manuscript, early 15th century, National Library of Wales, Aberystwyth)

The headline of this text reads "here bygynneth the book of the tales of caunterbury," which – except for the archaic third-person singular ending – translates straightforwardly into Modern English. Then follows the text of the prologue: "Whan that averill with his shoures soote the droghte of march hath perced to the roote …," which translates into Modern English: "When April with its sweet showers has pierced the drought of March to the root." Unlike the preceding Old English text, here it is probably more difficult to decipher the writing than to get the basic message. Of course, little traps remain. Note, for example, that the neuter possessive pronoun *its* did not exist yet, and the reference to April is by means of *his*. This was normal grammar in those days and has nothing to do with metaphorical personification.

Early Modern English period (c. 1500 – c. 1750)

12.1.3

Early Modern English

For England, this was the period of the Renaissance, the Reformation and the beginnings of colonial expansion, which all left their impact on the history of the language. The renewed interest in the classical languages, Latin and Greek, brought many borrowings which added a whole new layer to the vocabulary of English, namely the "hard words." These are words which are usually not found in informal speech but allow speakers to express fine nuances of meaning in more formal situations and in written texts. Readers wishing to prove this point are welcome to look up words such as *pathos, pathetic, sympathy, empathy, sympathetic, empathetic, sympathise* or *empathise* in their dictionary or to test whether they can spot the difference between *discrete* and *discreet*.

Among the noteworthy grammatical innovations of the Early Modern period were the introduction of the auxiliary verb *do* in questions and negations and the establishment of the modal auxiliaries as the distinct grammatical category that they represent now.

Phonetically, the Early Modern English period is the heyday of the *Great Vowel Shift*, a series of inter-connected sound changes which affected all long vowels and diphthongs. For example, the Middle English long monophthong [iː] in *time* [tiːm] turned into the modern diphthong [aɪ] via the intermediate stage of [əɪ]. As English spelling conventions were largely fixed before the Great Vowel Shift, there is considerable mismatch between pronunciation and spelling in standard English today. The standardisation of English spelling received a further boost from the introduction of the new printing technology into England by William Caxton in 1476, and the prestige of English grew steadily, for example because it replaced Latin in the religious services of the Church of England. Towards the end of the Early Modern English period Dr. Samuel Johnson published his monumental *Dictionary* (1755), a further landmark both in lexicography and the standardisation of English.

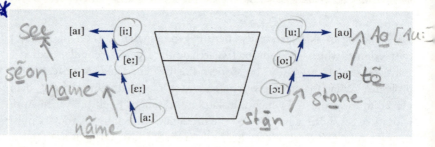

Fig. 12.4 | Great Vowel Shift

Facsimile of 18th century manuscript

The student of Early Modern English has plenty of printed material to use as data. For some purposes, however, manuscript sources – such as informal handwritten letters – remain important. This is what a late-18th-century manuscript looks like.

The text is easy to read: "And for the support of this declaration we mutually pledge to each other our lives[,] our fortunes, and our sacred honour." It is interesting to note that this version preserves a spelling <honour> which today would be considered British. Note, incidentally, that as you have this text in front of you, you are looking at the historical origin of the American idiom "put your hancock here" (for "could you please sign your name here"). John Hancock's forceful signature clearly outshines the other Founding Fathers.'

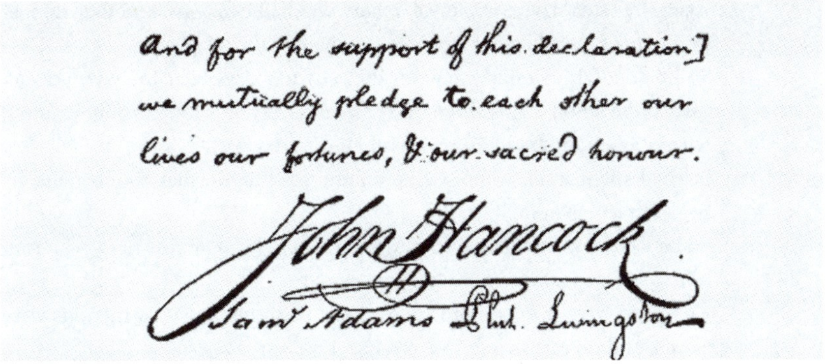

Fig. 12.5 Draft version of the United States Declaration of Independence, 4 July 1776, signatures of John Hancock, Sam Adams and Philip Livingston (National Archives and Records Administration, Washington DC)

12.1.4 Modern English

Modern English period (since c. 1750)

There are no drastic changes marking the transition from Early Modern English to Modern English. What we find is a reduction of variability in the grammar of the standard and the elaboration of analytical grammatical structures, particularly in the tense and aspect system of the verb. Thus, while in Early Modern English forms such as *I do not know* and *I know not*, or *I read* and *I am reading*, were still in variation, this was cleared up in the 18th century. *I know not* disappeared (or survived as a stylistic archaism) and the use of the auxiliary *to do*, a new and increasingly common option in the preceding period, became obligatory in Modern English in questions and negations involving main verbs. The expanded form *be reading*, on the other hand, ceased to be a stylistic variant of the simple form *read* and came to express the aspectual notion of an activity in progress.

Widespread literacy, increasing access to education and increasing social mobility all helped strengthen the position of standard English. With the advent of the audiovisual media (radio, television), standardisation increasingly affected the way English was spoken – at least in the public domain. As has become obvious in Unit 10, there is now a plurality of standard accents, and from being the language of the majority of the population of the United Kingdom English has developed into the pluri-centric world language that it is today.

12.2 Demonstration/discussion

Analysis of parallel texts – working our way back into the history of the English language

Among the texts which have been translated into English at all stages of its recorded history is, of course, the Bible. A comparison of parallel translations thus opens an interesting window on the history of the language. This is the text of the parable of the prodigal son (Luke 15, 11 ff.) in Modern English, followed by an Early Modern English, a Middle English and an Old English version (all from *The Bible in English*, CD-ROM, Chadwyck-Healey Ltd):

Text 12.1
New English Bible
(1960s)

11f. Again he said: 'There was once a man who had two sons; and the younger said to his father, "Father, give me my share of the property."
13 So he divided his estate between them. A few days later the younger son turned the whole of his share into cash and left home for a distant country, where he squandered it in reckless living.
14 He had spent it all, when a severe famine fell upon that country and he began to feel the pinch.
15 So he went and attached himself to one of the local landowners, who sent him on to his farm to mind the pigs.
16 He would have been glad to fill his belly with the pods that the pigs were eating; and no one gave him anything.
17 Then he came to his senses and said, "How many of my father's paid servants have more food than they can eat, and here am I, starving to death!"

Text 12.2
King James Bible
("Authorised Version"; 1611)

11 And hee said, A certaine man had two sonnes:
12 And the yonger of them said to his father, Father, giue me the portion of goods that fall**eth** to me. And he diuided **vnto** them his liuing.
13 And not many dayes after, the yonger sonne gathered al together, and tooke his iourney into a farre countrey, and there wasted his substance with riotous liuing.
14 And when he had spent all, there arose a mighty famine in that land, and he beganne to be in want.
15 And he went and ioyned himselfe to a citizen of that countrey, and he sent him into his fields to feed **swine**.
16 And he **would faine haue** filled his belly with the huskes that the swine **did eate**: & no man gaue **vnto** him.
17 And when he came to himselfe, he said, How many hired seruants of my fathers haue bread inough and to spare, and I **perish** with hunger?

Demonstration/Discussion — Unit 12

Text 12.3
John Wycliffe (Early; c. 1390s)

11 Forsothe he seith, Sum man hadde tweye sones;
12 and the yongere seide to the fadir, Fadir, gyue to me the porcioun of substaunce, ethir catel, that byfallith to me. **And the fadir departide to him the substaunce.**
13 and not aftir manye dayes, alle thingis gederid to gidre, the yongere sone wente in pilgrymage in to a fer cuntree; and there he wastide his substaunce in lyuynge leccherously.
14 and aftir that he hadde endid alle thingis, a strong hungir was **maad** in that cuntree, and he bigan to haue nede.
15 and he wente, and **cleuyde** to oon of the citeseyns of that cuntree. And he sente him in to his toun, that he schulde feede **hoggis**.
16 And he coueitide to fille his **wombe** of the **coddis** whiche the hoggis eeten, and no man yaf to him.
17 Sothli he turned agen in to him silf, seyde, Hou many hirid men in my fadir hous, 'han plente of looues; forsothe I perische here thurgh hungir.

Text 12.4
West Saxon Gospels, 10th century

11 He **cwæð** soðlice. Sum man hæfde twege sunes.
12 þa cwæð se ylder to his fader. Fader syle **me minne dæl minre ehte. þe me to gebyreð. Ða dælde he him his ehte.**
13 Ða æfter feawa **dagen** ealle his þing ge-gaderede se gingre sune. & ferde wræclice on **feor landen**. & for-spilde þær his ehte libbende on his gælsan.
14 Ða he hyo hæfde ealle amerde. þa **warð** mycel **hunger on þam rice**. & he warð wædle.
15 Ða ferde he & **folgede** anen burh-sittenden men on þare rice. **þa sende he hine to his tune þæt he heolde his swin.**
16 Ða ge-wilnede he his wambe fellen of þam bean-coddan þe þa swin æten. & him man ne sealde.
17 Ða be-þohte he hine & cwæð. Eala hwu fela erdlinga on **mines** fæder huse **hlaf** genoh hæbbeð. & ich her on hungre for-wurðe.

King James Bible

On the whole, we can read and understand text 12.2 fairly well. There are minor differences in spelling – for example the use of the letter <u> for <v>, and vice versa – which take some getting used to, but they are not a major obstacle to comprehension. There are obvious grammatical differences to modern English usage, particularly with the verbs. The third-person singular ending *-eth* (as in *falleth*) has now gone out of use. In two places ("the swine did eat," "I perish"), we would have to use the progressive obligatorily today. Note also that in the expression "the swine did eat" the auxiliary *do* is used not in its modern contrastive-emphatic sense, but vacuously. This was fairly common during the experimental period in which *do* was gradually establishing itself in questions and negations. The modal idiom "would faine haue" (= "would be glad to have") has fallen out of use, and so has the preposition *unto*. As for semantic and lexical change, the passage has a few cases, though none is particularly drastic. The word *swine*, for example, is not usually used in its literal sense today to denote pigs, but metaphorically, as a term of abuse.

John Wycliffe

In contrast to the King James Bible, text 12.3 is no longer immediately comprehensible to a modern reader. The spelling conventions take some more getting used to than in the 1611 version here. For example, it takes some time to realise that in *cleuyde* the <u> stands for <v> and that *clevyde* therefore corresponds to modern *cleaved*; or that *maad* is an alternative spelling for *made*. Somewhat surprisingly, the grammar of the text corresponds to modern usage rather closely. What is difficult, though, is the vocabulary. *Hoggis*, the term used to denote the pigs, is still in current use, especially in American English ("large pig kept for its meat"). The term *cods* (*coddis*, in our text) (for *husks*), however, has vanished from Standard English and barely survives in some traditional dialects (as in *peascods*, for example). *Womb(e)*, whose meaning today is restricted to the sense of "uterus," still had the much more general sense that is today preserved in the German *Wampe*. The verb *depart*, meaning "leave" today, is used in the transitive sense of "divide" in this text.

West Saxon Gospels

The sense of alienation created by this text, however, is nothing in comparison to what faces the modern reader who is confronted with an Old English text, e.g. text 12.4. Grammatically, this is a synthetic language, with elaborate inflections and free word order. Note, for example, the contrasting forms of the possessive pronoun *my* (Old English *min*). It has an accusative masculine singular ending in *minne dæl*, a feminine genitive singular ending in *minre ehte*, and a masculine genitive singular ending in *mines fæder huse*. Another nice example of a fully inflected noun phrase is *on þam rice*, the dative singular of *se rice*. Old English word order is very different from later stages of the language, and in fact rather similar to modern German, in that the finite verb is very often placed in second position in main clauses, as is shown by *Ða dælde he him his ehte* ("then dealt he him his share") or *þa sende he hine to his tune þæt he heolde his swin* (= "then sent he him to his town that he held his swine"). We also find another typically "German" word order, the clause-final position of the finite verb in subordinate clauses, for example in ... *minre ehte þe me to gebyreð* (= "of my share which to me belongs").

In the lexicon, there is considerable continuity, which however is often hidden by strange spelling conventions, extensive sound changes and some grammatical change: *dagen* → *days*, *dæl* → *deal*, *dælde* → *dealt*, *hunger* → *hunger*, *feor landen* → *far lands*, *folgede* → *followed*, *hlaf* → *loaf*, etc. Some words, however, have disappeared from the language. *Cwæð*, from *cwedan* ("say"), barely survives in the archaism *quoth*. *Warð*, from *weorðan* ("become," cf. German *werden*) has died out completely.

Problems and challenges

| 12.3

There is no reason to assume that the types of linguistic change which have characterised the history of English in the past should have come to a halt in the present. Change is still going on all around us – except that, as participants, we are less likely to perceive it clearly. But it is not just that some changes escape our notice. In those instances (they are none too rare) in which speakers are aware of ongoing diachronic developments and see them as decay and corruption of the language, the responses can be very emotional and exaggerated, and out of all proportion to the often trivial linguistic stimulus. All this makes the observation of changes in progress a challenge which any student of English should eagerly take up – all the more so as, with the present plentiful supply of corpora and other digital archives and databases, the infrastructure for the systematic study of such developments has never been better.

The story goes on ... – changes in progress in contemporary English

Change is not decay

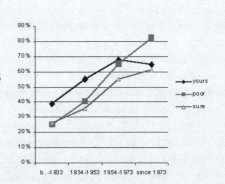

the decline of /ʊə/

- /ʊə/ gradually gets replaced by /ɔː/...
- so that *yours* sounds like *yaws*...
- *poor* like *pour* (or *paw*)...
- and *sure* like *shore*

| Fig. 12.6
The decline of the diphthong /ʊə/ in British English R. P. (source: http://www.phon.ucl.ac.uk/home/wells/)

As an illustration of ongoing sound change, consider the pronunciation of words such as *poor* or *sure* in present-day British R. P. Older speakers prefer a diphthong ([pʊə]), whereas younger speakers tend to use a long monophthong

Ongoing phonetic change

([pɔː]). John Wells, who offers a very attractive web-resource documenting ongoing changes in British pronunciation, has investigated the phenomenon systematically.

What this diagram shows is a reversal of preferences which took place in the very recent past, around the middle of the 20th century. People born before 1933 prefer the diphthongal pronunciation in all cases. Those born between 1934 and 1953 prefer it for the two lexical words *pour* and *sure*, but have shifted to [ɔː] in the grammatical closed-class item *yours*. The monophthongal pronunciation is the preferred one for all items for everybody born since 1954, with the trend gathering force for the youngest speakers. Extrapolating from these data, we can venture the prediction that the formerly dominant diphthongal pronunciations will disappear entirely as the speakers using it pass on.

Ongoing lexical change

Lexical innovation is where linguistic change in progress is most obvious to the lay observer. It is also an area in which corpora have long been used systematically, both as resources for the regular updates of dictionaries and in academic linguistic work on new words. As an illustrative example, consider the very short history of the proper name/noun *Google* and the even shorter history of the verb *to google*, derived from it by conversion.

Google is best known as the name for the popular web search engine created in 1998 by former Stanford students Larry Page and Sergey Brin. In the span of a few years, the word developed an additional verbal use through conversion or zero-derivation, the highly productive modern English word-formation process effecting change of part-of-speech class without corresponding form change on the base, and a generic use. As is shown by pairs such as *Hoover/to hoover* and *Xerox/to xerox*, this twofold extension – from proper name to common noun and from noun to verb (which need not necessarily have occurred in this order) – is not without precedent in the recent history of English.

In coining the name, the developers of the search engine may have been inspired by an existing word, which the OED lists as *googol*, an informal term for ten raised to the one-hundredth power (10^{100}). The entry has a 1990 citation which credits the term to one "Dr. Kasner's nine-year-old nephew [...] who was asked to think up a name for a very big number." Whether the millions of users who popularised the Google search engine in a very short time were aware of the established use of a very similar term in the mathematical community may, however, be doubted.

As for the verb *to google*, it has developed two distinct senses in its very short career: (1) "to search for information on the Internet/World-Wide Web (mostly but not always implying use of the Google search engine)," and (2) "to use the web to find out information about a particular person (as in *to google someone on the Web*)." As most corpora of present-day English were compiled before the term became popular, its current usage is best analysed on the basis of web-data. Below you find the first ten instances of *googled* culled from the BBC website during a recent search (21 December 2007):

PROBLEMS AND CHALLENGES   Unit 12

BBC China | 地道英语 Real English | To google 搜索 Google
Jo: To google means to use a search engine like google or yahoo to find information. Jo: Yes I do, I google all the time.

News - Health - Google 'aids doctors' diagnoses'
A team of Australian doctors **Googled** the symptoms of 26 cases for a study in the New England Journal of Medicine. Google searches found the correct diagnosis in just over half of the cases.
10 Nov 2006

News - Asia-Pacific - Google 'saved' Australian hostage
Iraqi kidnappers "**Googled**" their Australian hostage to check his identity before letting him free..
19 Oct 2004

News - UK - Google calls in the 'language police'
People now talk about "googling" and "being **googled**". I've since been told: 'That girl **googled** you because she knows who you are now.'
20 Jun 2003

Radio 1 - News - Is it right to check the details of potential staff on the internet?
Amit you google your employer when looking for a job. They google you when looing for an employee. what were you expecting?

Programmes - Click - ClickBack
Apparently, we're not allowed to say "I **googled** it", we have to say "I conducted a Google search on it". The Google itself probably looked like the image on the right.
15 Sep 2006

News - Science/Nature - Fame or misfortune beckons for weblogs?
Blogger fits with the Google way of doing things," he said. Catch-up With Google's backing, Blogger's future suddenly looks much brighter, irrespective of Google's motives.
18 Feb 2003

News - Business - Can Yahoo revive its digital dreams?
Compared to market leader Google, Yahoo is nearly an also-ran. No wonder people say that they have "**googled**" something.
19 Jun 2007

Programmes - Click Online - Search engine race gets personal
Google's Lorraine Twohill says: "We started with 10 TV networks. First came the MSN no-frills Search, and now we have Yahoo's new-look search, which has unashamedly been **Googled**."
12 Aug 2005

Slink - Sex, Love & Life - Agony Aunt Dr Mel
So I **Googled** it and someone had the same problem and they were told to put their finger up the hole and if it felt rough then you had this type of cancer. Katy, 15 A: Dear Katy Google is great.

Fig. 12.7
Uses of *googled* on the BBC website
(www.bbc.co.uk)

Note that many of the citations are about the use of the new verb itself – a sure sign that not all speakers are comfortable with this innovation yet. Some spell it with a capital <G>, some with a lower-case <g>, and some use distancing quotation marks.

Traditional corpora are more than sufficient to study ongoing grammatical change, which is usually much slower than lexical innovation. Take, for example, the interesting case of modern English *wanna*, a contraction from *want to*. In most cases, the contracted form has the same meaning as the full form. Consider, for example, the following instance from the British National Corpus:

Ongoing grammatical change

"Ma, you **wanna** hear me sing my song?"

Here, *wanna* can, of course, be replaced by *want to*: "Ma, (do) you **want to** hear me sing my song." The sentence can easily be put into the past tense: "Ma, did you want to hear me sing my song?" The meaning of *want* in this sentence is roughly equivalent to "wish": "Ma, (do) you wish to hear me sing my song?"

201

Now consider the following conversational exchange, also from the BNC:

> Hugh: I think the process we should go through is [unclear]
> Terry: You **wanna** be careful there because I'm not tak- I'm not necessarily taking [...]

As in the example above, *want to* can replace *wanna*: "You **want to** be careful ...". However, an interpretation of *want* as "wish" is not appropriate. Terry is not interested in what Hugh wishes or desires, but tells him that he **should** or **ought to** be careful. In other words, the lexical verb *want* has moved some way towards becoming a modal idiom expressing an obligation – weaker than *must* and about as strong as *should*. This is why it does not make sense to put the sentence into the past tense. Modals have no past tense. "You wanted to be careful" loses precisely the modal meaning which is at stake here and reverts to the lexical meaning of "wish, desire," which does not fit.

Similar processes – lexical items developing grammatical functions – are very common in the history of languages and generally referred to as **grammaticalisation**. Grammaticalisation processes are usually reflected in increasing discourse frequencies, which is exactly what we get when we look at corpora. These are the frequencies for the use of *wanna* by age-group in the BNC:

Table 12.4 Frequency of *wanna* in the BNC ("spoken-demographic sub-corpus") by age group (frequency represented as x per 1,000,000 words)

Age	Frequency
0–14	1178
15–24	700
25–34	496
35–44	368
45–59	330
60+	159

As in the case of the pronunciation of the vowel in the *poor*-class of words, we get a perfect age-gradient. The younger a speaker is, the more likely he or she is to use *wanna* instead of the full form *want to*. As we have seen above, it is not the case that the emerging modal use of *want* necessarily requires the use of the contracted form *wanna* in each and every case, but there clearly is a statistical correlation which shows up in the data.

In popular prejudice, especially in Britain, *wanna* is commonly regarded as an Americanism, or as an instance of sloppy articulation. A little bit of linguistic theory (grammaticalisation) and some hands-on corpus analysis has shown us that this is a very superficial way of looking at complicated and systematic developments. In your studies, you're gonna wanna look at similar instances of linguistic change, but you gonna gotta be careful in doing so.

References and further reading

An easy-to-read introduction to language change is

Aitchison, Jean. 2002. *Language change – Progress or decay?* 3rd ed. Cambridge: CUP.

The two standard histories of the English language are:

Hogg, Richard, and David Denison. 2006. *A history of the English language.* Cambridge: CUP.

Mugglestone, Lynda, ed. 2006. *The Oxford history of English.* Oxford: OUP.

For an introductory treatment of the subject which has been popular with generations of students compare:

Baugh, Albert C., and Thomas Cable. 2006. *A history of the English language.* 5th ed. London, New York: Routledge.

Recent and ongoing changes are surveyed in:

Mair, Christian. 2006. *Twentieth-century English: History, variation, standardization.* Cambridge: CUP.

Practice

|12.4

1 Consult a corpus of present-day English of your choice and list the senses of *swine* which figure prominently in your data. How does what you find in **your** corpus compare to a typical entry for the word in a major dictionary?

2 The Wycliffe translation of the parable of the prodigal son (text 12.3) contains the following sentence, which is puzzling at first sight:

> Fadir, gyue to me the porcioun of substaunce, ethir catel, that byfallith to me.
> (Father, give me the portion of substance, or cattle, that belongs to me.)

Consult the OED entry for *cattle* to make sense of this passage.

3 Consider this passage from Shakespeare's *As You Like It*:

> Touchstone: He sir, that must marry this woman. Therefore, you clown, abandon – which is in the vulgar leave – the society – which in the boorish is company – of this female – which in the common is woman. Which together is, abandon the society of this female, or clown thou perishest; or to thy better understanding, diest; or to wit, I kill thee, make thee away, translate thy life into death, thy liberty into bondage. [...] (*As You Like It*, V, 1, 47ff.)

Shakespeare has Touchstone use synonyms in a way that is clearly intended to produce a humorous effect. Explain the joke.

Consult an etymological dictionary to find out which of the synonyms used are of Germanic/Old English, French or Latin origin. How does origin relate to stylistic level?

4 The following quotations are from classic works of English literature:

(1a) Shakespeare, *Richard* III, I, ii

Anne [to Gloucester]: Either heaven with lightning strike the murderer dead
Or earth, gape open wide, and eat him **quick**.

(1b) Shakespeare, *Othello* I, i

Roderigo [to Brabantio]: Your daughter, if you have not given her leave;
I say again, hath made a gross revolt;
Tying her duty, beauty, wit, and fortunes,
In an **extravagant** and wheeling stranger
Of here and everywhere. […]

2. Defoe, *Moll Flanders*

I was really with child.
This was a perplexing thing because of the Difficulty which was before me, where I should get leave to Lye Inn; it being one of the **nicest** things in the World at that time of Day, for a Woman that was a Stranger, and had no Friends, to be entertain'd in that Circumstance without Security, which by the way I had not, neither could I procure any.

3. Shelley, *Prometheus Unbound*, I, 625 ff.

The good **want** power, but to weep barren tears.
The powerful goodness **want**: worse need for them.
The wise **want** love; and those who love **want** wisdom;
And all best things are thus confused to ill.

Look up the words printed in **bold** in the *Oxford English Dictionary* to determine the meanings presumably intended by the authors. Which semantic changes do you notice, and how would you explain them?

5 Use corpora and digital text data-bases documenting various stages in the history of English to study preferred choices between the following variable forms:

dream – dreamed – dreamed	vs.	dream – dreamt – dreamt
kneel – kneeled – kneeled	vs.	kneel – knelt – knelt

Have you (any money left)?
Do you have (any money left)?
Have you got (any money left)?

Which trends do you notice?

6 The recently coined word *co-opetition* (or *coopetiton*) is a blend between *cooperation* (or *cooperative*) and *competiton*. Check dictionaries, corpora and the World-Wide Web to find out as much as possible about the precise date and place of its origin. How solid is the evidence that you have been able to identify?

7 Below you find an early 20th-century advertisement for a much used washing soap. Look for a present-day advertisement for a detergent and comment on the changes in language structure and textual conventions that you notice.

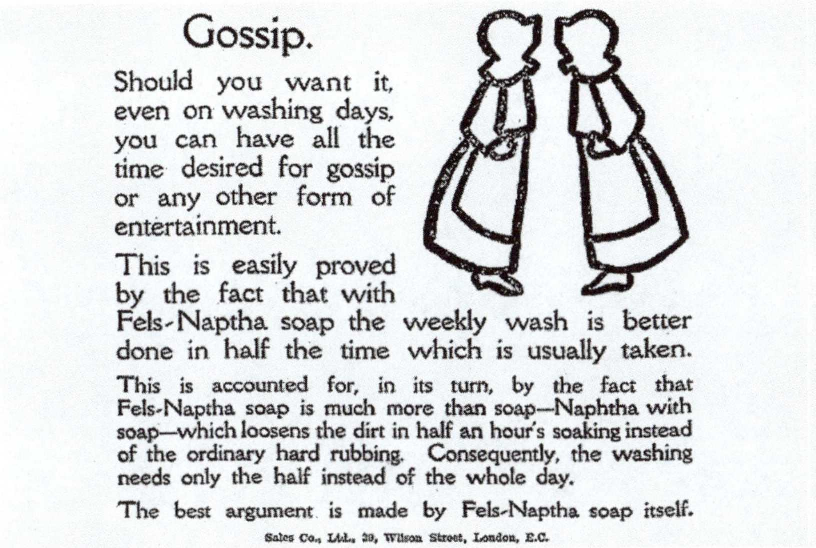

Gossip.

Should you want it, even on washing days, you can have all the time desired for gossip or any other form of entertainment.

This is easily proved by the fact that with Fels-Naptha soap the weekly wash is better done in half the time which is usually taken.

This is accounted for, in its turn, by the fact that Fels-Naptha soap is much more than soap—Naphtha with soap—which loosens the dirt in half an hour's soaking instead of the ordinary hard rubbing. Consequently, the washing needs only the half instead of the whole day.

The best argument is made by Fels-Naptha soap itself.

Sales Co., Ltd., 39, Wilson Street, London, E.C.

Fig. 12.8
Advertisement for Fels-Naptha Soap, *The Times*, 31 Dec. 1915, 15

8 As was pointed out in the Introduction to this Unit, historical and genetic relationship between languages is proved by systematic phonetic correspondences. State the regularity apparent in the following pairs of words:

ten – zehn
token – Zeichen
town – Zaun
water – Wasser
bite – beißen
write – reißen

Can you account for the following apparent exceptions to this rule?

stone – Stein
strike – Streich

Finally, do you note any parallels between these and the following, which seem to be relevant to a discussion of the /p – pf, f/ correspondence discussed above?

spin – spinnen
spring – springen

Past masters, current trends – theorising linguistics for students of English

Orientation

Every systematic description of a language requires a theory which specifies the terminology, categories and procedures to be employed. In our exposition so far we have occasionally encountered points of disagreement between various theoretical approaches. In grammatical description, for example, some analyses assume that the verb is the structural nucleus of the clause (and that the subject and the object are therefore both dependents of the verb), whereas others argue that the clause falls into two immediate constituents – a noun phrase "subject" and a verb phrase "predicate." In semantics, there are also (at least) two major rival approaches: a "structuralist" one which aims to describe meaning exclusively within the framework of the linguistic system itself, by decomposing complex meanings into constituent features, and a "cognitive" one which aims to identify prototype categories which are holistic and plausible in terms of human psychology.

On the whole, however, theoretical disagreements of this type have been backgrounded in the discussion, and our aim has been to present the facts of English in a way that is compatible with most current theories in linguistics. In other words, we have not done linguistics without theoretical foundation, but we have proceeded in a way that is as "theory-neutral" as possible. The present Unit will change this perspective. This is important, as you need to become aware that particular theories encourage particular research questions and discourage others, that particular theoretical models were fashionable at some stages in the development of linguistics and then went out of fashion and that, finally, one and the same set of data may receive different interpretations depending on the theoretical framework it is analysed in. To give an example: to the sociolinguist studying present-day English, multiple negations of the type *I don't know nothing about it* are an example of a stigmatised non-standard grammatical structure. For a typologist, on the other hand, the interesting fact about such multiple negations is not that they happen to be stigmatised in present-day English but that they are so common in other languages – as can be demonstrated by Spanish examples such as *no sé nada* or Russian examples such as *ya nichevo ne znayu* (both literally translating as "I don't know nothing").

Ultimately, a good feel for such connections between theoretical assumptions and analytical practice is necessary to save students from one naïve assumption, namely that there is one correct and comprehensive linguistic

| 13.1

No linguistic description without theoretical foundation

theory that holds the answers to all the many interesting questions which are raised by the complexities of language structure and language use.

13.2 | Demonstration/discussion

The history of linguistics since c. 1900

The best way of introducing you to the main currents of linguistic thought is probably to follow the history of the field since the early 20th century – that is the time when alternative approaches to the then dominant historical-comparative "Indo-Europeanist" paradigm began to emerge.

Ferdinand de Saussure and linguistic structuralism

As was already mentioned in Unit 1, the founding father of modern, synchronically orientated linguistics is generally considered to be the Swiss scholar Ferdinand de Saussure (1857–1913).

His central place in the history of the field is secure and well deserved, although there is the danger that singling him out might overshadow the achievement of other 19th-century scholars who never fully aligned themselves with the historical-comparative orientation and also cast a long shadow into the twentieth century. One such figure is Wilhelm von Humboldt (1767–1835), who will be briefly mentioned below.

Fig. 13.1 | Ferdinand de Saussure (1857–1913)

To his contemporaries, de Saussure's present fame would have come as a surprise. They valued him primarily for his research in historical linguistics which he carried out while teaching at the universities of Paris (1881–1891) and Geneva (1891–1913). In fact, his revolutionary introduction to general linguistics, *Cours de linguistique générale,* was not even published in his lifetime but posthumously, in 1916, by Charles Bally and Albert Sechehaye, two former students of his, who reconstructed their professor's ideas from lecture notes.

Synchrony vs. diachrony

What de Saussure apparently aimed for in his lectures delivered from 1906 to his death was to define the essential core of a language – that which remains after everything has been stripped away which is accidental and not central to such a definition. These accidental properties include first of all the history of the language, because speakers are obviously capable of using the language competently even if they are not aware of its history. As will be remembered from the discussion in Unit 1, this is the idea which motivated de Saussure to re-orientate the study of language from a diachronic to a synchronic perspective. The language we study is no longer seen as the product of a long and often convoluted process of historical evolution but as a system of communication which needs to function "synchronically" at a given point in time.

Langue vs. parole

But even after this re-orientation, our view of the essence of a language is still obscured by many distorting factors. In terms of the structure of English, a simple hypothetical spoken utterance – such as *I would like to briefly mention another topic* – remains the same whether it is spoken quickly or slowly, with a raspy voice or a clear voice, with a number of hesitation phenomena

(*I would ehm like to ehm mention another topic*) or without such interruptions, with or without a stutter on the final word (*t-t-topic*), and so on. In the written language, the corresponding sentence is "the same" at this level regardless of changes in type size (*I would like to briefly mention another topic*) or font (`I would like to briefly mention another topic`). That people talk with an accent, that they occasionally confuse or merge grammatical constructions because of tiredness, lack of concentration or problems with their short-term memory, that they display hesitation phenomena ("hemming and hawing") because they are embarrassed, that they get their spelling wrong, etc.: all this is interesting stuff to research for educators, psychologists, sociologists but will not reveal the true nature of language to the linguist. To capture this insight, de Saussure coined another dichotomy, using the French terms *langue* and *parole*. *Parole*, which might be rendered as "speech" in English or "Rede" in German, refers to the external, material "raw" manifestation of the linguistic data in their actual communicative context, whereas *langue* ("language system," "Sprachsystem") denotes the basic underlying system of structured oppositions which makes it possible to produce and understand such contextualised instances of *parole*. The cover term "structuralism" captures the fact that the language system is a complicated web of inter-connected but abstract structural oppositions between linguistic signs.

This is a complicated idea whose point usually is not immediately apparent to beginners. But consider the game of chess. We know that chess-pieces are of certain standard shapes and may be made of wood, ivory, plastic or a number of other materials. This is not the proper way to define the game, though. For if we know about the basic structure of the game and are short of one piece, we could easily take a button to replace a missing knight. The structural opposition would still function. Let us move on to a related example from a proper linguistic domain – the lexical-semantic field *smile, sneer, grin, smirk* in contemporary English. We can take each verb in isolation and think for a long time how we could define *smirk*, for example as "to smile in an unpleasant way to show that you are pleased by someone else's bad luck or think you are better than other people," as is done in the *Longman Dictionary of Contemporary English*. We could then judge how this compares to *sneer*, defined as "to smile [...] in a very unkind way that shows you have no respect for someone or something" in the same dictionary. However, the structuralist approach to a solution of this problem would be different: we would look at the entire field as a system of structured options and define each by what it is not. The specific meaning of *smirk* is thus precisely that which cannot be expressed by any of the other three, and so on.

The linguistic sign in its turn was defined by de Saussure as a conventional pairing of sound (or, using his French expression, the signifier or *signifiant*) and meaning (that which is signified, the *signifié*).

Structural oppositions in the linguistic system

The linguistic sign, and the place of linguistics within semiotics

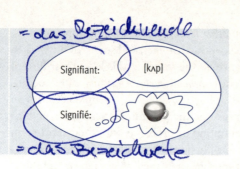

Fig. 13.2 | Ferdinand de Saussure's conception of the linguistic sign

As was already pointed out in Unit 1, the relationship between the sound and the meaning is an arbitrary one, which makes language such a powerful tool for the symbolic manipulation of concepts or meanings. Conventional form-meaning pairs are, of course, not restricted to language but permeate human social behaviour at all levels. There are road-signs. There are institutionalised and culturally specific systems of gestural signs. At a pinch, a signalling function could be attributed even to dress codes and fashion statements of similar kind. This is why, for de Saussure, linguistics, after it has ceased to be a historical science, finds a new home as one branch of a general science of communication through signs, which he calls *semiotics* (from the Greek for "sign").

Paradigmatic and syntagmatic relationships

It is easy to see how this radical abstraction away from everything that is historical, contextual, social, psychological or otherwise external about language, and the concomitant concentration on the essentials of the linguistic sign and the structural system it is a part of, lead to clarity and simplicity. In Unit 2, for example, we saw how de Saussure's idea, applied to the confusing complexity of speech sounds, helps us to identify precisely those very few (usually between 20 and 60) phonemic oppositions which matter to the distinction of meaning in a given language. In the field of grammar, de Saussure reduced the myriad rules and regularities to a basic distinction between two kinds of relationship: **paradigmatic relations** (A substitutes for B) and **syntagmatic relations** (A determines, agrees with or correlates with B). Thus, in the frame:

> They looked at [the picture]

the picture is in a paradigmatic relationship with the following phrases:

> They looked at {
> the picture(s)
> the book(s)
> the table(s)
> me/you/him/her/etc.
> mine/yours/etc.
> what emerged from behind the wall
> how the workers carried the piano through the narrow doorway
> }

The following paradigmatic relationships, by contrast, are ruled out and marked as ungrammatical:

$$\text{* They looked at} \begin{cases} \text{I, he } etc. \\ \text{my, your } etc. \\ \text{that the janitor locked up the building} \end{cases}$$

To illustrate how syntagmatic relations operate, contrast the following two sentences, one acceptable and the other ungrammatical:

They are looking at themselves.
* They is looking at oneself.

Even in the highly analytical grammar of present-day English, *they* must agree with the verb *to be* in number, as must the reflexive pronoun *themselves*. Therefore, the second version of the sentence does not work.

De Saussure's 1916 *Cours de linguistique générale* inspired several structuralist schools in linguistics which dominated the field for the first six decades of the 20th century. Beyond his own immediate circle of students, Saussure's ideas had a profound impact on the work of the Prague Linguistic Circle, founded in 1926. One member of this group, count Nikolay Trubetzkoy (1890–1938) perfected structuralist phonology and gave it the shape in which it is still taught to undergraduates today (cf. Unit 2). Another centre of linguistic structuralism emerged in the United States, around Leonard Bloomfield (1887–1949) of the University of Chicago, the author of an extremely influential textbook (*Language*, 1933). In addition to developing linguistic theory, many American structuralists showed that their method was effective in recording and describing the many native American languages which were fast disappearing at the time.

_{Structuralism after Saussure}

De Saussure's basic insight, finally, proved an inspiration for scholars working outside the field of linguistics who were attracted to linguistic structuralism because it seemed to offer a good way of reducing the irritating complexity, unpredictability and sheer chaos of human behaviour to a simple and clear constellation of basic contrasts and oppositions. For example, vexed with the many ways in which human societies defined "family", regulated who was to be considered a "relative," or what types of "brothers-in-law" were to be distinguished, French anthropologist Claude Lévi-Strauss (b. 1908) devised a "grammar of kinship," a system of basic oppositions which both delimited the range of allowed (or "grammatical") family structures and described the forbidden or impossible ones. Noting the many recurrent patterns, he later even extended the method to the study of the world's myths and legends. Saussurean notions of the *arbitraire du signe* (i. e. the fact that relationship between *signifiant* and *signifié*, sound and meaning, is both arbitrary and a convention) have been taken up in literary theory – sometimes in ways which surprise Saussure's disciples in linguistics. Almost 100 years after his death, Ferdinand de Saussure has thus remained a living influence both in linguistics and outside the field. Some of his insights, such as the separation of synchronic and diachronic

Structuralism outside linguistics

language study, his model of the linguistic sign, the distinction between *langue* and *parole* or the very concept of a language as a system of abstract oppositions have become commonplace notions.

Even those present-day linguists (and there is a growing number of them) who argue that synchronic and diachronic linguistics should be more closely integrated or that *parole* deserves systematic attention in sociolinguistics, pragmatics or psycholinguistics honour him by challenging him in his own terms.

Noam Chomsky and generative linguistics

Fig. 13.3
Noam Chomsky
(b. 1928)

Competence vs. performance

From the 1950s onwards, first in the United States and soon internationally, the various structuralist traditions in linguistic research began to be superseded by the *generative school*. This new research tradition in linguistics was inaugurated by the American linguist Noam Chomsky (b. 1928), who in addition to his many scholarly works has published numerous polemics against American foreign policy since the Vietnam War.

There were some tenets of structuralism which Chomsky never repudiated. Like the structuralists, he believed that a concentration on the details of surface data, or *parole*, obscured rather than revealed the true nature of the linguistic system. For *parole*, he used the term *performance*, which, however, he did not oppose to *langue* (a decontextualised abstraction of the linguistic system of a community) but to *competence*, which he viewed as a cognitive module of the individual speaker's mind, ultimately based in the neuronal networks of the speaker's brain.

The term *generative*, which originated in mathematics, was used to refer to what Chomsky regarded as the foremost design feature of human language, namely its capacity for unlimited creativity through the application of a limited number of productive (or "generative") rules on an equally limited number of linguistic forms. In plain terms this means that no single speaker, nor even a whole community, will ever be able to exhaust the full richness of their language; everybody is able to produce utterances which have never before been used by anyone, and every listener is able to understand such sentences.

Over the half century of its existence generative linguistics has developed its own highly formalised and abstract terminology and descriptive conventions, which in addition is subject to rapid changes. Whether such complexity is appropriate to the subject of investigation is a controversial issue, and it would certainly be a hopeless task to try to introduce the elements of this formalism in the framework of a single chapter of an undergraduate introduction. What we can do, however, is to point out a few fundamental insights and challenges which can be traced as leitmotifs in Chomsky's thinking on language which every linguist – regardless of his or her theoretical persuasion – needs to confront.

Language acquisition from imperfect input

One thing Chomsky has never tired of emphasising is the almost miraculous speed and efficiency with which children acquire their native language. This cannot just be "learning", in the sense that we learn how to ride a bicycle or how to do sums – in a process of being shown, imitating and hard practice which very slowly and gradually builds up competence. There are things in the core grammar of any language which it is difficult to see as "learnable" skills in this sense. The following sentences, for example, differ in that an adverbial of place, an object and the subject are "extracted" from the subordinate clause through questioning. Practically all native speakers of English agree that only the first two options are grammatical, and the third one is not:

1) Where did he say that we should meet?
2) Who did he say that we should meet?
3) * Who did he say that wants to meet us?

An additional complication is presented by the fact that as soon as we drop the conjunction *that*, all three sentences are fine:

4) Where did he say we should meet?
5) Who did he say we should meet?
6) Who did he say wants to meet us?

It is difficult to imagine children learning this subtle pattern through imitation of linguistic input data they get from their environment or some kind of drill-like practice routine.

The radical solution to the puzzle advocated by Chomsky is to assume that far more in language is innate than we would have thought. What is innate is thus not only our general ability to speak (which few people would have doubted), but also a large portion of the specific design features of the grammar themselves. Humans are born with a "Universal Grammar," a kind of genetically wired instinct to recognise and work with grammatical structures, and language "learning" is thus not accumulating experiental knowledge in the mind but activating and specifying this latent or sleeping "Universal Grammar" in such a way that the resulting output corresponds to the particular language which has to be mastered.

It will be noted that in Generative Linguistics the focus is very much on the formal properties of language rather than on message, content or language in use. In addition, generative linguists have developed a very complex formalism for stating and representing their rules which is partly inspired by the notational conventions of mathematics and philosophical logic. This is why generative linguistics and some related models are very often subsumed under the heading of **formalist linguistics**.

If the phonology, the grammar and to some extent even the semantic structure of a language are seen as resulting from a human language instinct, a part of the individual's genetic endowment, of his or her "nature," then the influence of society and the environment on the development of language are of course minimal and largely restricted to the level of performance. The linguistic system, at the level of competence, is autonomous and well-defined, and

"Universal Grammar" (UG) as an innate human capacity

Formalist linguistics – the autonomy of the linguistic system many apparently common-sensical explanations for why linguistic structures are shaped the way they are become suspect.

In particular, Chomsky has ridiculed attempts to explain grammatical structure by resorting to meaning or communicative discourse needs. He has been similarly dismissive of claims that frequency of use has an influence on the shape of the grammatical system, arguing for example that a sentence such as "I was born in New York City" will naturally be more common than "I was born in Akron, Ohio," but that this is a trivial fact of performance with no relevance whatsoever for linguistic theory.

The "functionalist" reaction to formalism

Over all, Chomsky's influence on the development of modern linguistics has been on a par with de Saussure's. However, this does not mean that the generative approach has dominated the field to the exclusion of others. From the late 1970s, some linguists began to challenge the formalist-generative orthodoxy on its own turf, so to speak, by arguing that the grammatical system is not necessarily well-defined and autonomous, but fuzzy and at least partly determined by language users' semantic and discourse needs in the communicative context. Unlike Chomsky, they maintained that a description of the formal properties of language should not be attempted without paying close attention to the functions of language in expressing meaning (semantics) and in communication (pragmatics). Form, their argument went, reflected function and was to a considerable extent determined by function. All the various theoretical schools and models elaborating this shared idea are today subsumed under the heading **functionalist linguistics**.

Note that advocates of fuzzy, context-sensitive, performance-based – in short: "functionalist" – models of grammar do not argue that linguistic structure is chaotic or that anything goes. Their claim is rather that in the context of human communication what is needed is a robust and reliable system which is not as precise as a well-defined mathematical algorithm but orderly up to a point. In this way, speakers get what they need for the practical needs of human communication, not a rigid computer programming language but a working tool which leaves speakers the margin of freedom and flexibility that they require to respond to new challenges and new situations.

Prominent functionalists

There is not a single individual which serves as a rallying point for functionalist linguistics in the way that Chomsky is at the centre of the generative movement or de Saussure was the inspirer of structuralism. Individual scholars in functionalist linguistics whose names deserve mention, however, include Joseph H. Greenberg (1915–2001), pioneer of functional typology, George Lakoff (b. 1941) and Ronald W. Langacker (b. 1942), who both developed functional-cognitive approaches to syntax and semantics, and Talmy Givón (b. 1936), who has done research on many languages to show how discourse patterns at the level of *performance*, or contextually motivated form-meaning pairings, ultimately solidify into grammatical rules over time. All three could be characterised as dissident generativists, i.e. scholars who had worked in the generative paradigm for a period, had shared generativists' interest in phonology and syntax and then developed dissatisfaction with the framework.

In addition, there are functionalist traditions whose roots are older than generative linguistics. One noteworthy example is the British contextualist school, which was started by John Rupert Firth (1890–1960) and whose major living representative is Michael A. K. Halliday (b. 1925). The hallmark of this school, which draws inspiration from anthropology, is that it avoids the type of instant abstraction reflected in the Saussurean and Chomskyan dichotomies between *parole* and *langue*, or *performance* and *competence*, and pleads for a study of language in its social and communicative contexts. In English linguistics, British contextualism has been influential in research on collocation (Firth). Halliday in turn has emphasised that we should not assume strict and arbitrary boundaries between the grammar and the lexicon but assume a unified lexico-grammatical continuum. Indeed, the insight that grammatical rules, such as the passive, are subject to lexical constraints and specification, and that words have more grammatical baggage than is typically apparent from the dictionary, is a useful one for the description of English (and, of course, other languages). In monolingual learners' dictionaries it has been put to practical use as these dictionaries are designed to show foreign learners (rather than native speakers who know this anyway) what the grammatical frames and lexical contexts are in which a particular word is used. Apart from these functionalist frameworks which confront generative linguistics on its home turf, there have been important new departures in linguistic theory which have focussed on precisely those performance-based aspects of language which tend to be neglected both by structuralism and generativism.

British contextualism: M. A. K. Halliday

All functionalists share an interest in the role of language in communication and human society. However, this interest is usually expressed in very general terms, and illustration is through individual case-studies and often unsystematic. One scholar who has brought rigorous statistical and quantitative methods to the study of social variation in language is William Labov (b. 1927), the pioneer of sociolinguistics and urban dialectology. Put briefly, Labov's aim was to document statistically significant correlations between independent social variables (e. g. regional background, class, ethnicity or sex) and dependent linguistic variables (e. g. accent, grammatical constructions), and in this he has found many followers. Studies in this tradition usually impress through their extensive field work, but there is a danger that the individual informant and his or her communicative intentions disappear behind the averages and statistics. More recently, there has therefore been a surge in qualitative interaction-based approaches in sociolinguistics, which of course establishes a new link between sociolinguistics and other branches of linguistics concerned with the study of language in use, such as conversation analysis and pragmatics.

William Labov and the rise of quantitative sociolinguistics

Qualitative interaction-based sociolinguistics, conversation analysis, pragmatics

Pioneers outside the linguistic mainstream – from Wilhelm von Humboldt to Benjamin Lee Whorf

Fig. 13.4 | Wilhelm von Humboldt (1767–1835)

Linguistics at the dawn of the 21st century – the state of the art

Corpus linguistics – the computer-assisted analysis of large amounts of language data

After sketching the history of linguistics in its major outlines, let us conclude by returning to Wilhelm von Humboldt, already mentioned above, and a few other figures who have contributed to the development of the discipline without ever becoming mainstream or starting movements. Wilhelm von Humboldt was a pioneer in research on non-Indo European "exotic" languages such as Basque or the Kawi language of Java and originator of highly original views on the mutual determination of languages and speakers' views of the world which have stimulated controversial debates inside and outside linguistics to the present day. In the latter half of the 19th century linguistics took a different turn from what von Humboldt would have wished, but his ideas were never forgotten completely. Among the people influenced by his views on the mutual determination between language, thought and culture were Edward Sapir (1884–1939) and Benjamin Lee Whorf (1897–1941), two linguists working on the indigenous languages of North America. Humboldt's original idea, that the structure of the language we speak determines what we can think and therefore express in our culture, is usually referred to as the Sapir-Whorf hypothesis in contemporary linguistics.

What is the state of the art then after almost a hundred years of work in linguistics with a synchronic orientation? On the positive side, we note that linguistics has been a booming field and that we now know more about more of the world's c. 5.000 languages than ever before in history. A somewhat problematical consequence of this quantitative growth has been a proliferation of terminologies and theories which has caused unnecessary confusion at times.

One factor which has contributed to progress in linguistics throughout the past century has been a purely external one – technological progress in the ways in which we record, store and transmit linguistic data. Recording live speech on site remained difficult well into the 1950s, and research on spoken language was much hampered by this fact. It is obviously far easier today. Neither sociolinguistic surveys of pronunciation nor conversation analysis would have become possible without these rapid advances in recording technology. *Corpus-linguistics*, that is the empirical description of languages on the basis of digitally stored spoken and written language, experienced its laborious and timid beginnings only in the 1960s and remained a minority pursuit in linguistics for at least two decades after that. Now corpora and the associated retrieval software are almost omnipresent, and the mere fact that such unprecedentedly huge masses of data are available has been a powerful driving force in the renewed interest in concrete language use and the development of usage-, *parole-* or *performance-*based theoretical models (see Unit 1).

My advice to students of English, who need to find a place for linguistics in their studies and may even think of specialising in the field, is to see the opportunities it affords them and not be intimidated by initial difficulties and confusion. English has a rich and well-documented history and is today's dynamically developing global language. As such, in some past or present variety, it can be used to study any language-related issue that you might be interested in. Interesting data are available to you – all around you out there in the field, in the shape of corpora and digital data bases, or at least in libraries and archives. It is these data which are the most direct link between linguistics and other, more general concerns of an English Studies course (cultural studies, literature, history, sociology, politics). The many sometimes difficult and inaccessible theories around in the field, on the other hand, lose much of their terror if you remind yourself of their proper role. Formalism and functionalism, or any other such fundamental dichotomy, do not primarily imply an abstract choice between right and wrong. Like all theories, they are tools which enable you to formulate interesting working hypotheses. You, and no one else, investigate these hypotheses on the basis of your own new and interesting data. And this is the exciting and worthwhile goal of linguistic research which you have started working towards in this introduction.

> **What the writers say:**
>
> "It is better to know less than to know too much that ain't so." ("Josh Billings" = Henry Wheeler Shaw, 1818–1885)

Problems and challenges | 13.3

As has been pointed out at the end of the "Orientation" section of this Unit, it is usually naïve to try and identify the single correct theory from a range of available ones. Rather than ask (and then fail to answer) the question of whether, for example, a formalist or a functionalist approach to the study of grammar is correct, we should start from the postulates of each approach and then see which working hypotheses they allow us to formulate. For example, most formalist approaches assume that the grammar and the lexicon of a language are best treated separately, whereas most functionalist frameworks advise an integrated treatment. *Prima facie*, neither of these assumptions is nonsensical and, depending on what we want to study, one or the other may provide the more practicable starting hypothesis.

A cognitive scientist implementing software for machine translation has a number of strong theory-independent motivations for treating the dictionary/lexicon and the grammar separately. The task facing him eventually will be to decide how far this initial working hypothesis has taken him. A foreign language teacher, on the other hand, knows from experience that purely lexical or purely grammatical errors are rare and that the lexico-grammatical contact zone (collocations, etc.) is the one which keeps causing most difficulties even to very advanced levels of teaching and learning. This may cause him to question the usefulness of traditional teaching and learning aids such as the grammar drill and the vocabulary book.

Just as a particular theory suggests particular research questions and makes it difficult to formulate alternatives, so particular sources of data are more

Different domains of investigation require different theoretical models

Methods for obtaining linguistic data

compatible with some theoretical frameworks than others. Today linguists derive their data chiefly from the following three sources: (1) the native-speaker's linguistic intuition (accessed through introspection or vicariously, through consultation of an informant), (2) experimental data obtained from informants through more or less systematic elicitation procedures, and (3) observational data collected (more or less systematically).

Data-gathering methods and their theoretical implications

To illustrate which data and research questions the various strategies of data collection lead us to, consider the following instance of divided usage in present-day English:

1a) Democracy means government by discussion, but it is only effective if you can stop people talking.

1b) Democracy means government by discussion, but it is only effective if you can stop people from talking.

Fig. 13.5
Clement Attlee
(1883–1967)

The original (1a) is an aphorism formulated by British Labour politician and Prime Minister Clement Attlee (1883–1967). (1b) is a possible variant.

Now consider what we would find out by appeal to introspection. Of the four theoretically possible constellations – a native speaker finding both ungrammatical, a native speaker finding both grammatical, a native speaker finding (1a) grammatical but (1b) ungrammatical, and, finally, a native speaker finding (1a) ungrammatical and (1b) grammatical – the first and the third can be discounted here as they are unrealistic. So chances are that we will get speakers accepting both options as possible (as would be the likely case with speakers of British or British-influenced varieties of English) or speakers who reject (1a) but accept (1b) (the expected response for speakers of North American English). In this type of research design we can easily refine the investigation by asking those informants who accept both versions whether the two forms are synonymous for them or whether they convey subtly different meanings. Further, we could think about reasons why in a grammar of American English sentences of the (1a) type are absent. An interesting question from a British English point of view would be which other verbs of prevention admit either one or both of the constructions, as there is a number of them:

ban, bar, block, delay, discourage, disqualify, dissuade, distract, divert, enjoin, exclude, exempt, forbid, hinder, hold back, inhibit, keep, preclude, prevent, prohibit, protect, restrain, restrict *(somebody from doing something)*.

As can be seen, we can describe one native speaker's internalised grammar in this way, or an abstract grammatical system; what we cannot do in this way, however, is to study linguistic variation and its social correlates. Whether (1a) or (1b) is the more common variant for a speaker who accepts both, or whether one form is more informal than the other, are questions beyond the scope of our method as informant self-reports on matters of statistics and contextually conditioned variation are notoriously unreliable.

218

The statistical dimension is, however, introduced the moment we turn to experimental work with a larger number of informants. Depending on how we construct the experimental task, we can test informants' judgment or their own performance, which are not necessarily the same. It seems that people often cultivate a sanitised image of how they speak, possibly for psychological reasons. This weakness is satirised in numerous jokes of the type: "I never say *ain't* myself because I know it ain't right." A recent study by Günter Rohdenburg (2006) on "Discrepancies between the rule formulations advanced by famous linguists and their own written usage" shows that linguists themselves are not immune to this weakness.

In closely controlled experimental conditions we can pursue hypotheses which are beyond the capacity of the introspective method to investigate. For example, we could systematically vary the length of the object noun phrase following *stop* to see whether the length of the object correlates with the likelihood of *from*. Given a sufficiently large and heterogeneous pool of informants, we could also study linguistic variation between British and American speakers, older and younger speakers, educated and vernacular speakers, or men and women. The one distorting factor which we will not get rid of is that such elicitation experiments yield data which are not entirely natural, because they are produced under artificial conditions.

Natural and authentic observational data are of course highly desirable but also most difficult to produce. If we require authentic instances of written usage, interesting data is usually available for present-day English. Surreptitious recording of other people's conversations, however, is considered unethical (though it has taken place in linguistics in the past). Traditionally, authentic examples were often collected unsystematically, for example by noting down examples of the phenomenon investigated from one's casual reading. Needless to say, this is very risky, because it introduces a bias. To stick with our example, an American observer is very likely to note the distinctly British usage represented in (1a), whereas the British observer is unlikely to note what is not used in American English. Given the recent phenomenal advances in the development and availability of digitised language corpora, unsystematic observation is, of course, no longer state-of-the-art. A corpus-based analysis of *stop* + NP (*from*) + V-ing will be very strong on variation. It will be very useful in checking hypotheses formulated on the basis of introspective or experimental data, and it will unearth patterns which are not previously suspected but open up promising avenues for further research. If, that is, the phenomenon is represented well enough in the corpus. The limits of corpus-based analysis are reached with low frequencies. If we have one or two instances, we cannot be sure whether they are occasional slips or performance-errors or authentic instances of a low-frequency option provided in the grammar. If we have none at all, this may be due to the fact that our corpus is too small, or it may be due to a construction's genuine ungrammaticality.

References and further reading

Amsterdamska, Olga. 1987. *Schools of thought: The development of linguistics from Bopp to Saussure*. Dordrecht: Reidel.
Harris, Roy, ed. 1988. *Linguistic thought in England 1914–1945*. London: Duckworth.
Harris, Roy, and Talbot J. Taylor. 1989. *Landmarks in linguistic thought.* Vol. 1: *The Western tradition from Socrates to Saussure*. London: Routledge.
Hoffmann, Ludger, ed. 1996. *Sprachwissenschaft. Ein Reader*. Berlin/New York: de Gruyter.
Hymes, Dell, and John Fought. 1981. *American structuralism*. The Hague: Mouton.
Joseph, John Earl, Nigel Love, and Talbot J. Taylor, eds. 2001. *Landmarks in linguistic thought*. Vol. 2: *The Western tradition in the twentieth century*. London: Routledge.
Matthews, Peter. 1994. *Grammatical theory in the United States from Bloomfield to Chomsky*. Cambridge: CUP.
Newmeyer, Frederick J. 1986. *Linguistic theory in America*. New York: Academic Press.
Newmeyer, Frederick J. 1998. *Language form and language function*. Cambridge MA: MIT Press.
Rohdenburg, Günter. 2006. "Discrepancies between the rule formulations advanced by famous linguists and their own written usage." In: Markus Kötter, Oliver Traxel and Stephan Gabel (eds.). *Investigating and facilitating language learning*. Trier: Wissenschaftlicher Verlag. 47–63.
Sampson, Geoffrey. 1980. *Schools of linguistics: Competition and evolution*. London: Hutchinson.

13.4 | Practice

1 To develop a feeling for language-specific structural constraints, try to work out a definition for the category "adjective" in English and German. Practically all available grammars agree that there are adjectives in English and German and that one of their major uses is to modify nouns in attributive position, typically in frames of the following kind.

```
a very_____[noun]
ein(e) sehr_____[Substantiv]
```

There is a core of adjectives which fit the frame both in English and German, for example items denoting qualities such as size, weight or colour. Beyond that, each language sets the limits differently on what it allows into this adjectival frame. For example, *a very South London voice* is possible in English, whereas *eine sehr Südlondon(er) Aussprache* is not. Find more contrasts of this kind.

2 One of the most productive word-formation processes in present-day English, namely part-of-speech class change without external marking (e.g. *bottle – to bottle*), was introduced as "conversion" in Unit 3 of the present book. Other sources treat similar phenomena under the heading of "zero-derivation," "syntactic homonymy," or similar

terms. Consult a few handbooks and give a comparative critique of the terminology they use and the phenomena they include in their treatment. Does the choice of terminology have an impact on the phenomena studied?

3 As the famous linguist Edward Sapir once remarked, "all grammars leak." For the linguist the problem is to decide whether an apparent exception to a rule can be interpreted as:

   1) a marginal instance in a fuzzy category
   2) rule-breaking which is licensed by the special circumstances of an individual utterance
   3) proper counter-evidence, which should lead to a modification or dismissal of a bad rule

Taking the widely accepted rule that "English has strict SVO order" as a starting point, comment on the status of the following apparent exceptions.

> * I speak well English.
> I speak well all those languages that I learned the natural way, and badly all those that I was exposed to only in school.
> This type of remark I really hate.
> [cf. * This type of remark really hate I.]
> On the wall hung a faded photograph of the previous owner of the place.

4 Which of the following claims by British contextualist M. A. K. Halliday are not compatible with the structuralist research agenda outlined by de Saussure, and why?

> We study language partly in order to understand language and how it works, and partly to understand what people do with it. The two questions are closely connected: the way language is organised has been determined, over the million and more years of its evolution, by the functions it is called on to serve. Like any other tool, it is shaped by its purposes. (M. A. K. Halliday and Ruqaiya Hasan, *Language, context and text: A social semiotic perspective*. Deakin University Press, 1985, repr. Oxford: OUP, 1989, p. 44.)

> Language, unlike mathematics, is not clearcut or precise. It is a natural human creation, and, like many other natural human creations, it is inherently messy. (M. A. K. Halliday, *Language as social semiotics: The social interpretation of language and meaning*. London: Arnold, 1978, p. 203)

For a start, you may find it helpful to consider how the Saussurean distinctions between *langue* and *parole*, or between the synchronic and the diachronic approach to the study of language, can be squared with the claims made in the first quotation.

Unit 14

Linguistics and the public – language myths, language politics, language planning and language rights

Orientation

There are many deep-seated beliefs about language, and about individual languages, including English. Who hasn't heard the opinion expressed that women talk more – or faster – than men, that American English is spreading everywhere, that English is easy to learn as a foreign language because it has no grammar, and so on and so forth? As for the first assumption, it is usually voiced without the support of systematically collected empirical evidence, though, of course, it is a hypothesis about language use which could be tested for individual languages in specific communicative situations in principle, for example on the basis of large corpora. As for the two English-specific claims, it should by now be obvious to readers of this book that they cannot be upheld in this blanket fashion. While American-English words and expressions are spreading everywhere, there is very little evidence that speakers of English in Britain, Australia or India are much influenced by American-English pronunciation. The appropriate punishment for anybody claiming that English has no grammar is to force them to work through Units 4 and 5 of the present book. One reward of "doing" linguistics as part of your university course in English studies is to put you in a position to view these and many other language myths with the scepticism they deserve.

On a more serious note, language is a central concern for many professions – educators, doctors, therapists, advertisers and lawyers, to mention just a few. In the school system, a lot of time is spent on teaching the reading, writing and general communicative skills required for success in the labour market. Doctors have to interpret patients' descriptions of their pain and ailments in the search for a proper diagnosis. Lawyers wrangle over details of verbal formulations in contracts. Experts, journalists, politicians and the general public together work out appropriate ways of referring to socially controversial issues of race, ethnicity or gender.

In addition, language plays an important role in many more specific political controversies and public debates. From the late 19th century, for example, the need to protect and, if possible, to revive the Irish language (also known as "Gaelic") has been a leitmotif of Irish nationalism. As a symbolic gesture, most important political institutions of the Irish Republic have been given Irish names: *Houses of the Oireachtas*, for the Parliament, *Dáil* for the lower house, *Seanad* for the upper house, *Taosieach* for the Prime Minister, and so on.

| 14.1

Language myths

Linguistic issues of interest to the general public

Symbolic use of Irish

Fig. 14.1 Official web-site of the Irish Parliament (source: http://www.oireachtas.ie)

As for Northern Ireland, Republican activists in their vast majority have always been English-speaking. Yet they too have invested the Irish language with great symbolic value. Their major political party goes by the name of *Sinn Féin* ("(we) ourselves"), Sinn Fein's weekly newspaper, mainly published in English, is called *An Phoblacht* ("the Republic"), and "Vótáil Sinn Fein" was the slogan used during a 2007 electoral campaign.

Fig. 14.2 *An Phoblacht* – masthead (source: http://www.republican-news.org)

"English Only" agitation in the US

In the United States, there is at present much concern about the perceived spread of the use of Spanish in public spaces, which by its opponents is seen as a threat to national unity. Pressure groups such as ProEnglish (http://www.proenglish.org/) have lobbied so successfully that more than half (to be precise: thirty) of the fifty states of the Union now have laws on their statute books which – in one way or another – provide for English to be the sole official language.

Fig. 14.3 US – 30 states with "official English" initiatives at state level (source: http://www.proenglish.org/issues/offeng/states.html)

In the German-speaking countries, many members of the public are worried about what they see as slipping standards of language teaching in schools. In addition, concerns are often voiced about a perceived unwillingness on the part of immigrants to learn German, which is feared to promote ghettoisation and social fragmentation.

High-profile language controversies in the German-speaking countries

Most of all, however, the language-conscious public seems to be worried about the world-wide domination of the English language. People resent the use of more and more English loan words in contemporary German (a phenomenon which will be illustrated and discussed below), with some even asking for language laws to protect the German language from too much foreign lexical influence, and they regret the decline of German as a foreign language taught in other countries and as an international language generally.

Linguistic experts and the public – a communication gap?

As this brief catalogue of issues has shown, there is no lack of public interest in language, the subject matter of linguistics. And indeed the whole range of issues – from the details of assimilating foreign words into a language to the social consequences of bilingualism – has been dealt with extensively in linguistic research. Nevertheless, linguists are frequently disappointed that very often the public does not seem to be interested in what they have to say. The public in their turn often accuse linguists of being out of touch with the real world and "academic" in the negative sense of the word (i.e. of not taking into account practical matters in their investigations). In brief: "Irrational prejudice!" is what the linguist very often says about lay opinions about matters of language structure and use, and "pointless theorising and impractical recommendations!" is what the public retorts when faced with expert opinion.

This communication gap between linguists and the public is satirically represented in Christopher Hampton's comedy *The Philanthropist*. Philip, a teacher of language history at a university, is milling about at a cocktail party and eventually faces Braham, who represents the general public, and the dreaded question of "what do you do for a living?" Philip's answer is somewhat evasive and apologetic:

Philip: No, the thing is, I teach philology which is sort of optional, and old texts and things like that, which she doesn't do because she's a graduate.
Braham: Philology?
Philip: Yes.
Braham: My God, I thought that went out years ago.
Philip: No.
Braham: I seem to remember it as the only subject which cunningly combined the boredom of the science faculties with the uselessness of the arts faculties.
Philip: Well ...
Braham: The worst of both cultures.
Philip: Most people seem to think that way. But I ... find it interesting.
Braham: Why? How?
Philip: Words. Words as objects. The development of words. Abuse of words. Words illustrating civilization. I mean, I can't go into it now, but all this new work that's being done in structural linguistics, I find absolutely fascinating.
Braham: Structural linguistics, what's that, a yet more complicated method of over-simplification?

(Christopher Hampton, *The Philanthropist: A Bourgeois Comedy*. London 1970: 34)

What seems to put Braham off philology and linguistics is a sense that the work carried out in these disciplines is extremely technical, specialised and generally far removed from the practical concerns of everyday life.

Aside from a possibly forbidding terminology, the major difficulty the public has with linguistics is its radically descriptive stance. The general public has no problem whatsoever with the notion that some languages, or some ways of speaking, are better than others, whereas linguists are extremely reluctant to make this type of judgment.

The public's problems with "mere" description

To give an example: A linguist looking at the phonology and grammar of English, German and Eipomek, a language of the Papua highlands in Indonesia, sees three different structural systems which are wonderfully complex each in their own way and have a comparably powerful expressive potential. Clearly, on this account none of the languages is superior to any other, and there is no need whatsoever to rank them according to their quality. The lay observer, on the other hand, sees two "languages," English and German, with long and distinguished written traditions and one "dialect," Eipomek, spoken by a few thousand people in a remote hinterland. The lay observer also knows from common-sense experience that in most places in the world English is more useful than German to the travelling tourist and that nowadays English is essential if you want to become a scientist or an airline pilot. As for the comparison between German and Eipomek, there are more reasons for learning the former as a foreign language than the latter, which – in fact – you require only if you decided to work among the Eipo people as a development worker or a missionary. In such a common-sense perspective, there is thus a clear hierarchy between the three languages, and one language may well be considered superior to another one.

The foregoing example was so clear and simple that it is not likely to give rise to misunderstandings between linguists and the public. The criteria applied are plain in each case, and uncontroversial. The interesting areas of disagreement are to be found in the middle ground, for example in cases in which a linguist sees language change, a normal and expected phenomenon, and members of the public see decay and degeneration. On a sociolinguistic level, similar issues may arise in the evaluation of certain types of non-standard multilingualism. For example, a sociolinguist who knows about covert prestige will instantly understand why an alienated adolescent of migrant background will **code-switch** between, say, German and Turkish or Russian or use the full range of partly offensive juvenile slang available to him or her. The explanation will be set forth in value-free terms. A teacher, on the other hand, may deplore the very same behaviour because he rightly sees it as potentially jeopardising the young person's success in school. But this very example shows how dialogue between the linguist and the teacher may be useful and productive. An awareness of the sociolinguistic background issues will certainly help the teacher in developing a more appropriate response to the pupil, and the linguist would be well advised not only to consider his informant's verbal creativity now but also his prospects in the future.

Whether after your studies you go into teaching or any other profession, not the least advantage of a training in linguistics should be for you to encourage such dialogue between expert and public opinion.

Demonstration/discussion

| 14.2

The role of Anglicisms, lexical borrowings from English, in German is viewed with increasing scepticism by many today. There is fear that English borrowings are pushing out perfectly useful German words and that a kind of German overloaded with Anglicisms will develop into an incomprehensible jargon. Depending on the context, business consultants, scientists, media personalities or adolescents fascinated by Anglo-American pop culture are made out as the main culprits.

"Anglicisms" in contemporary German

Lobby groups such as the *Verein für deutsche Sprache* have formed in order to raise awareness of the problem (and – it needs to be added – also for their own activities). For more than ten years now an annual award (currently dubbed "Sprachpanscher des Jahres") has been on offer for members of the German political, academic and business establishment. Winners have included the following luminaries: Jil Sander, fashion designer (1997); Ron Sommer (1998) and Klaus Zumwinkel (2002), business executives; media executive Markus Schächter (2004) and politician Günther Oettinger (2006). In every single case from 1997 to the time of writing (2006) the award has been for the use of English instead of German, parallel use of both languages in code-switching style, or for relabelling objects or institutions with English names. Reading the citations, it is indeed difficult not to sympathise with the *Verein* members' disgust at the awardee's pompous and self-important drivel. This, for example, is the award-winning performance by Jil Sander, the first laureate:

Language purism – keeping the language "clean"

> Ich habe vielleicht etwas Weltverbesserndes. Mein Leben ist eine giving-story. Ich habe verstanden, daß man contemporary sein muß, das future-Denken haben muß. Meine Idee war, die hand-tailored-Geschichte mit neuen Technologien zu verbinden. Und für den Erfolg war mein coordinated concept entscheidend, die Idee, daß man viele Teile einer collection miteinander combinen kann. Aber die audience hat das alles von Anfang an auch supported. Der problembewußte Mensch von heute kann diese Sachen, diese refined Qualitäten mit spirit eben auch appreciaten. Allerdings geht unser voice auch auf bestimmte Zielgruppen. Wer Ladyisches will, searcht nicht bei Jil Sander. Man muß Sinn haben für das effortless, das magic meines Stils. (Magazin der FAZ, 1996, as quoted on the VdS at http://vds-ev.de/denglisch/sprachpanscher/sprachschuster.php)

If the *Verein's* aim merely was to criticise or ridicule a particular individual's pompous utterance, there would be no quarrel with linguists. They would regard the statement as an instance of language in context, Saussurean *parole*, which calls for an analysis in terms of pragmatics. Why did Jil Sander use so many English terms – to impress an audience? – to show off? – or just unselfconsciously, because she is used to moving in an international Anglophone environment? The *Verein's* assumption, however, goes further: this is supposed to be a threat to the German language, and this is where the linguist has to contradict the argument.

A dispassionate look at the linguistic facts suggests that the situation is harmless enough. First, it seems safe to say that *combinen* and *searchen* are not about to fully replace the established German verbs *kombinieren* (itself a loan word) and *suchen* in the foreseeable future. *Searchen* has established a marginal hold in colloquial German in the context of computer or web searches. Thus, an utterance such as *Ich bin schon seit Wochen am Rumsearchen* is conceivable. The example raises numerous linguistically interesting issues about the phonetic, orthographic and morphological integration of the new verb. Whatever one may think about the beauty of the new addition to the wordstock of German, however, one thing is clear: what we have is not replacement of a German term by an English one, but the addition of an English word to the vocabulary for greater semantic differentiation, and this is the usual course of developments.

Differentiation rather than decay

A survey of similar cases soon shows that full replacement of a German word by an English one is extremely rare, and that semantic differentiation, i.e. lexical enrichment, is really the name of the game. Thus, *Kulturevent* has not replaced or pushed out *Kulturereignis* but merely serves to mark a certain type of commercially inspired performance with a high media profile. As such, a hybrid form such as *Eventkultur* is even very helpful in talking about specific features of contemporary cultural life.

Another argument against English borrowings, particularly adjectives and verbs, is that they are difficult to integrate into the German inflectional paradigms, eventually leading to a "pidginisation" of German. In a popular book on present-day German, *Deutsch und anders: Die Sprache im Modernisierungsfieber*, the well-known journalist Dieter E. Zimmer surveys a long list of English verbs recently added to the German vocabulary and claims that several among them:

> [...] scheinen ein für allemal unkonjugierbar zu sein, und wenn ihnen in einer Notsituation einmal ein Konjugationsaffix angeheftet wird, stehen sie damit da wie am Pranger. Wie auch immer man es macht, es sieht einfach unmöglich aus, und zwar ganz im Wortsinn. [...] Wir haben das Material *recycled? recycelt? gerecycelt? regecycelt?* (Dieter E. Zimmer, *Deutsch und anders: Die Sprache im Modernisierungsfieber.* Reinbek 1997: 60)

On the face of it, this seems to be proved by Jil Sander's "diese refined Qualitäten," where refined lacks the plural ending -*en* that would be found in expressions such as *diese neuen Qualitäten* or *diese beeindruckenden Qualitäten*.

Again, however, we note that if an English word stays around long enough, the problem is solved. While we may be unclear about the inflectional endings of *refined*, most Germans have now incorporated *recyceln*. A search in the digital archives of Zimmer's own newspaper, *Die Zeit*, shows that by now the vast majority of writers prefers the participle form *recycelt*, and all of the alternatives occur extremely rarely if at all. The few English verbs and adjectives that genuinely resist morphological integration, such as *sexy* in attributive use, for which it is indeed difficult to formulate a comparative or superlative (cf. *ein sexy Kleid, ein sexier/sexieres Kleid, das sexiste/sexieste Kleid*) will join an existing group of "outcasts" such as *lila* (*ein lila Kleid*), where they will do no lasting harm to the language.

In the heat of the argument about the current wave of English lexical borrowings, it is well to remember that German survived previous "onslaughts" by Latin and French without long-term damage. And for every Latin and French loan which 16th-century and 18th-century speakers of German permanently added to the vocabulary there certainly is one which later generations discarded. Based on this experience, we can rest assured that many of the anglicisms which are currently being used experimentally will have disappeared within a few years' time. In the meantime, the safe assumption is that the people who criticise the influx of English words into contemporary German are in fact criticising something else – the new ways of doing business and the new lifestyles and (pop-)cultural developments which first emerged in the English-speaking world and are now influencing life everywhere. Such a critical posture is legitimate. However, it should be expressed directly, and not indirectly through linguistic arguments which do not hold water.

The long-term view: English taking over as donor language from Latin and French

What the above discussion has aimed to make clear, by contrast, is that a dialogue between linguistic experts and the public is useful because it allows both parties to state the issues more clearly, upon which the incriminated linguistic developments usually reveal themselves to be far less comprehensive and apocalyptic than appears at first sight.

Problems and challenges

14.3

The integration of lexical borrowings in a language is a fairly narrowly defined problem which can be solved largely by means of linguistic analysis. Matters are more complex in the case of linguistic diversity in the world – an issue in which linguistic technicalities are inextricably mixed up with the analysts' stance on matters such as the rights of minority groups or the social goals of devleopment. At the end of the 20th century a total of ca. 5,000 languages were spoken in the world. Of these, ca. 3,000+ languages had less than a few thousand speakers, which of course makes their survival through the present

Linguistic diversity – English as a "killer language"

century unlikely. Linguistic diversity in the world is vanishing fast, and English is often accused as being a "killer language" in this process.

The easiest way of finding out about linguistic diversity in the world is to consult the Summer Institute of Linguistics' *Ethnologue: Languages of the World* database (http://www.ethnologue.com/). This database also offers the following interesting map:

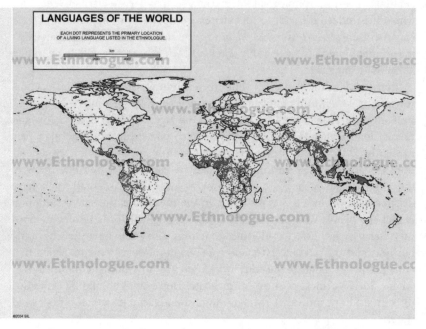

Fig. 14.4 | Linguistic diversity in the world (SIL, 2004)

Linguistic diversity: focal regions

This map makes two points: (1) we still live in a multilingual world, as is witnessed by the many dots on the map, but (2) some regions in the world are more multilingual than others – tropical West and Central Africa, Central America, the remoter parts of South America, the Himalayas and interior regions of South East Asia and – most obviously of all – the Island of New Guinea, which comes out as one shaded blot. Linguists, who tend to be natural champions of a multilingual world (and, if the author be granted the right to voice his personal view here, have every right and duty to be so), are faced with an uncomfortable message. Multilingualism is most evident in economically and technologically disadvantaged regions of the world, and linguistic homogenisation, up to a point at least, seems to be an inevitable by-product of societal modernisation.

Linguistic diversity and development

Reversing the argument, linguistic homogeneity seems to be the hallmark of those regions of the world – such as North America, Australia, or Siberia – which were most effectively colonised by large-scale European settlement. Historically, English and other European colonial languages may therefore well have been "killer languages." As for the present, however, a slightly different interpretation suggests itself. Usually, small languages are not under threat directly from a world language, but rather from a neighbouring mid-sized language. In that sense, the linguistic diversity of the Arctic region is threatened by Norwegian and Finnish as much as by French, Russian and English.

How can we protect the linguistic and cultural rights of minorities in such a situation, as UNESCO, for example, is committed to doing (cf. its 1996 "Universal Declaration on Linguistic Rights")? If possible, as a first step people should be offered access to primary education and literacy in their mother tongue. However, this is obviously difficult for languages which have never been written down, and people are only motivated to learn how to write and read a language if at the end of the process there is enough in the language that is worth reading. Another problem encountered is the high degree of geographical mobility that the modern lifestyle demands. How can speakers keep up the links to their local languages when economic pressure forces them to move to far-away urban centres? Pointing out these many difficulties does not mean that protecting linguistic diversity is not a worthy goal, but we see that it is a very difficult and costly one.

On the other hand, the rapid reduction in linguistic diversity in the world has a price, too. Individually, it leads to unnecessary suffering, whenever speakers of minority languages are discriminated against or forced to assimilate. Culturally, the loss of a language also implies losses of other kinds. In their "primitive" languages, "primitive" peoples have accumulated valuable knowledge of their environment which is stored in ethno-botanical classification systems. Modern science, including modern ecology, may find it difficult to re-construct this knowledge once it has been lost. Similarly, a community's store of folk-lore, song, myth and story-telling often does not survive the shift to another language, which may lead to a total loss of a valuable oral tradition.

Fig. 14.5
UNESCO position paper on education in a multilingual world – written in English

As for the guilty parties, however, as has been pointed out, it is simplistic only to blame the world's big languages such as English. Recently, there has been much concern about the dominance of (American) English not just in geographical space but also in "cyberspace," on the Internet. On reflection,

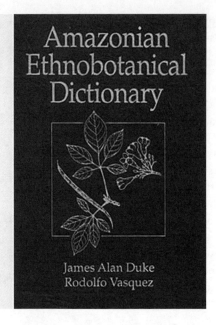

Fig. 14.6 | *Amazonian Ethnobotanical Dictionary* – cover

however, this is not really the dominance of the language, but the dominance of the powerful economy of the English-speaking US, which was the first nation in which large portions of the population started to use the new medium on a habitual basis. There is still a vast "digital divide" in the world today, separating the world's poor, who have no easy access to the new technology, from the rich who have. But as more nations are entering the digital age, the Web is becoming more multi-lingual. In fact, the one language in the world which probably does not need a boost from the Web is English. For many other languages, though, the Web may be one means of ensuring their survival. The world's communicative economy is not a closed one, where the gain of one language automatically means the loss of another. As new channels of communication are being opened, there are opportunities for growth for all languages. In an age of unprecedented global migration, for example, it is possible for people all over the world to remain readers of newspapers in their own language everywhere and thus to maintain their heritage languages.

In the present connection, it is also interesting to reflect on the continuing role of former colonial languages such as English in independent post-colonial nations such as India, Nigeria or Singapore. In all three countries English is more important for more people now than in the days of colonial rule, and in all three English continues to serve as one of the countries' official languages.

Fig. 14.7 | Gandhi, photographed at Downing Street 10, Seat of the British Prime Minister (1931)

This is puzzling, for in the days of colonialism, the English language was frequently felt to be an alienating force, undermining the colonial subjects' pride in their own linguistic and cultural traditions. This idea is succinctly expressed in the following statement by Mohandas K. Gandhi (1869–1948), the famed leader of the Indian Independence movement:

> To give millions a knowledge of English is to enslave them. [...] Is it not a painful thing that, if I want to go to a court of justice, I must employ the English language as a medium; [...] and that someone else should have to translate to me from my own language? [...] Am I to blame the English for it or myself? It is we, the English-knowing men, that have enslaved India. The curse of the nation will rest not upon the nation but upon us. (quoted in Richard W. Bailey, *Images of English*. Cambridge 1992: 144)

If colonialism and imperialism are political, economic, cultural and linguistic, by this logic true freedom will not be not achieved until the English language is reduced to the status of a useful foreign language in the new nation. This is, in fact, the position taken by Kenyan writer Ngugi wa Thiong'o, whose native language is Kikuyu, a Bantu language spoken by ca. 5 million of Kenya's inhabitants:

Rejecting English as a strategy of combating cultural imperialism?

> I believe that my writing in Gikuyu language, a Kenyan language, an African language, is part and parcel of the anti-imperialist struggles of Kenyan and African peoples. In schools and universities our Kenyan languages – that is the languages of the many nationalities which make up Kenya – were associated with negative qualities of backwardness, underdevelopment, humiliation and punishment. We who went through that school system were meant to graduate with a hatred of the people and the culture and the values of the language of our daily humiliation and punishment. I do not want to see Kenyan children growing up in that imperialist-imposed tradition of contempt for the tools of communication developed by their communities and their history. I want them to transcend colonial alienation. (Ngugi wa Thiong'o, *Decolonising the Mind: The Politics of Language in African Literature*. London 1986: 32)

It is difficult to find fault with the emancipatory impulse underlying this pronouncement, and such liberationist rhetoric has remained common in contemporary academic discourse – for example in post-colonial cultural studies, a booming subfield which students of English are sure to encounter in the course of their studies.

What such comments fail to take into account, however, is that languages are not "products" which are exported to other regions of the globe or forced on unwilling "customers." In the history of British colonialism and American imperialism have undoubtedly been economic exploitation and political oppression. However, it is difficult to find evidence for a rigid and ruthless policy of linguistic assimilation. On close sociolinguistic inspection, the spread of English thus becomes a process in which both coloniser and colonised were agents. Colonial settlers, missionaries and administrators passed the language on, but what eventually became of it in the mouths of the

Fig. 14.8 Ngũgĩ wa Thiong'o, cover of *Decolonising the Mind* (1986)

recipients would have baffled many of the donors. As was demonstrated in Unit 9, wherever English continued to be spoken and written in the de-colonising world, new varieties emerged – some of them standards in a pluricentric polyphony of voices and even more of them non-standard varieties responding to local life and local experience.

There are no blanket answers to the question whether the use of English in post-colonial societies is a good or bad thing. The following Table summarises the complex network of opposing factors, and how this dynamic plays itself out will differ from country to country.

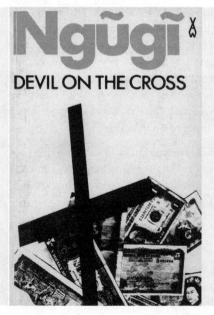

Fig. 14.9 Fig. 14.10 Ngũgĩ wa Thiong'o, cover of Kikuyu original and English translation of *Devil on the cross*

Table 14.1 Advantages and disadvantages of the use of English as an official language

Use of English as official language is good because …	Use of English as official language is bad because …
… it contributes to a sense of national unity in multilingual and multiethnic societies	… it serves the needs of a small local elite and excludes the masses from participation in public life
… it promotes modernisation and international contacts	… it corrupts traditional social structures and cultures
… it saves money spent on translation (of teaching materials etc.)	… it prevents the development of writing, written standards and publishing in the local languages
… it is a culturally, politically and ethnically neutral link language	… the continuing use of the coloniser's language entrenches European cultural values in developing societies ("cultural imperialism", "colonialism of the mind")
… it is what people want if they are allowed a choice	… use of foreign languages in the educational system slows down pupils' academic progress

Singapore, now a prosperous city state, was founded and developed by the British. The majority of its population came from elsewhere – predominantly from Southern China. In fact, it would have been difficult to force the majority of Chinese to embrace English as an official language and, increasingly, also as a family language. However, in this particular climate, the economic benefits to be derived from the use of English and the integrative function of English in a multilingual and multiethnic society led to generally positive attitudes towards English. In addition, a functioning and highly developed educational system ensures almost universal access to English. In contemporary Nigeria, by contrast, there is a much more violent rift between an English-trained modern elite, on the one hand, and the masses of rural and urban poor which are denied access to English, on the other. Although – as in Singapore – English is probably here to stay, too, the role of the language remains much more divisive in this sort of social constellation.

What the study of linguistics can contribute to a deeper understanding of such social, political and cultural issues is this type of differentiated analysis, based on an appreciation of the fact that global English today is no longer a one-way street. "The Empire Writes Back" was a slogan coined in response to a growing number of authors from former colonies achieving global prominence alongside British and American writers – for example Wole Soyinka from Nigeria or Derek Walcott and V. S. Naipaul from the Caribbean, to mention just three winners of the Nobel Prize for literature. "The Empire Talks Back," we might go on to say, so as to recognise that English has been appropriated by its non-European users and changed to reflect their own experiences.

Appropriating English as a strategy of combating cultural imperialism?

Fig. 14.11 | Fig. 14.12 | Brixton, South London, 1981 (http://www.fb10.uni-bremen.de/anglistik/kerkhoff/DubPoetry/DubQuest/Brixton.gif) and 2000s

As a result of the current wave of global migration, the Empire now talks back even in the very heart of the former motherland, as is shown by the following observation of a British-based writer of Nigerian descent. The locale is Brixton, a multi-ethnic South London neighbourhood:

> I was sharing Brixton with a number of 'right-on' white friends and acquaintances from university, but here was the funny thing. In all my years there, we almost never found ourselves in the same social space. And though they, with their ethnic beads and accessories, and the pot they bought from the Rastaman in their pub, thought they were all part of some multicultural paradise, many knew little of what was truly going on in their communities. They weren't noticing, from their eyries in trendy Notting Hill and Brixton, how deeply young urban Britain was changing around them. How it had become increasingly black-inflected. How average white, Greek or Asian kids on the streets where they lived, were pronouncing 'ask' like 'arks', Caribbean-style, and had a ready grasp of patois. And how, in the whiter suburbs, there were others too who wanted a piece of this new action. (Diran Adebayo, "Young, gifted, black … and very confused," *Observer*, 25 November 2001)

While the pronunciation [ɑːks] may indeed signal Jamaican Creole or British Black English to contemporary Londoners, it is good to remind ourselves that this pronunciation has been around since Old English. As the OED puts it in its entry for the verb: "*Acsian, axian*, survived in *ax*, down to nearly 1600 the regular literary form, and still used everywhere in midl. and south. dialects, though supplanted in standard English by *ask*, originally the northern form." It was also the form African slaves picked up during creolisation in Jamaica in the 17th and 18th centuries – and which their descendants brought back to London. Linguistic history has come full circle.

References and further reading

Adger, C. T., C. E. Snow, and D. Christian, eds. 2002. *What teachers need to know about language.* Washington DC: Center for Applied Linguistics.

Aitchison, Jean. 2001. *Language change: progress or decay.* 3rd ed. Cambridge: CUP.

Bauer, Laurie, and Peter Trudgill, eds. 1998. *Language myths*. Harmondsworth: Penguin Books.
Cameron, Deborah. 1995. *Verbal hygiene*. London: Routledge.
Heeschen, Volker. 1998. *An ethnographic grammar of the Eipo language spoken in the central mountains of Irian Jaya (West New Guinea), Indonesia*. Berlin: Reimer.
Nettle, Daniel, and Suzanne Romaine. 2000. *Vanishing voices: the extinction of the world's languages*. Oxford: OUP.

Practice

|14.4

1 Consult the *Ethnologue: Languages of the World* database (at http://www.ethnologue.com) and use it to draw up linguistic profiles of the United Kingdom, Canada and Nigeria. What is the role of English in each country? How many linguistic minorities are there? Try to find out – at least for some of them – whether any measures are taken to safeguard their rights.

2 Consult the catalogue of your university library and the MLA bibliography for published linguistic work on the Eipomek language mentioned above. Be careful to use both "Eipo" and "Eipomek" as search terms to get complete coverage. Do you notice any obvious gaps in our knowledge of this language? How does what we know about Eipo(mek) compare to what we know about English or German?

3 Below you find a selection from the *Verein für deutsche Sprache*'s list of anglicisms. All words and expressions marked "3" are considered to be pushing out their proper German equivalents and therefore proscribed. Those marked "2" are considered "differenzierend," while "0" stands for proper names and "1" (not attested in the present selection) for "ergänzend."

air bag:	2	Prallkissen (**air bag** ist eine irreführende Bezeichnung, da beim Aufprall in den **bag** nicht Luft, sondern ein Explosionsgas einschießt) [→]
air base:	3	Fliegerhorst, Militärflugplatz
air brake¹:	3	Bremsklappe (am Flugzeug)
air brake²:	3	Luftdruckbremse
airbrush:	2	luftpinseln, sprühmalen; Spritzpistole, Spritztechnik
Airbus:	0	(EN) AIRBUS
air-condition:	3	Klimaanlage, auch in
air-conditioned:	3	(voll-)klimatisiert
air-conditioning:	3	Klimatechnik, Klimatisierung
aircraft:	3	Flugzeug, siehe auch **airplane** [→]

|Table 14.2
From *Anglizismenliste* published and maintained by Verein für deutsche Sprache e.V. (http://http://www.vds-ev.de/anglizismenindex/suche2.php)

air crane:	3	Luftschiffkran, siehe **cargo lifter** [→]
aircrew:	3	Flugzeugbesatzung
airfield:	3	Kleinflugplatz, Sportflugplatz
airflow:	3	Luftströmung
air force:	3	Luftwaffe	Luftstreitkräfte
airframe:	3	Flugzeugzelle
air hole:	3	Luftloch
airless[1]:	3	atemlos, stickig (in geschlossenen Räumen), windstill
airless[2]:	2	Vollgummireifen	Vollwandreifen
airline:	3	Fluggesellschaft, Fluglinie
airliner:	2	(großes) Passagierflugzeug
airmail:	3	Luftpost, Luftpostbrief
air place:	3	Sendeplatz
airplane:	3	Flugzeug, siehe auch **aircraft** [→]
airplay:	3	Radio-, Fernsehausstrahlung
airport:	3	Flughafen
air safety:	3	Flugsicherheit
airship:	3	(Starr-)Luftschiff, Zeppelin, siehe auch **blimp**[2] [→]
air show:	3	Flugschau
airsick:	3	flugkrank, luftkrank
air terminal:	3	Abfertigungshalle, Terminal
air ticket:	3	Flugschein
airtime:	3	Gesprächsdauer, Sprechzeit (z. B. Telefon)

How current are the incriminated anglicisms? What evidence can you provide to back up your view? How do you assess the usefulness of the suggested German alternatives.

4 Consult digitised text bases for the study of German, for example the corpora held at the Institut für deutsche Sprache (IdS) in Mannheim (http://www.ids-mannheim.de/kl/corpora.html) or electronic newspapers for uses of *einkaufen* and *shoppen*. Are the two verbs used interchangeably or is there a clear semantic differentiation? Look for forms such as *shoppt, shopt, geshoppt* etc. to find out whether the English verb is orthographically and morphologically integrated into the German language.

5. This is a much-quoted statement by Nigerian writer Chinua Achebe, in which he justifies his use of English as a medium of literary expression.

> The real question is not whether Africans *could* write in English but whether they *ought* to. Is it right that a man should abandon his mother tongue for someone else's? It looks like a dreadful betrayal and produces a guilty feeling.
>
> But for me there is no other choice. I have been given this language and I intend to use it. I hope, though, that there always will be men, like the late Chief Fagunwa, who will choose to write in their native tongue and insure that our ethnic literature will flourish side by side with the national ones. For those of us who opt for English, there is much work ahead and much excitement.
>
> Writing in the London *Observer* recently, James Baldwin said: 'My quarrel with the English language has been that the language reflected none of my experience. But now I began to see the matter another way. ... Perhaps the language was not my own because I had never attempted to use it, had only learned to imitate it. If this were so, then it might be made to bear the burden of my experience if I could find the stamina to challenge it, and me, to such a test.'
>
> I recognize, of course, that Baldwin's problem is not exactly mine, but I feel that the English language will be able to carry the weight of my African experience. But it will have to be a new English, still in full communion with its ancestral home but altered to suit its new African surroundings.

Text 14.1
Chinua Achebe, "The African Writer and the English Language." In Chinua Achebe, *Morning Yet on Creation Day.* New York 1975 [1965], 103

Consult works by Achebe, such as his first novel *Things Fall Apart* or the later *Anthills of the Savannah*, to find out more about the ways in which he has altered English to suit its African surroundings.

6. In Canada, a sizable French-speaking minority population has long felt itself to be marginalised culturally and economically by an Anglophone majority. Recently, since the 1960s, it has asserted its linguistic rights forcefully, to the point of separatism. The following passage from Canadian writer Margaret Atwood's novel *Surfacing* encapsulates within the space of a few paragraphs several fault lines of this conflict:

What the writers say

The woman looks at me, inquisitive but not smiling, and the two men still in Elvis Presley haircuts, duck's ass at the back and greased pompadours curving out over their foreheads, stop talking and look at me; they keep their elbows on the counter. I hesitate: maybe the tradition has changed, maybe they no longer speak English.

"Avez-vous du viande haché?" I ask her, blushing because of my accent.

She grins and then the two men grin also, not at me but at each other. I see I've made a mistake, I shoud have pretended to be an American.

"Amburger, oh yes we have lots. *How* much?" she asks, adding the final H carelessly to show she can if she feels like it. This is border country.

Text 14.2
Margaret Atwood, *Surfacing.* Toronto/New York 1972, 27 f.

> "A pound, no two pounds," I say, blushing even more because I've been so easily discovered, they're making fun of me and I have no way of letting them know I share the joke. Also I agree with them, if you live in a place you should speak the language. But this isn't where I lived.
>
> She hacks with a cleaver at a cube of frozen meat, weighs it. "Doo leevers," she says, mimicking my school accent.

The liberal Anglo-Canadian narrator is caught in a double bind. In full sympathy with French Canadians' quest for linguistic and cultural rights, she wants to accommodate, by speaking her – atrocious – French. The French-speaking shop assistant proves to be better qualified in practical linguistic battles. Explain her tactics, using the explanatory concepts provided by sociolinguistics.

Glossary of linguistic terms

1) Socially or regionally typical pronunciation, e. g. "English with a Scottish accent" or "British urban working-class accents." Note that the term *accent* refers to deviations from the standard in terms of pronunciation; if reference is also to grammatical or lexical features, the terms → *dialect* or (*non-standard*) *variety* are used. 2) In phonetics/phonology, *accent* is sometimes used synonymously with word or sentence stress → *regional accent*. **Accent**

In languages which express grammatical relations within the sentence by means of a case system (e. g. in Latin and to a large extent also in German) the case typically used for the verb's direct object; cf. German *der Mann* (nominative) and *ich sehe den Mann* (accusative). English does not inflect nouns for the accusative; the distinction between a *common case* and an *object case* is only possible for some personal pronouns and – optionally – the interrogative pronoun *who* (cf. *he/him* and *who/whom*). **Accusative**

A type of complex word which consists of the initial letters of its components, e. g. *BASIC* (derived from "**b**eginners' **a**ll-purpose **s**ymbolic **i**nstruction **c**ode") or *WASP* (= **w**hite **A**nglo-**S**axon **P**rotestant). In contrast to *alphabetisms* where each letter is pronounced separately (e. g. *USA*), acronyms are pronounced like single words. Acronyms coinciding with existing words (as the two examples above) are classified as motivated, due to their better memorability and possible semantic associations; acronyms such as *NATO* (= **N**orth **A**tlantic **T**reaty **O**rganisation) are not motivated. **Acronym**

A part of speech typically describing the characteristics of a noun. Adjectives can be qualified by adverbs and are gradable: *a cheap meal/the meal is cheap, an extraordinarily cheap meal, a cheaper meal, the cheapest meal*. Some adjectives fulfil these criteria only partially; cf. e. g. *the child is ill* but **an ill child*, *the *illest child*. **Adjective**

An optional constituent of a clause. → *complement*. **Adjunct**

A part of speech chiefly used for modifying the verbal predicate, e. g. by specifying manner, cause or spatial and temporal dimensions: *Sue draws **beautifully**, they sell flowers **here sometimes***. Adverbs can also be used to modify adjectives: *a **sometimes** boring film, a **really** stupid remark, a **beautifully** crafted basket*. Note that the term *adverb* refers to the part of speech, not to its function within the sentence (cf. → *adverbial*). **Adverb**

A → *constituent* denoting the spatial, temporal and other concomitant circumstances of the state of affairs expressed in the basic clause (i. e. the subject, predicate and complements). Structurally, adverbials can take the shape of adverbs, noun phrases, prepositional phrases, or subordinate clauses: *I'm working **now**, I work **all day**, I've been working **for three hours**, I have been working **since you left***. In a substitution test, *when, where, how, why*, etc. are the typical interrogative pronouns used to ask for adverbials. Typically, adverbials are optional constituents or adjuncts. In exceptional cases, they are obligatory constituents or complements (e. g. the adverbial of place in *I put the book on the shelf*). **Adverbial**

An adverbial indicating the manner in which an action or event unfolds: *The meeting was dispersed **violently**, the proposal was rejected **in the clearest possible terms***. **Adverbial of manner**

An adverbial indicating the place of an action, event, or state: *I wear this t-shirt **on the beach**, it is rather humid **outside***. **Adverbial of place**

An adverbial indicating the point of time or duration of a verbal action, e. g. *I read Oliver Twist **last year*** or *I read Oliver Twist **in eight hours***. **Adverbial of time**

Cover term for the most important classes of bound morphemes used in derivation and inflection. Prefixes attach to the beginning of a word (e. g. *loyal/disloyal*), whereas suffixes attach to the end of words (e. g. *warm/warmth, bring/brings*). A third possibility, infixation, is marginally attested in English in emphatic-emotive language: *kangaroos* → those *kanga-bloody-roos!, fan-fucking-tastic!* **Affix**

GLOSSARY OF LINGUISTIC TERMS

Agentive noun   A noun derived from a verb which denotes the person or instrument/object conceived of as performing an action, e.g. *cleaner* (from *to clean*).

Allomorph   The realisational variant of a morpheme (cf. → *morpheme*). The three past-tense forms *attacked, frightened,* and *insulted* show that the regular past-tense morpheme can be realised in three ways, depending on the phonetic environment – as /t/ following voiceless sounds except /t/, as /d/ following voiced sounds except /d/, and as /ɪd/ following /t, d/. The allomorphs of a morpheme are in complementary distribution, i.e. where /ɪd/ occurs, /t/ and /d/ are excluded, and vice versa.

Allophone   The realisational variant of a phoneme (cf. → *phoneme*). In the British English standard pronunciation → R.P. ("Received Pronunciation"), the phoneme /l/ is realised in three ways depending on its position within the word: "clear" [l] before vowels (as in *lip* or *million*), "dark" [ɫ] word-finally and before consonants (*feel, called*), and voiceless [l̥] after voiceless stops (*place, click*). For transcriptions, diagonal slashes (/) are used for phonemes, square brackets ([]) for their allophonic realisations. Typically, the allophones of a phoneme are in complementary distribution, i.e. in places where clear [l] occurs, the dark and voiceless variants are excluded, and vice versa. If this were not the case, the relevant sounds could potentially occur in → *minimal pairs* and thus develop a phonemic contrast.

Analogy   Irregular forms are regularised by assimilating them to regular and synchronically productive patterns. In the history of English, for example, many noun plurals ended in *-n*. Most of these were assimilated to the dominating plural pattern ending in *-s*, cf. e.g. Middle English *shoon* and modern *shoes*, so that only very few irregular *-n* plurals remain today (*oxen, children*).

Analytical   In languages of the analytical type, the grammatical relations between constituents are primarily expressed by constituent order and function words and not by case endings. Languages using case endings to express grammatical relations in a sentence are called "synthetic". Compared to German, English is more analytical; cf. e.g. *ich widme mich der Musik* (dative) and *I devote myself to music* (function word plus noun).

Anaphora   A word or expression referring to a previous mention, e.g. *this* in *she made me wait for twenty minutes; **this** made me nervous*. Cataphoric expressions, by contrast, refer to material following in the discourse: *what I wish to emphasise is **these** three qualities: reliability, flexibility and a sense of commitment*.

Antonym   In the broad sense, any word expressing the opposite of another word, e.g. *single* vs. *married* or *to open* vs. *to close*. In the narrow sense, antonyms refer to gradable oppositions such as *cheap* versus *expensive*, which allow intermediate stages.

Aphasia   A speech disorder caused by organic damage of the brain.

Arbitrariness   Central concept of Ferdinand de Saussure's theory of the linguistic sign. The phonetic form of a word is not causally related to its content, i.e. the relationship between the two sides of the linguistic sign is in principle a random (= arbitrary) social convention. So-called onomatopoetic word forms are no exception to the claim that the relation between sound and meaning in the linguistic sign is arbitrary because they, too, are conventionalised in individual languages – cf. German *kikeriki* and English *a-cock-a-doodle-doo*.

Article   A word indicating whether the noun it modifies is definite or indefinite, specific or general; cf. ***the*** *new book* and ***a*** *new book*. In both German and English a distinction is made between *definite* and *indefinite* articles.

Aspect   A grammatical category of the finite verb (others are *tense* and *mood*) which exists in English but not in German. Aspect provides information about the manner and duration of the verbal action. Since Early Modern English, an obligatory grammatical distinction has been in place between *simple forms* and *progressive* (or *continuous*) *forms* of the verb, e.g. *what do you read?* (general habit of reading) versus *what are you reading?* (present reading).

Assimilation   The influence of one sound on the articulation of another sound. In *ten bottles*, for example, /n/ in *ten* can be pronounced as /m/ in rapid speech due to the influence of the following labial sound.

Attribute   Modification of a noun by means of adjectives/adjective phrases or participles/participle phrases which are used in adjectival function: *a new car, a recently excavated temple*.

Glossary

A verb with dominantly grammatical function, usually co-occurring with another verb (the "main" verb), which bears the core semantic content of the verb phrase. English has the primary auxiliaries *be, have,* and *do,* used to form compound tenses, progressives, passives, questions and negations, and a class of modal auxiliaries (*can, may, must, ...*). In addition, English is particularly rich in semi-auxiliaries, i. e. verbal idioms which do not share the typical formal-grammatical characteristics of auxiliaries but perform very similar functions. Cf., e. g., *this **is not going to** happen* (≈ *this **will not** happen*), *you're **not supposed to** smoke in here* (≈ *you **shouldn't** smoke in here*).	**Auxiliary**
A word-formation process in which a base form is created which originally did not exist. The English verb *edit*, for example, is the result of a back-formation from *editor* because the suffix *-or* could be interpreted as a spelling variant of the derivational morpheme *-er* as present in *baker, singer*, etc.	**Back-formation**
A research tradition in psychology restricted to the analysis and measurement of observable behaviour. Some linguists attempted – unsuccessfully – to explain language acquisition and even meaning on the basis of behaviourist models of stimulus-and-response.	**Behaviorism**
A complex word created by fusing its two components (*education + entertainment* → *edutainment*); in the broader sense each compound based on abbreviations of the original words (e. g. *modulator + demodulator* → *modem*).	**Blend**
A dominant school of thought in American linguistics, named after Leonard Bloomfield (1887–1949); it had its heyday between 1930 and 1950. This approach aimed at developing rigorous and exact methods for recording and describing the sound systems and grammars of languages. Its orientation towards behaviorist psychology proved an impediment when dealing with questions of semantics.	**Bloomfieldian structuralism**
A category of noun inflection which indicates the grammatical function of a noun phrase within the sentence. English retains only two nominal cases, *common case* and *genitive*. In recent linguistic theories, the term is also used in a broader sense, i. e. to denote the semantic role of the person or object involved in the verbal action. In such models, "dative" describes the person who is affected by the verbal action, e. g. ***ihm** lief die Frau weg*/*his wife walked out **on him***. In this broader sense, English has a dative case even if, as in this example, it is realised analytically, as a prepositional phrase. → *dative*	**Case**
→ *anaphora*.	**Cataphora**
A complex grammatical construction expressing that someone or something brings about a specific situation, or causes someone else to do something. In many languages, causativity is expressed morphologically (e. g. through verb inflection); in English, it is typically expressed syntactically: *They got us to work, they had us work(ing), they made us work*, etc. Causativity is important also in word-formation and the lexicon, to account for word-formation patterns such as *rational* → *rationalise* (= "cause to become more rational").	**Causative construction**
A rhetorical stylistic device based on the cross-over of elements (pattern: ab-ba), e. g. *when the going gets tough, the tough get going* or – to quote the motto of a well-known US motorcycle maker – "Live to ride. Ride to Live."	**Chiasmus**
→ *sentence*.	**Clause**
A syntactic construction in which one constituent is emphasised by separating it from the rest of the sentence: *I met my cousin Angela in Paris* → *it was in Paris that I met my cousin Angela*. Neither parts of constituents nor more than one constituent can be highlighted in this way. In order to determine whether a part of a sentence is a constituent or not, the "cleft sentence test" can therefore be applied: cf. **it was my cousin that I met Angela in Paris* and **it was my cousin Angela in Paris that I met*.	**Cleft sentence**
Abbreviated word forms which originate from omitting the beginning or end of words, e. g. *exam* (from *examination*) or *bus* (from *omnibus*).	**Clipping**
A bilingual speaker's use of more than one language within the same utterance or text. Note that some shifts or switches from one language to the other are conditioned by objective external factors (for example, the linguistic competence of a specific addressee or the topic of a conversation), other instances of code-switching are more difficult to predict and categorise and may even occur at certain points within a clause. A common classification thus distinguishes between intra-sentential code-switching (within a clause or sentence) and inter-sentential code-switching (at more "expected" points, such as, for exam-	**Code-switching**

ple, the end of a sentence or an utterance). In a loose sense, the term is sometimes applied to switches between standard and non-standard forms of a language, or between any two or more varieties of a language.

Coherence	Texts are coherent if they make sense in terms of their content → *cohesion*.
Cohesion	Formal and structural links between the sentences of a text, e.g. lexical variation and pronominalisation: **Al Capone** knew that his power was threatened. **The wily gangster** reacted promptly. On 25 October **he** called a meeting just outside Chicago ... Other important cohesive devices comprise conjunctions and adverbials with linking function: *The fridge did not work.* **Therefore,** *we had a chicken dinner from the hamburger place round the corner* → *coherence*.
Collection of citations	→ *corpus*.
Collocation	The tendency of words to co-occur in ways that go beyond grammatical and logical semantic restrictions. In English, for example, *a flock* collocates with *birds* and *sheep*, but not with *cattle*, which collocates only with *a herd*. Goats, however, can co-occur with both (*a flock/herd of goats*). A phenomenon related to collocations are *idiomatic expressions/idioms*, e.g. *to spill the beans on someone* ("reveal information"). The main distinguishing criterion is the fact that the meaning of a collocation results from the sum of the individual meanings of its components, which is not the case for idioms. Cf. also → *idiomatic, phraseologism*.
Communication	The purposeful transmission of meaningful contents. Languages are the most important and most highly differentiated systems of communication in human communities. However, communication can take place also through other channels, e.g. gestures and facial expressions. Conversely, there are formal aspects of languages which are not directly connected to their communicative function.
Competence	According to Chomsky a native speaker's ability to assess the well-formedness of example sentences, recognise ambiguities and produce and understand an infinite number of sentences; the opposite of *performance*, where non-linguistic aspects (e.g. loss of concentration or the inability to find the proper word) lead to impaired competence.
Complement	A constituent whose presence is necessary for a sentence to be complete. Depending on the type of verb, the number of complements ranges from one to three. The verb *sleep*, for example, requires only a subject (cf. *she is sleeping*). The verb *put*, however, requires a subject, an object, and an adverbial of place (*she is putting the kettle on the table*). Additional optional constituents are called *adjuncts* (e.g. *she put the kettle on the table* **carelessly/with a flourish/five minutes ago/...**). In some descriptive models of English grammar, the term *complement* has a narrower meaning, referring to the predicative specification of subjects and objects, as in *She is* **stupid** (complement of the subject) or *She called him* **an idiot** (complement of the object).
Complementary distribution	→ *allophone*.
Complex sentence	→ *sentence*.
Compound word	A word assembled from at least two free morphemes, e.g. *bedroom, apple pie, to short-change (someone)*.
Conjugation	→ *inflection*.
Conjunction	Subordinating conjunctions like *that* or *although* introduce subordinate clauses; co-ordinating conjunctions like *and, but* or *or* serve to link main clauses or other coordinated syntactic elements.
Connotation	→ *denotation*.
Consonant	A sound produced with an obstruction (occlusion or friction) of the air flow, e.g. /p/, /t/, /k/, or /m/. Consonants can be classified according to place and manner of articulation and voicing. Thus, /p/ is a voiceless, bilabial stop.

Glossary

Constituent
An element of a complex syntactic structure which can be determined by means of semantic or formal criteria. For example, the clause *the tourist lost the key to his hotel room* can uncontroversially be analysed as consisting of a noun phrase *the tourist* and a verb phrase *lost the key to his hotel room*. This verb phrase falls into the two constituents *lost* and *the key to his hotel room*. Of these, the noun phrase *the key to his hotel room* is complex in itself and can be divided further into its constituents.

At clause level, the most important formal tests for constituent structure are substitution tests, movement tests, question tests and transformation tests. In order to determine whether *in New Guinea* in the sentence *I read a book about the customs of some native tribes in New Guinea* is a constituent or part of a long object noun phrase, several tests, such as the following, are possible. If it is a constituent, *in New Guinea* can be placed at the beginning of the sentence without change of meaning (*in New Guinea I read a book about the customs of some native tribes*); the necessary question pronoun is *where* (*where did you read a book about ...?*); it can be replaced by an adverb of place such as *there*; furthermore, a → *cleft sentence* can be applied to put *in New Guinea* into focus (*it was in New Guinea that I read a book about ...*).

Constituent order
The position of constituents within the clause, inaccurately also called *word order*. In English, the basic constituent order in simple sentences is subject – predicate – object (SVO); in German, the finite verb occurs in second position (*verb-second*) in the main clause and in final position in subordinate clauses.

Conversation analysis
A linguistic sub-discipline mainly concerned with investigating how → *cohesion* and → *coherence* are established in everyday conversations. Conversation analysis was inspired by ethnomethodology, a sociological movement which aims at gaining insights into how members of particular communities construct their social reality through regular interaction.

Conversion
→ *zero-derivation*.

Corpus
A collection of texts compiled for the purposes of linguistic analysis. Today, most corpora are available in machine-readable form. Corpora are provided either as plain text or with various types of coding or annotation (e.g. for grammatical part of speech or for speakers' social or regional background). Various types of retrieval software are available to make possible linguistically sophisticated quantitative and qualitative analysis of the material.

Creole
Any language which developed on the basis of a → *pidgin*. Pidgins are reduced auxiliary languages with limited communicative functions which are not spoken as native languages by any of their users. Creoles, by contrast, despite their origins in such pidgins, are fully fledged natural languages – and thus in principle no different in their expressive potential from languages with an unbroken historical transmission. The quick development of creoles within a short period of time (1–2 generations), and the related impressive degree of structural expansion, still mystifies linguists. Most creoles developed in the Caribbean and in East Asia and the Pacific in the wake of European colonialism.

Dative
In languages which express grammatical relations within the sentence by means of cases – e.g. in Latin and to a large extent also in German – the case which is typically used for the indirect object of the verb: *ich gebe **dir/der Frau** eine Orange*. In this sense, the dative case does not exist in English. Some grammarians use the term nevertheless to denote the indirect object in general, speaking of a *dative shift* when dealing with word order variability of the type *give her the book – give the book to her* → *case*.

Declarative clause
The declarative clause (*You're cleaning my room*) is one of the three fundamental sentence types. The other two are the *interrogative clause* (*Are you cleaning my room?*) and the *imperative clause* (*Clean my room!*).

Declension
→ *inflection*.

Deixis
Cover term for all linguistic devices serving to anchor an utterance in its context. The most important deictic expressions are personal pronouns, those spatial or temporal adverbs whose meaning is context-dependent (e.g. *here/there* or *now/then*), demonstrative pronouns (*this/that*, etc.), and the tenses of finite verbs. The meaning of the sentence *President Yeltsin spoke to the Queen on 3 March 1996* is independent of the speech context. The sentence *you are speaking here now*, on the other hand, merely states that the person addressed is talking at the same place and point in time as the speaker. Its full meaning can be deduced only from the specific context.

Demonstrative pronoun	A pronoun allowing the reference to extra-linguistic or textual contexts. The most important demonstrative pronouns of present-day English are *this/these* and *that/those*. *This woman* refers to a woman close to the speaker, *that woman* to a woman positioned further away. Metaphorically, distance may come to express a negative evaluation.
Denotation	Denotation refers to the "objective" meaning of a word or expression for the person(s), object(s), concept(s) or attribute(s) it may refer to in some segment of extra-linguistic reality. *Connotation*, on the other hand, refers to the "subjective" aspects of meaning such as the stylistic level or the emotional associations of a word. Both *he's gay* and *he's queer* denote the same sexual preference; only the latter expression, however, carries a pejorative undertone or connotation.
Derivation	A word-formation process where a new word is created by adding at least one bound derivational → *morpheme* to the base; cf. *dress* → *undress*, *think* → *thinkable* → *unthinkable*. → *inflection, morphology, word-formation*.
Determiner	→ *pronoun*.
Diachronic	The historical analysis of linguistic facts → *synchronic*.
Dialect	A regionally specific variety of a language differing from the standard language in terms of pronunciation, grammar, and lexis. If the deviation affects only pronunciation, the term (*regional*) → *accent* is used.
Diphthong	A vowel sound which changes its quality, e.g. from /a/ to /ʊ/ as in /aʊ/; *monophthongs* do not change their quality during articulation (e.g. /u:/).
Discourse	1) A synonym for "text"; 2) situation-specific communication, e.g. "classroom discourse"; 3) the generic term for speech conventions which are socially and historically typical of an era, e.g. "the nationalist discourse in post-communist Eastern Europe".
Dissimilation	A sound change where the same or similar sounds become different, e.g. /r/ becomes /l/ as in *pilgrim* or *marble* (from Latin *peregrinus* and Middle English/Old French *marbre*).
Distinctive feature	A limited number of features used in the description and distinction of phonemes. The phoneme /t/, for example, can be described as the set of the distinctive features "stop", "voiceless", and "alveolar place of articulation"; other phonemes differ from /t/ in terms of one or several characteristics: /d/, for example, with respect to voicing, /p/ with respect to the place of articulation, and /b/ with respect to both voicing and place of articulation. If all universally valid distinctive features – a limited and in fact rather small number – are agreed on, it is possible to describe the sound systems of all natural languages in a very economical way.
Dysphemism	→ *euphemism*.
Elicitation	Collection of primary language data by questioning informants. Elicitation techniques vary from informal interviews with a single informant to systematic test series with statistically representative random samples of informants.
Error Analysis	A branch of applied linguistics which uses the analysis of learners' errors as the basis for investigating foreign language acquisition.
Etymology	A sub-discipline of historical linguistics concerned with the origin of words and the change of their meanings. From the etymological point of view, the present-day English word *daisy*, for example, is an amalgamated compound (Middle English *daies eye* "day's eye"). The most authoritative source of reference for English etymology is the *Oxford English Dictionary* (OED), which aims to document the entire vocabulary of present-day English from the earliest attestation of a word to the present with detailed attention to all recorded changes in meaning.
Euphemism	A pleasant-sounding and positive substitutive term for a potentially offensive word, e.g. *pass away* instead of *die*. Opposite: *dysphemism*, e.g. *croak* instead of *die*.
Final devoicing	Voiced consonants such as [b] or [z] are devoiced in German when they occur word-finally or syllable-finally (cf. the pronunciation of *rauben* and *Raub* or *Gräser* und *Gras*). In English, on the other hand, voicing is distinctive also in word-final position (cf. minimal pairs like *cap/cab*, *tap/tab*, *rack/rag*, *rice/*

Glossary

rise, rich/ridge). The mistaken transfer of final devoicing from German to English is one of the most characteristic features of a German accent.

A verb form agreeing in person and number with a subject or signalling grammatical tense, e.g. *she **lives** here* or *she **lived** here*. In compound tense forms such as *she **has been** living here*, the first verb is finite, the others are non-finite. In English, modal verbs are always finite → *non-finite verb form*. **Finite verb form**

The semantic or morphological analysis of a word which, historically, is unsustainable. The word *penthouse*, for example, goes back to *appendix* (albeit through several intermediate stages); the analysis of the last syllable as *-house* is a later folk etymological interpretation by speakers who were no longer aware of the connection between *penthouse* and *appendix*. **Folk/popular etymology**

→ *functionalism*. **Formalism**

A word which, having lost its specific lexical meaning, has come to serve to express grammatical relations within a sentence. The preposition *to* in *come to me*, for example, is not a function word because it describes the direction of movement. In *scholars attribute the painting to Giotto*, on the other hand, *to* is a function word because here it no longer expresses a direction of movement but merely serves to mark the following noun as an object. The importance of function words in English has increased since the decline of noun → *inflection*. **Function word**

A model developed to describe the information structure of a sentence. Sentences are split into the "theme/topic" and the "rheme/comment". The "theme" provides known, contextually given or otherwise lower-order information, whereas the "rheme" provides new or higher-order information. The typical sequence is "theme" before "rheme", as exemplified by the second sentence of the following text: *I went to visit the town's museum. It had been built in the middle of a spacious park*. Note that if we place the rheme before the theme in the second sentence, stylistic oddity results: *I went to visit the town's museum. In the middle of a spacious park it had been built*. **Functional sentence perspective/FSP**

The collective name for linguistic schools of thought which argue that grammatical form is wholly or partly shaped by meaning/semantics and speakers' communicative needs/pragmatics. On such a view, the important feature of the grammatical category "subject", for example, is not that it agrees with the predicate in number but that it usually expresses the semantic role "agent" and the pragmatic-textual function of "theme." Functionalism is opposed to *formalism*. The central tenet of formalism is that natural language grammars function as autonomous formal systems. **Functionalism**

The branch of linguistics which, in contrast to the study of individual languages such as German or English, is primarily concerned with the study of the similarities among human languages and the properties of human language in general. **General/theoretical linguistics**

A theory of grammar, developed by Noam Chomsky, whose major tenet is that the grammars of natural languages are formal systems. **Generative grammar**

A non-finite English verb form which – like the present participle – is formed by adding the suffix *-ing* to the base of the verb. Some *gerund*-constructions, such as *the hunting of rare animals*, can be analysed as complex noun phrases – *hunting* is pre-modified by the definite article and post-modified by a prepositional phrase. Other gerunds can be considered as clauses with a verb, e.g. *he strongly objects to tourists hunting rare animals*. This *gerund*-construction can be interpreted as a clause in which *tourists* functions as the subject and *rare animals* as the object. Note that such clausal gerunds may have a passive variant: *he strongly objects to rare animals being hunted*. As the modern English present participle also ends in *-ing*, further issues of demarcation arise. **Gerund**

Vowels are articulated without, consonants with an obstruction of the air flow (e.g. by occlusion or friction). The glides/semi-vowels [w] and [j] are borderline cases which do not fit either classification. **Glide, semi-vowel**

The description of structural rules for combining words into → *constituents* and clauses. Grammar encompasses the grammatical component of word-formation (*inflectional morphology*) as well as *syntax*. Basically, all languages use the same four strategies – albeit to different degrees – to express grammatical relations: 1) inflection, 2) constituent or word order, 3) function words, and 4) intonation → *syntax*. **Grammar**

247

Hendiadys	A stylistic device where two nouns linked by *and* are used instead of a more common "adjective + noun"-combination, e.g. *in iron and chains* instead of *in iron chains*. In the broader sense also used for similar kinds of intensification by means of duplication, e.g. *the room was nice and warm* (instead of *nicely warm*).
Historical-comparative linguistics	The branch of linguistics concerned with the reconstruction of older states of languages and the study of the relationship among languages which have developed from a common source. The study of Indo-European is the most advanced branch of historical-comparative linguistics, partly because linguists have studied this family of languages longest and partly because the documentary evidence is richest.
Homography	Words which are spelled the same but have a different pronunciation and different meanings, e.g. *tear* ("rip" [tɛə] and "a drop of the clear salty liquid produced by the lachrymal gland of the eye" [tɪə]).
Homonymy	Words which are spelled and pronounced in the same way but have different meanings, e.g. *ear* ("organ of hearing" and "part of a cereal plant"). Cf. also → *polysemy*.
Homophony	Words which have the same pronunciation but different meanings and spelling, e.g. *pain* and *pane*.
Hypercorrection	In foreign-language learning research and contrastive linguistics, the tendency of learners to make excessive use of structures which are identified as typical of the foreign language; e.g. *[weɪɪ] for [veɪɪ]. In sociolinguistics, hypercorrection occurs when prestigious structures are over-represented or used in inappropriate contexts. As some speakers believe that the form *me* in *he's more interested in soccer than me* is incorrect and should be replaced by *I*, hypercorrect expressions such as *she gave it to my wife and I* can occur. The prestigious form *I* is thus also used in cases where it is impossible according to grammatical rules.
Hyperonym and hyponym	Super- and subordinate terms; *fruit* is the hyperonym of *apple*, *apple* is the hyponym of *fruit*.
Idiom	→ *collocation*.
Idiomatic	Those restrictions on the combinability of words which are neither logically nor grammatically motivated. An example is the English expression *to summon* (or *pluck up*) *courage* (cf. German *Mut fassen*), although theoretically a number of different verbs could combine with the noun. Because of their multitude and lack of systematicity, idiomatic restrictions present a major problem for foreign language learning and teaching → *collocation*.
Implication	One statement implies another statement if the latter can be deduced from the former. In contrast to *I asked him to stop smoking*, *I forced him to stop smoking* entails that "he" did indeed stop smoking – the verb *force*, unlike the verb *ask*, implies that the action described in the subordinate clause actually takes place.
Implicature	If, on the basis of existing speech conventions, an utterance conveys meaning beyond its literal denotation, this is referred to as *implicature*. The expression *have you got a watch?* will usually be interpreted as a – somewhat impolite – variant of *could you tell me the time?*, not as a question about the actual ownership of a watch.
Infinitive	A non-finite verb form which, in English, is identical to the base and which is introduced by *to*, *in order to* or *so as to* in specific syntactic contexts.
Inflection, inflexion	In both Latin and German, nouns, adjectives, pronouns, articles, verbs, and sometimes also adverbs have grammatical (= inflectional) endings in order to express grammatical relations within a sentence. In the case of nouns, pronouns, articles, and adjectives, inflection is called *declension*, in the case of verbs, *conjugation*. Present-day English nouns are inflected only for plural and genitive. For some pronouns, an "object case" is relevant (e.g. *them* versus *they*). Further inflectional endings are present tense *-s* for the third person singular and *-ed* for *past tense* and *past participle* of verbs. For the comparison of most mono- and some disyllabic adjectives, inflectional endings are used as well (e.g. *simple, simpler, simplest*) → *morphology*.
Interference	The influence of native-language competence which leads to errors in the foreign language, also called "negative transfer". In **I have met her only yesterday*, modelled on German *ich habe sie erst gestern*

Glossary

getroffen, similarity of use is mistakenly inferred from the similarity of tense forms. In sociolinguistics and dialectology, the term is occasionally used in the broader sense to describe the influence of foreign languages on language use in language contact situations.

Intonation Pitch movement in spoken utterances. A common way to analyse intonation is to split utterances into *tone groups*, which are arranged around an accented syllable (*nucleus, head*). The most important criteria for classifying tone groups are *pitch range*, relative *height*, and the progression of *pitch movement*. The major types of tone groups in English intonation are *fall, rise, fall-rise* and *rise-fall*. On the one hand, intonation has grammatical function – e.g. marking a question by rising pitch height –; on the other hand, it can be used in an expressive and rhetorical way and also in order to structure a text. Languages like Chinese, where the pitch range is distinctive lexically (i.e. where two phoneme sequences have different meanings depending on the pitch range) are called tone languages. Intonation and → *stress* are the major objects of investigation in suprasegmental phonology (suprasegmental: extending beyond the individual sound segment or phoneme).

Intransitive Verbs without objects or predicative complements, e.g. *I'm sleeping*. Many verbs can be used both transitively and intransitively (e.g. *I'm surviving* vs. *I barely survived the accident*), although the meaning can change.

Introspection Descriptive linguistic data are obtained and investigated by resorting to one's own native-language intuition.

Isogloss A line drawn on a map marking the spread of a dialect feature. When several isoglosses fall together in one place, a dialect boundary emerges which is often noticeable also for non-linguists.

Langue (French "language"): According to Ferdinand de Saussure, the linguistic system of a specific speech community, in contrast to its realisation in individual speech acts (*parole*) or the general human capacity of speech which goes beyond individual languages (*langage*). According to de Saussure, *langue* is the true object of analysis of linguistics.

Lexeme A linguistic term formed in analogy to → *phoneme* and → *morpheme* which designates the smallest distinctive unit of a language's vocabulary. The term lexeme, although usually used synonymously with the more common *word*, sometimes allows a more precise linguistic description. The words *good, well*, and *better*, for example, can be described as different realisations of a single abstract lexeme.

Lexical field A number of partly synonymous words which define each other mutually and which, when taken together, cover an entire conceptual/semantic area. The meaning of a specific lexeme thus does not always have to be defined by the link to an extra-linguistic referent. An example of a lexical field is the English verbs for laughter/smiling: *smile, grin, sneer, snigger, snicker, laugh, guffaw*, etc.

Lexico-grammar A term going back to the linguist M.A.K. Halliday intended to make clear that the boundary between the lexicon and the grammar of a language may be clear in theory but will usually be fluid in the data.

Lexicography A branch of applied linguistics concerned with designing and producing dictionaries. Although lexicography and → *lexicology* have much in common, lexicography is more practically oriented and deals with problems going beyond purely linguistic aspects (e.g. criteria concerning the selection of dictionary entries, the order of different meanings of polysemous entries, etc.).

Lexicology The description of a language's vocabulary and its inherent structure.

Linguistic sign The nature of the linguistic sign is to assign meaning (*signifié* according to de Saussure) to sounds (*signifiant* according to de Saussure). Such sound-meaning pairings are arbitrary, i.e. there is no causal relation between the sound sequence /haʊs/ and the meaning "building consisting of several floors accommodating people". Once the match between sound and meaning is established in a language, it becomes obligatory for the members of the respective speech community.

Linguistic universal An element or structural principle present in all languages of the world; *implicational universals* are formulated as "if-then" statements, such as the following: "If, in a specific language, the demonstrative pronoun follows the noun, then also the relative clause follows the noun" – a generalisation which has not been disproved so far. Until proven otherwise, languages in which the relative clause precedes the noun while the demonstrative pronoun follows it must be considered impossible. (The other three logically possible constellations are all attested → *universals*.)

249

Glossary of linguistic terms

Linguistic variation This term captures the fact that all living languages are variable – diachronically with time, or synchronically according to a speaker's social or regional origin, other types of group membership, or the communicative situation.

Linguistics The scientific description of natural languages. Essential research areas are *historical-comparative linguistics* – often called → *diachronic linguistics* or, if literary problems are addressed additionally, *philology* – and → *synchronic-descriptive linguistics*. Diachronic linguistics investigates the history of languages and historical relationships among languages deriving from a common source. In synchronic linguistics, languages are viewed independently from their historical development and described as structural systems at a specific point in time. Further linguistic sub-disciplines are concerned with regional and social variation (*dialectology* and *sociolinguistics*) or the link between language, cognition and the physiological activity of the brain (*psycholinguistics*).

Main clause → *sentence*.

Manner of articulation One of the most important criteria for classifying sounds (in combination with the → *place of articulation*). A vowel is produced if the air flows freely; if the air flow is obstructed, a consonant is produced. Depending on how the air flow is obstructed, consonants are classified into *stops, fricatives, nasals,* and further subgroups.

Markedness Structural oppositions in language are often not symmetrical: one member of a pair is treated as neutral, whereas choice of the other needs specific motivation. Thus, the question *how tall is she?* is open, whereas *how short is she?* implies that she is shorter than average or than expected. By the same token, active verb phrases can be considered as unmarked, whereas there needs to be a special motivation for the use of the passive. Unmarked members of a pair of structural oppositions are usually morphologically simple, frequent in discourse and common cross-linguistically, whereas marked categories are morphologically more complex, less frequent in discourse and rare across the languages of the world.

Maxim of conversation The philosopher H. P. Grice (1913–1988) assumes that we are guided by a fundamentally co-operative mindset in communication and conversation, both when we formulate our own utterances and when we interpret the utterances of others. His four maxims claim to spell out the basic co-ordinates of this mindset. The *maxim of quality* states that we only claim what we believe to be true or what we have sufficient proof for. The *maxim of quantity* controls the amount of information. We use as much information as the particular context requires, and neither more nor less. Thus, a typical answer to the question "what time is it?" would be "a quarter past two," but not "evening" or "three o'clock, three minutes, twelve seconds and nineteen milliseconds". Further maxims are the *maxim of relevance* and the *maxim of manner*.

Metaphor The transfer of meaning – an expression is used in a context in which its literal meaning does not apply, e. g. *this crime cries out for revenge* or German *schreiendes Unrecht*. Recent research in cognitive linguistics has emphasised the fact that metaphor is not just verbal ornament but central to human language at all levels. For example, expressions of time routinely involve metaphors based on space (*long time, face an uncertain future*), and talk about emotions and cognition involves metaphors based on the human body (*the news upset me; I'm feeling down; can't you see my point?*).

Metonymy A term is substituted by a part or an attribute of it, e. g. *we are several hands short* (instead of *we are several workers short*).

Middle English The English language from the end of the 11th century to c. 1500.

Minimal pair Two words with different meanings varying in no more than one sound; e. g. *cat – mat*. Cf. → *phoneme*.

Modality The linguistic expression of degrees of probability and obligation/permission. In English, modality is primarily expressed by means of modal verbs, but also by adverbs and other constructions. Examples expressing probability are *she may be asleep, probably she's asleep, chances are she's asleep*; *you must wait* and *you're obliged to wait* are examples expressing obligation.

Monophthong → *diphthong*.

Morpheme The smallest linguistic unit carrying meaning. A distinction is made between free morphemes on the one hand, and bound (inflectional and derivational) morphemes on the other. The word *weaknesses*, for

example, consists of a combination of three meaningful elements – the free morpheme {weak}, the bound derivational morpheme {-ness} and the bound inflectional morpheme {-es} expressing the grammatical category "plural". If the addition of bound morphemes to the base causes a different pronunciation (e.g. *delete/deletion*), "morpho-phonological" processes are at work.	
The branch of linguistics concerned with describing the structure of words, generally separated into → *inflection* and → *word-formation*.	**Morphology**
A vowel or consonant which, due to the lowered position of the soft palate, is produced with all or some of the air flow escaping through the nose.	**Nasal**
A new word in a language.	**Neologism**
Verb forms which are not inflected for tense and person; cf. → *gerund*, → *infinitive*, → *participle*. Non-finite verb forms are necessary for compound verb phrases (*is **singing**, has **done***), they may modify nouns (*a **sleeping** child*) or function as the verbal nucleus of non-finite subordinate clauses (*I hate **people** interfering with me*) → *finite verb form*.	**Non-finite verb form**
→ *restrictive relative clause*.	**Non-restrictive/non-defining relative clause**
In the narrow sense, the standard form of a language as codified in reference grammars and dictionaries and as used by educated speakers in formal written and spoken language use. In the broader sense, the language form appropriate in a specific context or communicative situation.	**Norm**
In English, *noun* denotes a part of speech which can be modified by articles, determiners and adjectives. Most nouns have a plural and many can be used in the genitive. Grammatically important distinctions are between (1) **proper** nouns (*Roger, Smith, Xerox, ...*) and **common** nouns (*girl, book, glory, ...*), (2) **concrete** nouns (*book, cup, ...*) and **abstract** nouns (*glory, shame, ...*), and – (3) finally – **count** nouns (*berry – berries, story – stories, ...*) and **mass** nouns (*water, advice, furniture, ...*), which in all or some of their senses have no plural. Multiple membership is common: thus, *glass* in the "container" sense is a count-noun ("two glasses of beer"), whereas *glass* in its "material" sense is a mass noun ("made of expensive crystal glass").	**Noun**
A syntactic structure with a noun as its head or nucleus; e.g. *my new coat, a recently retired friend of mine, the new one* (where *one*, a so-called *prop-word*, forms the nucleus); noun phrases can also be realised by → *pronouns*.	**Noun phrase**
The core of a tone group, i.e. the stressed syllable where pitch movement sets in, e.g. *SEEN* in *I've never even SEEN him*.	**Nucleus**
A grammatical category of noun and verb inflection, distinguishing between *singular* and *plural*: e.g. *one book – several books; she sing**s** – they sing*.	**Number**
A constituent complementing a transitive verb. If a verb has two objects, a distinction is made between *direct* (directly affected by the action) and *indirect* object (indirectly affected by the action, e.g. as beneficiary or injured party), e.g. *I bought my daughter* [indirect object] *a tricycle* [direct object]. Formally, objects can be realised as noun phrases, prepositional phrases (= prepositional objects), or non-finite or finite subordinate clauses: *he asked me, he asked for help, he asked me to help him, he asked that I should help him* → *subject*.	**Object**
The English language from its beginnings in the sixth century to c. 1100.	**Old English, Anglo-Saxon**
A type of semantic analysis starting from real-world objects or situations and studying the lexical concepts used to refer to them or talk about them. The reverse procedure – starting from the study of linguistic concepts and then moving on to real-world referents – is called *semasiological*.	**Onomasiological**
A rule-governed pattern is extended and used in inappropriate contexts; over-generalisation is a typical feature of child language (cf. **goed* instead of *went*) and of foreign learners' language (**I avoid to eat that* instead of *I avoid eating that*).	**Over-generalisation**

Part of speech	The traditional classification of words as nouns, adjectives, pronouns, articles, verbs, adverbs, prepositions, and conjunctions has been in use since antiquity. This classification is based on a number of formal and semantic, but partly intuitive criteria. Although specific parts of speech, e. g. numerals, elude a clear-cut categorisation, the main features of the traditional classificatory system are still accepted.
Passive (voice)	A clause with a transitive verb can be turned into the passive by changing the verb form and making the object of the active verb the subject of the passive sentence. Cf. e. g. *the soldiers burned the house* → *the house was burned by the soldiers*.
Performance	→ *competence*.
Philology	In the broader sense, the scholarly analysis of the language and literature of a specific cultural area (e. g. English philology, Romance philology); in the narrow sense, studies based on detailed linguistic analyses of written – mainly medieval and/or literary – texts. Specific interests of philology go beyond the purely linguistic domain (e. g. editing texts, the study of handwriting styles in manuscripts, and the like). In English, the expression *historical-comparative philology* is frequently used synonymously with *historical-comparative/Indo-European linguistics*.
Phoneme	A sound which distinguishes meaning. By means of minimal pairs (e. g. *cat – mat*), it is possible to establish whether two sounds have phonemic status in a given language. Cf. also → *allophone*.
Phonetic transcription	A system of writing in which each sound is unambiguously assigned no more than one character, making possible the precise representation of an utterance's phonetic form. Our standard orthographies are unsuitable for this purpose, as they usually preserve older stages of pronunciation. In addition, the letters of the Latin alphabet are not sufficient for recording all relevant sound differences in many languages. The most widely used phonetic alphabet is that of the *International Phonetic Association* (IPA).
Phonetics	The description of the sounds of human language as physical phenomena, aided by technical recording devices and analytical methods from the natural sciences. There are three different approaches – *articulatory phonetics* studies sound production; *acoustic phonetics* is concerned with measuring sound, and *auditory phonetics* addresses the perception of sound on the hearer's part.
Phonology	The description of the sounds of human language as the smallest units of a particular system. The focus is on a sound's ability to distinguish meaning within the linguistic system (→ *phoneme*) and not on its precise physical description.
Phonotactics	The description of possible phoneme combinations occurring in a language. In both English and German, for example, the sound sequence /sr/ does not occur word-initially.
Phrasal verb	A verb category prolific in English consisting of a verb and one or two prepositions or adverbial particles, e. g. *to put (someone) up* (= "accommodate") or *put up with (someone/something)* (= "tolerate"). In contrast to verb-preposition/adverb sequences which are only loosely connected, "real" phrasal verbs behave like a single lexical unit when submitted to syntactic tests; cf. *I ran down the hill/*the hill was run down by me* versus *the car ran down the cyclist/the cyclist was run down by the car* where *run down* behaves like the one-word verb *hit*.
Phrase	Any grammatical structure larger than the word and smaller than a clause → *constituent*.
Phraseologism	The collective name for multi-word lexemes (e. g. *take advantage of*, *difficult-to-use* [as in *a difficult-to-use dictionary*]), established collocations (e. g. *need something badly*), and fixed phrases (e. g. *to face the music*) → *collocations, idiomatic*.
Pidgin	An improvised and structurally reduced contact language used for basic communication in multilingual settings → *creole*.
Pitch movement	A criterion to classify tone groups; pitch movement sets in with the syllable carrying the main stress.
Place of articulation	In conjunction with → *manner of articulation* one of the most important criteria for classifying sounds. Vowels are primarily classified according to the position of the tongue. As for consonants, the place of articulation indicates the position in the oral cavity where the air flow is obstructed. In English, the places of articulation are *labial* (with both lips), *labio-dental* (lower lip at the upper row of teeth), *dental* (tongue at the upper row of teeth), *(post-) alveolar* (tongue at or just behind the teeth-ridge), *palatal* (at the hard

Glossary

palate), *velar* (at the soft palate), and *uvular* (at the uvula). The so-called *glottal stop* is articulated in the glottis.

→ *number*. — **Plural**

A special case of semantic ambiguity. Polysemy occurs when the various meanings of a single word can be derived from each other or when they go back to a common component; e.g. *glass* (= name of a substance, "drinking-vessel", "binoculars"). → *Homonymy* occurs if two unconnected meanings are represented by the same sounds (e.g. *can* "be able", "metal container"). Although this distinction is reasonable in theory, in practice, it is not unambiguously applicable. — **Polysemy**

The linguistic sub-discipline concerned with analysing the rule-governed aspects of language use. — **Pragmatics**

The verbal core of a sentence. The sentence *the caretakers have been able to find you a chair* can be split into two immediate constituents, viz. the noun phrase *the caretakers* and the verb phrase *have been able to find you a chair*. Some linguists call this verb phrase, consisting of the verb and its complements, the predicate. The present book, in line with many other descriptions of present-day English, reserves the term *predicate* for the verbal core of the verb phrase – in the present example *have been able to find* → *verb, verb phrase*. — **Predicate**

In contrast to an object, a predicative complement does not introduce a new participant in the verbal action, but specifies an existing one. A distinction is made between *subject complements* – e.g. *they are fools, they are stupid* – and *object complements* – e.g. *she called him a fool, she called them stupid*. — **Predicative complement**

→ *affix*. — **Prefix**

A part of speech used to mark the relationship between verbal or adjectival predicate and noun phrases and between component noun phrases of a complex noun phrase: *I depend **on** you **for** help, I'm keen **on** sports, uncertainty **about** the future **of** higher education **in** this country*. Typical prepositions are *at, on, in*; an example of a compound preposition is *in spite of*. Contrary to their name, some "pre"-positions follow their reference word (*hours ago*) or surround it (*for heaven's sake*). — **Preposition**

A syntactic structure introduced by a preposition, e.g. *into trouble* or *after several hours of waiting*. Typically, prepositional phrases function as objects (*talk to you*) or adverbials (*leave because of the noise*), or serve to modify nouns (*a book about Ireland*). — **Prepositional phrase**

The aim of a prescriptive grammar is not the description of actual language use, but the formulation of rules for "good" language use, i.e. speech and writing in accordance with the educated, prestigious standard. An example of a prescriptive rule in English is the recommendation to use the genitive or possessive with gerunds functioning as objects: *do you mind **my** smoking/**your wife's** smoking?* – rather than the object or common case: *do you mind **me** smoking/**my wife** smoking?* The latter option is of course in common use among English native speakers and would therefore be accepted as normal in a descriptive grammar. — **Prescriptive**

The term *productive* refers to those word-formation patterns which still give rise to new forms, such as, for example, the derivation of adjectives from verbs by means of the morpheme *-able* (cf. *to xerox* → *xeroxable*). The word-formation pattern [adjective + morpheme *-th* → noun (*warm* → *warmth*)], on the other hand, is no longer productive, even though such words are still transparent as derivations. The productivity of morphological processes is subject to many constraints and therefore very much a matter of degree. — **Productivity**

A part of speech including all elements which can take the place of noun phrases or refer to them, i.e. *personal pronouns, interrogative pronouns* (e.g. *who, what, why*, etc.), *demonstrative pronouns, possessive pronouns, reflexive pronouns* (e.g. *myself*, etc.), *indefinite pronouns* (e.g. *somebody/someone*), and *relative pronouns*. Elements which do not replace the entire noun phrase but are part of it – such as the possessive pronoun *my* in *my car* or the indefinite pronoun *any* in *at any price* – are usually called *determiners* rather than *pronouns* in recent English grammars. Forms replacing or repeating constituents which extend beyond a noun phrase – such as *do so* in *everybody else has finished their papers, and you should do so, too* – are called *pro-forms*. — **Pronoun**

Prosody	Cover term used in (suprasegmental) phonology to refer to variations in pitch/intonation, loudness and rhythm.
Prototype semantics	A semantic prototype is a typical representative, or ideal cognitive model, of a class of objects to which a term refers. An apple, but not a tomato, would be prototypical of the category *fruit*. Prototype semantics is opposed to structural semantics, which assumes that the meaning of words can be described by decomposing a complex meaning into its constituent features.
Raising/fused construction	Complex sentence structures in which the clause boundary is blurred because the grammatical status of one constituent is ambiguous. For example, in *I'd hate my children to see me there*, the noun phrase *my children* could be regarded as the object of the verb *hate*, as it is in the proper object position and could be replaced by the object form of the pronoun (*them*). Semantically and logically, though, *my children* belongs into the subordinate clause, as a kind of implicit subject or agent, for clearly the sentence does not imply that "I'd hate my children" (SVO), but is roughly equivalent to "I'd hate it if my children saw me there." Speaking metaphorically, we could say that a constituent of the subordinate clause has been extracted from its clause and raised into the superordinate one. Other common types of raising constructions in present-day English are illustrated by *she seems to be innocent* (cf. *it seems that she is innocent*) and *this book is difficult to translate* (cf. *it is difficult to translate this book*). Depending on the theoretical framework, more specific terms are used to refer to some or all such constructions, such as *ECM* (= empty case marking) *constructions* in some versions of Chomskyan generative grammar.
Received Pronunciation (R. P.)	The national pronunciation standard of British English which historically developed in the Southeast of England. Today, it is no longer tied to a specific locality and dominant in England and Wales. In addition, it is one of the two important reference accents in foreign-language teaching. Note that R. P. identifies a pronunciation standard only. To refer to standard grammar and vocabulary, the term *standard English* is used. Although R. P. pronunciation usually goes with vocabulary and grammar that is standard English, the reverse does not hold – standard English can be pronounced with accents other than an R. P. one, for example a Scottish or an Irish English one → *standard, Standard American English*.
Reference	The relationship between the linguistic expression and the object it denotes.
Regional accent	A regionally specific pronunciation of a language; not restricted to genuine regional → *dialects* but also commonly encountered in varieties which are close to the standard in vocabulary and grammar → *accent*.
Register	A variety of language determined by the communicative situation or domain, e.g. "informal/conversational English" or "the English of cricket reportage".
Relative clause	A subordinate clause which does not depend on a super-ordinate verb or clause but specifies a nominal head, e.g. *whom you talked to* in *the man whom you talked to*. Finite relative clauses are usually introduced by relative pronouns (*who/which, that*). In English, non-finite relative clauses are common, such as *toys for children to play with* (= "toys that children can play with").
Restrictive/defining relative clause	A relative clause defining the number or type of objects to which the preceding noun refers. Thus, in *all those students who wish to take the final exam this year* the relative clause singles out a specific subgroup of students from the total. This is different in non-restrictive relative clauses: cf. *my wife, who is a historian* (i.e. in a monogamous marriage, *my wife* refers unambiguously to a specific person, and *who is a historian* is additional information). In English, restrictive and non-restrictive relative clauses can be distinguished by means of intonation, punctuation and a number of grammatical properties.
Rheme	→ *functional sentence perspective, theme*.
Semantics	A sub-discipline of linguistics concerned with the description of word meaning and contextually independent aspects of sentence meaning.
Semasiological	→ *onomasiological*.
Semiotics	The study of how meaning is generated and conveyed by means of sign systems. Linguistics deals with the most complex of all human sign systems, thus representing the core area of semiotics. In principle, however, any system of conventional signs – graphic symbols, fashion, or hairstyles – can be the object of semiotic analysis. Fashion statements, for example, hold a message, too.

Glossary

In English, it is useful to distinguish systematically between the terms *sentence* and *clause*. *Sentence* is a commonly used term which is usually not specific enough for linguistic analysis. In linguistics, particularly in grammatical analysis, the term *clause* is preferred to denote a single grammatical unit with a verbal core. A *simple sentence* is a clause with a single verbal core. *Compound sentences* are sentences consisting of two or more clauses in co-ordination; *complex sentences* are sentences with at least one dependent clause (= *embedded clause, subordinate clause*). The following examples illustrate the three sentence types in the order of mention: 1) *I'm falling asleep*, 2) *I'm slaving away, but he's sitting in front of the stupid box*, 3) *while I'm slaving away, he's sitting in front of the stupid box* (with sub-ordinate clause followed by main clause) or *I would like you to persuade her to join us for dinner tonight* (with the main clause followed by two embedded non-finite object clauses).	**Sentence, clause**
→ *number*.	**Singular**
A linguistic structure with two or more realisations which correlate with speakers' social status. In New York City, for example, the social variable "post-vocalic /r/" has two variants – [r] and [zero] – which correlate with middle-class/educated and working-class/vernacular usage, respectively.	**Social variable**
A linguistic variety specific to a social class or group. The systematic distinction between regional varieties (dialects) and social varieties (sociolects) may be reasonable from a pedagogical point of view. In practice, however, a sharp differentiation is not always feasible because many, particularly urban, dialects are avoided by middle and upper class speakers resident in a region.	**Sociolect**
In the narrow sense, the branch of linguistics studying quantitative-statistical correlations between independent social variables such as social class, ethnic or regional background and dependent linguistic variables (sounds, grammatical forms and constructions, words), as pioneered by William Labov. In a wider sense, any enquiry into the role of language in social life.	**Sociolinguistics**
In German and English, speech rhythm is primarily based on the sequence of stressed and unstressed syllables.	**Speech rhythm**
The prestigious norm of a language which is codified in reference grammars and dictionaries, propagated in the educational system, used in public and in the media on formal occasions, and taught to foreign learners. The standard is the dominant variety in writing; spoken usage is not subject to standardisation to the same extent.	**Standard**
The prestige norm of American English, spread by the media and geographically mobile educated speakers. It differs from British standard English minimally in grammar, more in vocabulary, but most in pronunciation. In addition to standard British English (with an R.P. pronunciation), standard American English is the second major reference standard in foreign-language teaching.	**Standard American English**
In contrast to variable sentence stress, which is based on considerations of emphasis and information structure (cf. *shé is talking to you* versus *she is talking to yóu*), word stress is usually fixed for polysyllabic words. Thus, the English word *category* is stressed on the first syllable in all cases. English, like the other Germanic languages, tends to stress the base syllable (*stánd, understánd, understándable, understánding*). Owing to an extensive history of language contact and borrowing from French and Latin, however, word-final (*políce, devóut*) and movable stress (*phótograph, photográphic, photógrapher*) is commonly found, as well.	**Stress**
In the tradition of literary criticism, the characteristic way in which the language is used in a particular text or by a particular author. In linguistics, style is usually defined as speech appropriate to a particular communicative domain (e.g. formal versus colloquial/informal style).	**Style**
In both German and English, the only complement of intransitive verbs and a necessary complement of others. The subject agrees with the predicate in number (*he takes – they take*) and is used in the nominative case (which in English affects only the personal pronouns). In semantic terms, the subject is associated with the role of *agent*, although not every grammatical subject has to express the role of semantic agent → *object*.	**Subject**
A subject that is realised as a finite or non-finite subordinate clause: *that he has apologised is gratifying*; *to realise my mistake took me some time*. Long constituents being rich in informational content, most	**Subject clause**

subject clauses are positioned clause-finally, which is commonly referred to as *extraposition*: *it is gratifying that he has apologised, it took me some time to realise my mistake.*

Subjunctive An inflectional category of the verb contrasting with the indicative ("form of reality") and imperative ("form of command"). In present-day English, the subjunctive occurs only in few constructions. (1) expressing wishes, particularly in certain slightly archaic and frequently fossilised phrases (*God save the Queen!*), (2) the past subjunctive, restricted to the verb *be* (*if I were you* ... besides the indicative *if I was you* ...), and (3) the present "mandative" subjunctive after verbs and adjectives expressing degrees of necessity or desire (*they demand that we be prepared*). In English as well as in German, the subjunctive is frequently paraphrased analytically, by means of modal verbs: *sie verlangen, dass wir vorbereitet sein sollen/ they demand that we should be prepared.*

Subordinate clause → *sentence*.

Substandard A regional or social variety of a language which deviates from the standard; also called *non-standard* if no valuation is intended.

Substitution test A grammatical test procedure intended to identify the status of a structure by replacing it by a simpler structure, e.g. *I hate people messing with me* → *I hate that*; as *people messing with me* can be replaced by *that*, it functions as an object.

Substrate A contact language whose speakers are in a socially subordinate position. If speakers of this language shift to the dominant language, a variety may develop which preserves substrate influences. This is likely for Irish English, which displays many features which can best be accounted for as influence from Irish Gaelic. A contact language with a higher social standing is called a *superstrate*. Most modern European languages, for example, have been affected by Latin as a superstrate. An *adstrate* has the same social status as its contact language.

Suffix → *affix*.

Syllabic consonant Although most syllables have a vowel nucleus, consonants can sometimes be syllabic, too, e.g. /l/ in *simple*.

Synchronic A linguistic approach which describes languages as functioning systems at a specific point in time; the opposite to → *diachronic*. The distinction between synchronic and diachronic approaches to the study of language was first explicitly made by Ferdinand de Saussure.

Synonym Words with the same meaning are called synonyms. Total synonymy does not usually occur in natural languages; synonymy is thus partial, with a core meaning being shared and each term differing in minor ways, or in emotional and stylistic connotation, as in *loneliness* versus *solitude*.

Syntax The study of the grammatical relations of words and constituents within a sentence. Essentially, all languages use four strategies to express syntactic relations: 1) inflection, 2) constituent or word order, 3) function words, and 4) intonation. Different languages use these strategies to different degrees → *grammar*.

Synthetic → *analytical*.

Tense A grammatical category of the verb relating it to situation-external time. The connection between the grammatical tenses and the three psychologically relevant temporal dimensions ("past", "present/now", "future") is far from clear-cut. One only needs to consider that both German and English have more than three tenses at their disposal.

Text In the narrow sense, a coherent written linguistic utterance of varying length; in the broader sense, the term can also be used for coherent spoken utterances or discourse sequences → *textlinguistics*.

Text type A category of texts distinct from other texts due to specific linguistic and functional features, e.g. weather reports or conversations between doctors and patients.

Textlinguistics/ discourse analysis A linguistic sub-discipline concerned with the description of linguistic structures which extend beyond the sentence level → *discourse, coherence, cohesion, text*.

Glossary

Cf. → *functional sentence perspective*. In contrast to *rheme*, the new information, *theme* is that part of a sentence or utterance which is already known or pre-supposed as given in a particular context.	**Theme**
The basic unit of analysis of intonation.	**Tone group**
Verbs which take at least one object.	**Transitive**
The classification of languages according to shared formal characteristics. In contrast to the classification of languages according to their common historical origin, such typological classifications are essentially synchronic in nature. A prominent traditional typology is based on the shape of the word in a particular language, distinguishing between isolating, agglutinating, fusional (or inflectional) and polysynthetic types. More recent research has attempted to classify languages on the basis of their neutral or preferred constituent orders, distinguishing, for example, SVO (**S**ubject-**V**erb-**O**bject) languages such as English from SOV languages such as Turkish or VSO languages such as Irish Gaelic. In general, research in typology is concerned with determining the limits of possible variation in human languages. Aspects which are not subject to variability are considered *linguistic* → *universals*.	**Typology**
A sound change in older Germanic languages (e. g. early Old English) where the phonemes /i/ or /j/ in the subsequent syllable caused the preceding stressed back vowel to develop a fronted articulation. Thus, the word *fōti* (plural of *fōt* "foot") came to be pronounced as *fœt(i)* and eventually as *fēt*, which is the ancestor of present-day English *feet*. In the history of English, the many irregularities in inflectional paradigms arising from i-mutation were largely eliminated through analogy apart from few remnants (e. g. *mouse – mice, foot – feet*). In German, by contrast, umlaut was charged with secondary grammatical functions (e. g. plural marking) and extended.	**Umlaut, i-mutation**
Properties or features shared by all natural human languages. We distinguish substantial universals ("All languages have numerals for 'one' and 'two'." "All languages have vowels and consonants." "All languages have pronouns.") from implicational universals, i. e. statements of the type "If a language has a dual [i. e. a grammatical category denoting exactly two items of a kind], then it also has a plural." In a strict sense, a property or feature is **not** a linguistic universal if there is just one attested counter-example among the languages of the world. Recent research in → *typology* and universals, however, has also drawn attention to important statistical generalisations. For example, among the six possible orderings of S, V, O (**S**ubject, **V**erb, **O**bject) three, namely SVO, SOV and VSO, are common, whereas OVS, OSV and VOS are very rare → *linguistic universal*.	**Universals**
A regionally, socially, functionally or otherwise specific form of a language.	**Variety**
A part of speech which – at least in German and English – functions as the carrier of tense marking and typically serves to express activities, actions, and states.	**Verb**
A grammatical structure consisting of a verb and those noun constituents directly dependent on it. The sentence *naturally, I did not talk about this* can thus be separated into the sentence adverb *naturally*, the noun phrase *I* and the verb phrase *did not talk about this* (which, in turn, consists of the verbal predicate and the prepositional phrase *about this*) → *predicate*.	**Verb phrase**
That variety of a language found in a community which is furthest away from the standard educated norm, i. e. traditional dialects in rural settings and highly stigmatised working-class or ethnic varieties in modern cities.	**Vernacular**
Sounds are voiced when, during their articulation, the vocal cords vibrate. All vowels and many consonants are voiced. Consonants which are not voiced are called *voiceless*. The activity of the vocal cords can be tested by putting a finger to the larynx. Whispering does not only mean speaking in a low voice, but also requires complete absence of any voicing.	**Voiced**
→ *voiced*.	**Voiceless**
Sounds whose articulation is not impeded by obstruction or friction so that the air can escape freely.	**Vowel**
→ *compound word, lexeme, morpheme*.	**Word**
Morphological processes that create new words. → *back-formation, compound word, derivation, morphology, zero-derivation*	**Word-formation**

257

Zero-derivation, conversion — A change of word class without change of word form, e. g. *petition* → *to petition*. The term *zero-derivation* is based on the assumption that the conversion is caused by a → *zero-morpheme*, i. e. a morpheme without phonetic realisation.

Zero-morpheme — An inflectional or word-formation morpheme lacking phonetic substance. One may assume a zero-morpheme changing the adjective *black* into the noun *(a) black* so as to avoid the – possibly unwanted – conclusion that *the blacks* is an adjective which has exceptionally taken a plural *-s*.

Index

Index of Names

Austin, John 113, 116

Bally, Charles 208
Bloomfield, Leonard 211
Bühler, Karl 110–112, 119

Chomsky, Noam 10–11, 212–215

Daneš, František 118
de Saussure, Ferdinand 6, 208–211, 214, 215, 217
Dieth, Eugen 160
Dirven, René 175

Firth, John Rupert 215

Givón, Talmy 214
Greenberg, Joseph H. 214
Grice, Herbert Paul 114, 115, 116, 119, 121

Halliday, M. A. K. 215

Jakobson, Roman 111–112
Jones, William 5–6

Labov, William 92, 163, 164, 172–175, 176, 180, 215
Lakoff, George 107, 214
Langacker, Ronald W. 214
Lévi-Strauss, Claude 211

McWhorter, John 179

Orton, Harold 160–162

Robins, R. H. 10–11
Rohdenburg, Günter 219

Sapir, Edward 10–11, 67, 216
Schlegel, August Wilhelm 67
Searle, John Rogers 113, 116
Sechehaye, Albert 208
Shaw, George Bernard 21, 26
Sinclair, John 100
Sweet, Henry 26

Trubetzkoy, Nikolay 211

von Humboldt, Wilhelm 67, 208, 216

Whorf, Benjamin Lee 216
Wittgenstein, Ludwig 112, 116

Subject Index

AAVE (African-American Vernacular English) 177–180
accent 7, 8, 9, 26, 27, 29, 30–31, 33, 34, 64, 69–70, 128–129, 142, 144, 147, 152–153, 156, 159, 160, 172, 176, 195, 209, 215
accusative 65, 189, 198
acronym 49, 159
adjective 40, 42–43, 45, 46–47, 48, 50–51, 54, 62, 64, 66, 68, 69–70, 73–75, 76, 78, 94, 96, 128, 190, 228–229
AdjP (adjective phrase) 75–76, 77–78
adjunct 80
adverb 12, 47, 50–51, 54, 73, 74–75, 119, 132
AdvP (adverb phrase) 75–77
adverbial 62, 69, 75, 77–79, 80, 83, 109, 132
adverbial of place 62, 76, 213
affix 40–41, 228
affricate 23, 31, 33
agglutinating language 67
allomorph 41–42
allophone 27, 28, 31
alphabetism 49
alveolar 22, 24, 30
analogy 11, 39, 50
analytical language 44, 68, 74, 78, 189, 192, 195, 211
anaphora 120
Anglicism 7, 227, 229
antonym, antonymy 96–97, 99
aphasia 127
approximant 22, 25
arbitrary, arbitrariness 3, 12, 21, 99, 100, 102, 210, 211, 215
article 30, 65, 73–75, 76, 117, 118, 189
aspect 74, 119, 177, 195
assimilation 30
attribute 69, 128
autosemantic word 73–74
avoidance 130–131

back-formation 49–50
bilabial 22, 23, 25
bilingual, bilingualism 180, 192, 225
blend 49
Bloomfieldian structuralism 211
BNC (British National Corpus) 14–16, 51–52, 70, 91, 95, 101, 117, 120, 202
"bottom up" 116

Canadian Raising 36
case 14, 65, 74, 189
cataphoric 120–121

259

chiasmus 112
clause patterns 77
click 23
clipping 49
cluster 28–29, 135, 177
coda 29–30
code-switching 172, 227
cognitive semantics 90–91, 93
coherence 109
cohesion 109, 117
collocation 99–103, 137, 149, 215, 217
communication 11, 12, 13, 49, 89, 90, 94, 110–112, 113, 114, 141, 142, 171, 175, 192, 208, 210, 214–215, 224–225, 232
competence 31, 100, 131–132, 134, 137, 212–213, 215
complement 62, 70, 77–79, 83–84, 118
complementary distribution 27
complex sentence 81
component/feature 91
compound sentence 81
compounding 45–46, 51
conative 110, 112
conjugation 103
conjunction 30, 73, 75, 81, 109, 116, 213
connotation 95
consonant 21–26, 29, 31–34, 37, 41, 48, 129, 134, 135, 146, 177, 188
constituent/phrase 58–61, 63–64, 69–70, 73, 75–82, 207
constituent order/word order 63–64, 66, 68, 69, 117, 198
contextualism 215
conversation analysis 116, 215–216
conversational implicature 115
conventional implicatures 115–116
conversion/zero derivation 45, 47–48, 200
cooperative principle 114
corpora, corpus linguistics 13–14, 34, 51, 70, 83, 96, 135, 137, 156, 199, 200–202, 216–217, 219, 223
covert prestige 174–175, 226
Creole 134, 236

dative 65, 68, 189, 192, 198
declarative sentence 57, 113
declension 65, 74
deixis 119–120
demonstrative pronoun 14, 74, 119
denotation 94–95
dental 22, 32, 192
derivation 40–43, 45, 46–47, 48, 50–51
descriptive approach 8
determiner/pronoun 13, 14, 30, 73–76, 109, 118–120, 193, 198, 211
diachrony, diachronic 6–7, 11, 67, 159, 174, 199, 208, 211–212
dialect 141, 142, 143–145, 159–161, 163–165, 171–174, 177, 182, 189, 190, 192, 198, 226, 236

diphthong 21, 25–26, 29, 31–32, 34–37, 148, 160, 175, 194, 199–200
discourse analysis 109–110, 116
discourse marker 124, 144
dysphemism 98

Early Modern English period 193–194
EFL (English as a Foreign Language) 152
embedding 80
endo-normative 152
ENL (English as a Native Language) 151, 152–156
error analysis 131, 137
ESL (English as a Second Language) 151, 153–155, 156
ethnic identity 176
ethnomethodology 116
etymological 49, 94, 147
euphemism 98
exo-normative 152

false friends 129
final devoicing/*Auslautverhärtung* 33, 135
finite verb 198–199
flapping/tapping 10
F-LOB (Freiburg-Lancaster-Oslo/Bergen Corpus) 18, 80, 83
focus 117
form (or category) 61–62
formalism 212–217
fricative 22, 23, 25–26, 30–33, 134–135, 192
function word 65–66
function 61–62
functionalism 216
functional sentence perspective (FSP) 116

general/theoretical linguistics 73, 127, 208
generative linguistics 212–213, 215
gerund 13, 58, 81, 132, 136
glide/semi-vowel 32, 160
glottal 22, 23
grammar 57
grammaticalisation 202
Great Vowel Shift 194

head 45, 75–76
historical-comparative linguistics 6
Hochdeutsche Lautverschiebung 188
homonym, homonymy 48, 94
hyperonym, hyperonymy 97
hyponym, hyponymy 97

ICE (International Corpus of English) 156
ICLE (International Corpus of Learner English) 102, 135–137
IDEA (International Dialects of English Archive) 165
idiom 63, 103, 131, 149, 190, 194, 198, 202
idiomatic 99, 132
illocution 113
imperative sentence 57
implication 115
implicature 115

Index

infinitive 58, 81, 82, 133, 136, 151
infixation 46
inflection, inflexion 40–43, 46, 48, 50, 57, 63, 64–65, 68, 74, 90, 189, 190, 192, 198, 228–229
inflectional (fusional) language 67–68, 78
initialism 49
interaction-based approach 176, 215
interference 128–131, 137
interrogative sentence 57
intonation 28–29, 63, 64, 66–67, 122
introspect 218–219
IPA (International Phonetic Association) 21–22, 23, 25, 26, 27, 29, 30, 31, 121
isogloss 159–161, 171
isolating language 67–68

labiodental 22
language purism 227–228
langue 208–209, 212, 215
lateral approximant 22, 23
lateral fricative 22
lemma 90
lexeme 90
lexical field 93, 98
lexicalisation 43, 90
lexicography 90, 194
lexicology 90
linguistic diversity 229–231
linguistic intuition/*Sprachgefühl* 11, 218
linguistic sign 110, 209–210, 212
linguistic variation 142, 171, 173, 175, 176, 177, 180, 218, 219
locution 113

main clause 58, 198
manner of articulation 25
markedness 96–97, 135, 137, 148
maxim of conversation 114–115, 119, 121
meronymy 97
metalinguistic 111–112
Middle English period 192–193
minimal pair 27, 32–33, 89, 173
Modern English period 195
modality 74
modifier 45, 75, 76
monophthong 25, 148, 160, 194, 199–200
morpheme 39–44, 45, 46, 47, 48, 50, 51–52, 63, 65, 67, 68, 100, 144, 148
morphology 39, 41, 57, 109, 150
multilingual, multilingualism 2, 154, 172, 180–181, 226, 230–231, 235
multiple negation 143, 207

nasal 22, 23, 24, 25, 31
non-finite clause 58, 81, 83
non-restrictive/non-defining relative clause 66
norm 131, 135, 141, 145, 148, 152, 154, 156, 165, 171, 172, 176

noun 39–48, 50–51, 59, 61, 62, 64, 65, 66, 69, 73, 74, 75, 76, 78, 97, 99, 101, 117, 128, 137, 146, 151, 189, 190, 200
NP (noun phrase) 59–61, 62, 66, 74, 75–77, 78, 101, 118, 198, 207, 219
nucleus 21, 29–30, 58, 59, 77, 207
number 65, 74, 78, 211

object 13, 14, 59, 62, 64, 69, 74, 76, 77, 78–83, 101, 102, 118, 207, 213, 219
OED (Oxford English Dictionary) 17, 49, 50, 200, 236
Old English period 7, 141, 188, 190–192
onomatopoeia 3
onset 29–30, 36–37
over-generalisation 131, 138
over-representation 130
overt prestige 174

palatal 22, 23, 25, 26, 27, 30, 31
parole 208–209, 212, 215, 216, 227
part of speech 48, 73–75, 200
passive (voice) 78, 82, 84, 118, 215
performance 134, 212–216, 219
perlocution 113
pharyngeal 22
phatic 112
phoneme 27, 28, 31, 32, 33, 35, 39, 41, 89, 100, 129, 130, 147, 192
phonetic alphabet 21, 22, 23, 121
phonetics 23–24, 27, 28, 30, 34
phonology 23, 27, 28, 30, 109, 211, 213, 215, 226
phonotactics 28
phrase 25, 39, 40, 49, 51, 57, 58–64, 66, 73, 74, 75–80, 101, 103, 114, 118, 124, 198, 207, 210, 219
pidgin/pidginisation 134, 228
pitch movement 29
place of articulation 23, 25, 26
plosive (or stop) 23, 25, 26, 27, 28, 31, 33, 34, 36, 147
plural 29, 40, 41, 42, 43, 48, 64, 65, 67, 74, 78, 89, 90, 91, 99, 103, 143, 145, 189, 192, 228
polysemy 94
polysynthetic/incorporating language 67
postalveolar 22, 30
postmodification 80
PP (prepositional phrase) 59, 61, 62, 64, 75–79
pragmatics 89, 90, 109–110, 112, 114, 116, 118, 119, 149, 212, 214, 215, 228
Prague School 116, 211
predicate 59, 77, 80, 207
prefix 46, 51
premodification 80
preposition 30, 47, 59, 65, 73, 74, 78, 192, 198
prescriptive approach 8
productivity 41, 42
pronoun 13, 14, 30, 73, 74, 75, 109, 118, 119, 120, 193, 198, 211
proto-Indo-European/*Ursprache* 5–6, 187, 189
prototype (semantics) 93, 207

261

Subject Index

qualitative approach 1, 176, 215
quantitative approach 1, 215

R. P. (Received Pronunciation) 28, 31, 144, 147–148, 152, 153, 160, 161, 172, 199
reference/denotation 94, 95
regional accent 144, 159, 160
register 52, 143, 174
relative clause 66, 82, 83, 93, 130
restrictive/defining relative clause 66
retroflex 22, 28
rheme 116–117

Santa Barbara Corpus 118, 121, 122
Sapir-Whorf hypothesis 216
SED (Survey of English Dialects) 160
semantics 89–90, 93, 94, 99, 109, 116, 118, 207, 214
semiotics 209–210
sense 94
signifiant 209–211
signifié 209–211
singular 40, 41, 64, 65, 74, 78, 89, 90, 99, 103, 114, 119, 189, 193, 198
social variable 176, 215
sociolinguistics 143, 172, 176–177, 179, 212, 215
sound law 188
source language 131
speech act 113–115, 121, 124
standard 3, 7, 9, 23, 33, 121, 129, 141–145, 147–148, 151–156, 159–160, 164, 171, 173–179, 190, 192, 194, 195, 198, 209, 224, 234–236
Standard American English 178
Standard British English 23
standardisation 127, 141–142, 152–156, 194, 195
stress 28, 29, 30, 34, 47, 48, 51, 147–148
structural semantics 90–91
structuralism 6–7, 208–209, 211, 212, 214, 215
subject clause 62, 117
subjunctive 74, 151
subordinate clause 58, 81, 151, 199, 213
sub-standard 141
suffix 46–47, 50–51
supra-segmental 28–30, 34
synchrony, synchronic 6–7, 11, 21, 67, 174, 208, 212, 216
synonym, synonymy 75, 95–96, 97, 99, 180, 192, 218

synsemantic word 73–74
syntax 57–58, 73, 99, 109, 118, 150, 214–215
synthetic language 68, 189, 190, 198

tap/flap 10, 22
target language 130–131
tense 40–41, 58, 64, 74, 81, 114, 119, 120, 124, 150, 151, 177, 195, 201, 202
textlinguistics/discourse analysis 109
theme 116–117
tone group 30
"top down" 116
transitive 198
translation 127, 129, 132–133
trill 22, 28
turn-taking 116, 124
typology 67–68, 214

UG (Universal Grammar) 213
umlaut/i-mutation 42
urban dialectology 172–173, 215
utterance 11, 13, 29, 43, 57, 84, 90, 100, 109, 111–121, 124, 172, 208, 212, 227, 228
uvular 22, 28

variety 1, 14, 141, 144, 150, 153, 154, 156, 159, 165, 174, 177, 179, 192, 216
verb 3, 12, 13, 15, 30, 40, 41, 44, 45, 46, 47, 48, 50, 58, 59, 68, 69, 73–76, 78, 79, 81, 98, 99, 102, 109, 112, 114, 115, 119, 130, 132, 137, 138, 143, 144, 150, 177, 190, 192, 195, 198, 199, 200, 201, 202, 207, 209, 211, 228, 236
velar/dark 22–23, 27, 28, 34
vernacular 171, 174, 175, 177–178, 190, 219
voiced 22, 25, 33–34, 36, 41, 48, 134–135
voiceless 25, 27, 30, 32–34, 36, 41, 48, 147
vowel 8, 10, 21–22, 24–26, 29, 31–34, 36, 37, 41, 135, 146, 147, 151, 176, 188, 191, 194, 202
VP (verb phrase) 59–61, 75–77, 78, 79, 207

word class 46, 73
word-formation 39, 45–51, 200
word order 63–64, 66, 68, 117, 198

zero-derivation/conversion 48, 200
zero-morpheme 48